MW00778622

The Yanks are Coming

THE YANKS ARE COMING

The American Invasion of New Zealand
1942–1944

Harry Bioletti

Century Hutchinson

This book is dedicated to the memory of those members of the United States of America Forces who knew New Zealand 1942–1944, gave their all, and were never to know it again.

Century Hutchinson New Zealand Ltd
An imprint of the Century Hutchinson Group
187 Archers Road, Glenfield, Auckland 10.

Century Hutchinson Ltd
62–65 Chandos Place, Covent Garden, London WC2N 4NW

Century Hutchinson Australia Pty Ltd
89–91 Albion Street, Surry Hills, Sydney, N.S.W. 2010

Century Hutchinson South Africa Pty Ltd
P.O. Box 337, Bergvlei 2012, South Africa

First published 1989
© Harry Bioletti 1989

Printed in Hong Kong

ISBN 1 86941 034 3

Contents

*Do you remember the time — Yes I remember the time; it was 1942
in November —*

Do you remember the place where we had gone?
Yes, it was New Zealand; Auckland and Wellington.

Do you recall the purpose it was for?
Certainly, we were an Army; it was War.

Tell me, then, what else do you remember
Of that time and country, that November?

I recall our first arrival there,
How beautiful the season was, how fair
The land, how kind the people were, and their ways,
How gracious was their welcome and the days
We spent among them, and the dignity
They faced their life with; the austerity
They met with humor, courage, character,
And strength, as much as they had vim to bear.

That was what I saw when I was there.

Merrill Moore (Major)
US Army Medical Corps.

From *Cross Currents: A Selection by Denis Glover of Sonnets by Merrill
Moore 1903–1957*, Pegasus Press, Christchurch, 1961.

PREFACE

'Americans? Americans? I didn't know there were any Americans round here,' I heard a teenage girl in my class say one day. I thought then it was time their story was told. This book tells that story: where the Americans came from, where they stayed in New Zealand, what they did while they were here, where they went to and what happened to them. More than that, it details the effects of the American presence and the ways in which the visitors were affected. New Zealanders of course knew all about America. Hollywood with its myth-making machine and the American radio serials of the day had set the scene for the US Forces when they arrived in June 1942. They fitted well into the role cast for them, not only as ambassadors for Uncle Sam but also as combat soldiers, sailors, airmen, and nurses, soon to be committed to jungle warfare in the Pacific.

Movies may have been an escape mechanism, but down-to-earth New Zealanders had known war for two and a half years, and suffered the agony of casualty lists. Since the Pearl Harbour bombing on 7 December 1941, the Americans had been at war for seven months, with barely a shot fired in anger.

Many ex-servicemen returning to New Zealand on a sentimental journey have explained the inner compulsion to see their old haunts again. 'Paekakariki was paradise after Tarawa,' said a returning Marine. 'I just had to come back and see it all over again. I have found it a very moving experience.'

A detachment of the 2nd Marine Division Association of the US Marine Corps made its sixth pilgrimage to New Zealand in February 1988, touring both the North and South Islands. Not only did their journey revive memories for the Marines, it also struck a nostalgic chord with New Zealanders, especially with thousands of middle-aged women who remember those times if not with a tear, then at least with a sigh. Other units, including representatives of the 43rd and 25th US Army Divisions, continue to come back. The Americans gave New Zealand a shake in those war years. Some would say that the reverberations have not ceased.

It seems an incredible abrogation of historical responsibility that no in-depth study of the American 'invasion' of New Zealand has ever appeared in over forty years. This book hopes to fill that gap in our recorded knowledge of history in modern times. For any sins of omission or commission the responsibility will lie solely at my door. This book does not purport to be a definitive study of the subject, mainly because there can be no such thing. Time plays tricks with memories after more than forty years, and it will always change our interpretation of the past. If I have captured in some small part the spirit of those fleeting days not just for those who knew them, but for a new generation too, I will have achieved my goal.

Harry Bioletti

ACKNOWLEDGEMENTS

For the contribution they have made to this story, I gratefully acknowledge the help given me by all those American ex-servicemen and their wives, too numerous to mention by name, most of whom live in New Zealand. Without them my record would have been bleak indeed, for so little has appeared in print about the American presence here in New Zealand. Similarly I hasten to thank a host of New Zealanders who cast their minds back to capture stories of their associations with the Marines, Army or Navy boys. Special thanks are due to Brian Collins, who generously placed at my disposal the many photographs of American servicemen taken by his uncle, Tudor Collins.

To the many librarians who have assisted me, including those of the Alexander Turnbull, the Defence Library (Wellington), Masterton, Pukekohe and Auckland Public Libraries, the Auckland Museum, Wellington Public Library, Wellington Maritime Museum, Auckland Harbour Board and National Archives, I tender my thanks. The Aviation Historical Society of New Zealand Inc., the Otaki Historical Society, and the New Zealand Military Historical Society have always been most co-operative. Where the New Zealand Defence Department has been able to help, it has always been forthcoming with information. Various American organisations of Veterans of Foreign Wars have been pleased to assist. I acknowledge the unfailing help of Danny J. Crawford of the Marine Corps Historical Center, Washington, DC, also the Chief of Military History, Department of the Army, Washington, DC. To those two young women, my editors, firstly Christine Price and latterly Harriet Bennett Allan, I proffer my thanks for the meticulous expertise they brought to the task of sifting and arranging my material. Then there are those interested people who, knowing of my study, volunteered information and stories. Finally I wish to thank my wife Joan, who fielded my phone calls, plied me with coffee, and was able to come up with the name of Franklin D. Roosevelt's black Scottish terrier and other Mastermind details.

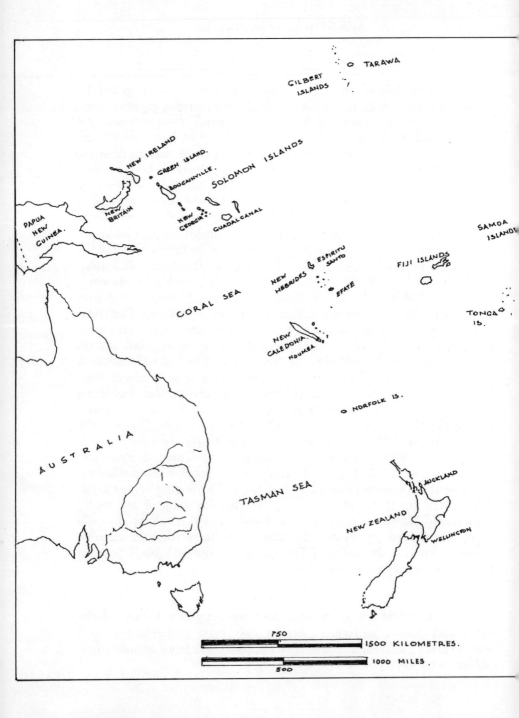

The Pacific region.

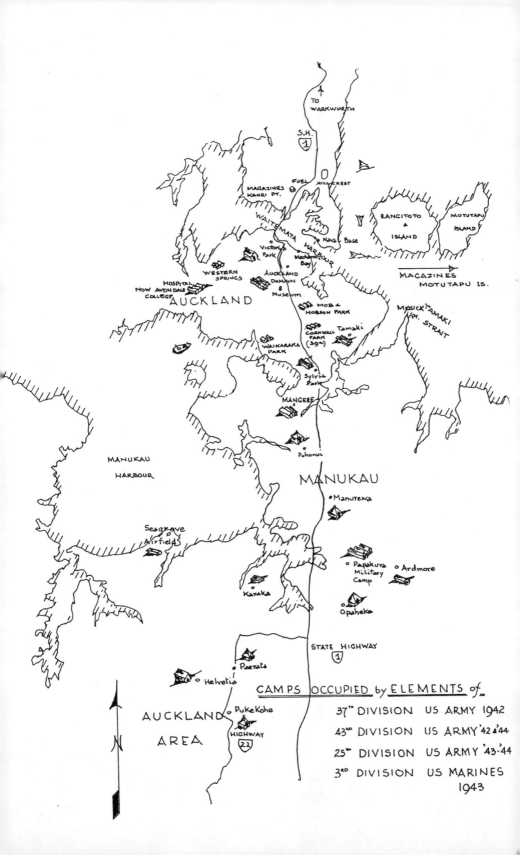

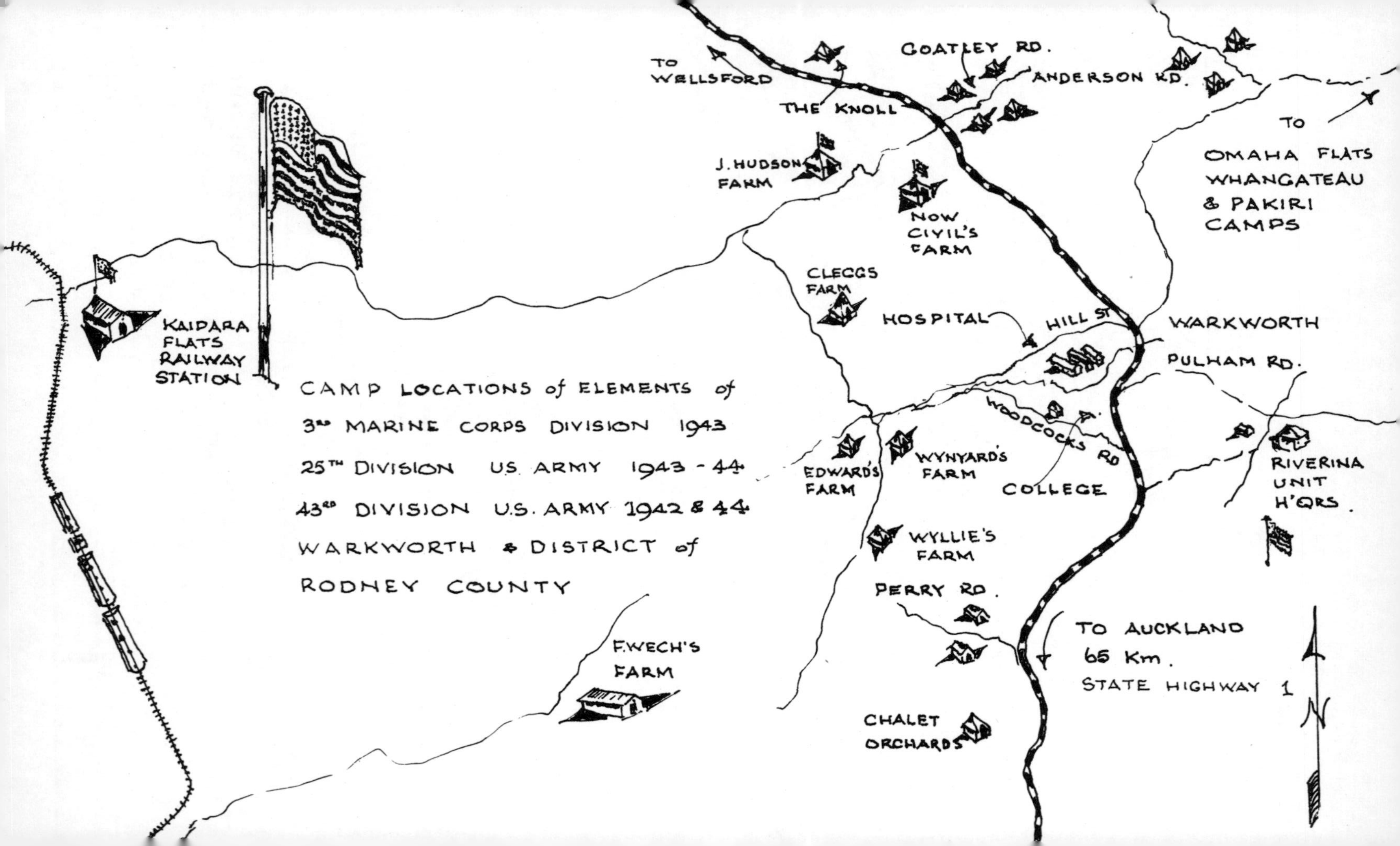

CAMP LOCATIONS of ELEMENTS of

3RD MARINE CORPS DIVISION 1943

25TH DIVISION U.S. ARMY 1943 - 44

43RD DIVISION U.S. ARMY 1942 & 44

WARKWORTH & DISTRICT of

RODNEY COUNTY

TO WELLSFORD

GOATLEY RD.

ANDERSON RD.

THE KNOLL

J. HUDSON FARM

NOW CIVIL'S FARM

CLEGGS FARM

HOSPITAL

HILL ST

WARKWORTH

PULHAM RD.

WOODCOCKS RD

WYNYARD'S FARM

COLLEGE

EDWARD'S FARM

WYLLIE'S FARM

PERRY RD.

CHALET ORCHARDS

RIVERINA UNIT H'QRS.

TO AUCKLAND 65 Km.

STATE HIGHWAY 1

N

F.WECH'S FARM

KAIPARA FLATS RAILWAY STATION

TO OMAHA FLATS WHANGATEAU & PAKIRI CAMPS

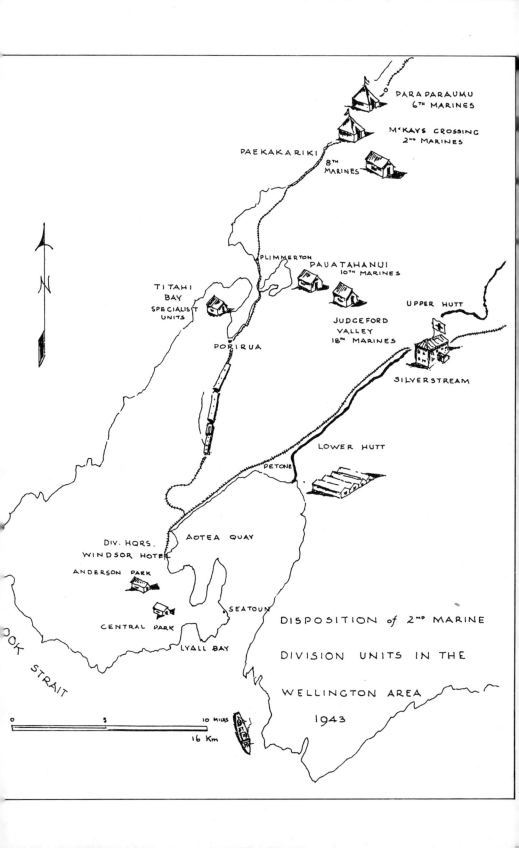

PARAPARAUMU
6TH MARINES

McKAYS CROSSING
2ND MARINES

PAEKAKARIKI

8TH
MARINES

PLIMMERTON

PAUATAHANUI
10TH MARINES

TITAHI
BAY
SPECIALIST
UNITS

UPPER HUTT

JUDGEFORD
VALLEY
18TH MARINES

PORIRUA

SILVERSTREAM

LOWER HUTT

PETONE

AOTEA QUAY

DIV. HQRS.
WINDSOR HOTEL

ANDERSON PARK

SEATOUN

DISPOSITION of 2ND MARINE

CENTRAL PARK

DIVISION UNITS IN THE

LYALL BAY

WELLINGTON AREA

COOK STRAIT

1943

0   5   10 MILES
16 Km

CHAPTER ONE

The Kiwi Meets Uncle Sam

Office workers in Auckland flew to their windows on that June wartime morning when the sound of military music blasted through their windows. They looked down to see soldiers marching up Queen Street. Some thought the Japanese had arrived, that the enemy was on the doorstep. But the music told otherwise: *Over there, over there, the Yanks are coming* . . . For some it was the most traumatic, for others the most exciting experience of the whole war. Uncle Sam was here, but why, what was it all about?

In the late afternoon of 12 June 1942, a convoy of vessels in battleship grey had nosed its way into Auckland's Waitemata Harbour, led by a US Navy cruiser, the 10,000 tonner USS *San Francisco*, escorting the troop transports USS *Uruguay, Santa Clara, President Monroe, Tasker M. Bliss*, and the *James Parker*. The USS *Farragut*, a US Navy destroyer, brought up the rear. On board were the 145th Regiment and auxiliary troops of the 37th US Army Division from Ohio. The convoy's entrance was not without incident, for escorting warships dropped depth charges on an alleged submarine. What was thought to be a periscope turned out to be the fin of a paravane towed by a minesweeper.

The following day the USS *Uruguay* (22,754 tons), with the com- mander of the American forces, Brigadier General Ludwig M. Connelly, aboard, tied up at Princes Wharf together with the USS *Santa Clara* and *President Monroe*. Present to greet the invading forces were Major General P. G. Bell, New Zealand Forces, US Military Attaché Colonel John H. Nankivell, and the Mayor of Auckland, Mr J. A. C. Allum. First Sergeant Nathan E. Cook of Company A, 145th Infantry, was selected as the first enlisted man to come down the gangway because his surname echoed that of Captain James Cook, re-discoverer of New Zealand.

'What town, where are we?' Hundreds of American servicemen were to ask this question when the troopship was pushed alongside Princes Wharf, which was to be used exclusively by the Americans in 1942 and 1943.

'Owckland! Where's that?'

'Noo Zillund — is that Orstralia?'

Cigarettes, oranges and coins showered down on the wharf as the ships were pushed into their berths by steam tugs. The regimental bands on deck blasted out 'Roll out the barrel', or, if there were Marines aboard, the Marine Corps hymn, 'From the halls of Montezuma, to the

1

shores of Tripoli . . .' The sousaphones swayed above the tightly packed blue uniforms and the olive drab of the soldiers. Somebody from the American advance party on the wharf shouted, 'No Scotch, two percent beer, but nice folks.' Four New Zealand military bands were on the wharves, playing tunes the Americans described as 'familiar American pieces with New Zealand accents'. The 'Buckeyes' retaliated from the upper decks of the transports with a swing version of the 'Beer Barrel Polka'. (Ohio is known as the 'Buckeye State' because of the abundance of buckeye trees, which are related to the European horse chestnut.)

An American serviceman of those days describes how, after marching through Auckland streets to the railway station, 'troops were jammed into the Toonerville-Trolley-like coaches of the miniature narrow gauge trains. The conductor tarried on the platform, puffed on a whistle and signalled "Ready" with a tiny piece of green cloth. The engine steamed out of the station and tugged the cars along at a snappy twenty miles per hour, interrupted only when it was necessary to stop and shoo wayward sheep off the railroad's contested right-of-way.'

On 19 June the Americans put on a show marching up Queen Street. Their arrival and presence had not been printed in the newspapers but word got around the parade was on. Next day the *New Zealand Herald* commented, without mentioning the word 'American', 'In the opinion of those able to judge, yesterday's military display brought larger crowds into Queen Street than ever before in the history of Auckland, not excepting the last three visits of Royalty . . . children's shrill cheers rose above the blare of the bands and encouraged older folk to shout as New Zealanders rarely do when a procession passes.'

Independence Day, fourth of July, had to be celebrated with a parade. The 145th Infantry Band played the Buckeyes up Queen Street. Wrote an American, 'Thousands lined the curbs waving American and New Zealand flags, demonstrating their fondness for the men from Up Over by celebrating one of the American holidays with the boys.'

At the same time as elements of the 37th Division of the US Army were arriving in Auckland, the first of the US Marine corps were about to descend on Wellington. On 13 June, the 23,000 tonner USS *West Point* (formerly the transatlantic liner *America*), with its sixty life rafts strapped to its sides, passed Pencarrow Head and entered the harbour. It had taken the 32nd US Army Division to Australia and was en route to San Francisco. But it is the USS *Wakefield* that Wellingtonians will remember. Formerly the transatlantic liner *Manhattan*, the 24,000 tonner carried the advance echelon of Major General Alexander Vandegrift's 1st Marine Corps Division. On 14 June the *Wakefield* berthed at King's Wharf, and the Marines came down the gangway. New Zealand was never to be quite the same again.

For the first time in New Zealand's history (apart from courtesy visits by various nations), foreign troops had landed on its shores. Naturally

Men of the US Forces march down Queen Street Auckland. St James Theatre is on the left. 25 November 1942. *NZ Herald*

a few officials were privy to the arrival of the Americans, but the vast majority of New Zealanders found themselves hosts to an ally without any prior notice. If they were surprised, they were also delighted; for the enemy, if not at the front door, might soon be coming up the path. Japanese midget submarines had breeched the boom defence of Sydney Harbour just a few days before the American invasion and had caused damage. One New Zealander remembers just how terrifying this threat was, 'One night Cyrus the local air-raid warden rang up. "Phyllis have you got your windows blacked out? There are Jap submarines out there off the coast." I nearly panicked. What shall I do if the Japs land? Shall I kill my children? We had heard they took the young women and killed the old and I had my mother with me at the time. I can tell you I said a few "Hail Marys" that night. It put the fear of God into me. I huddled all the children into one room. And then the "All Clear" came over the phone.'

3

The arrival of the Americans was also a culture shock New Zealand needed, because for too long the country had been cushioned from outside influence by its isolation. No newspaper or radio station of the day recorded that eventful time, for the dissemination of critical information on troop movements was strictly censored. Indeed, mention of the American presence was banned in the press for almost a year. The New Zealand press were most annoyed when Prime Minister Peter Fraser, during a visit to the United States, commented publicly on the presence

The US Marines arrive in the middle of winter, June 1942, Aotea Quay, Wellington. *Alexander Turnbull Library*

of American forces in New Zealand. Everyone knew in any case, including Tokyo Rose, the Japanese radio propagandist.

Surprise it may have been to office workers, but the arrival of the Americans was no secret to that small organising group which had to have camps in place to house thousands. Suddenly, in April 1942, the Public Works Department was given instructions to construct camps in the Paekakariki area to bed down 20,000 men, and given six weeks to do it. Troops began to pour into the Auckland area, and camps from Warkworth in the north to Pukekohe in the south sprang up to cope with newly arrived Marines, soldiers and sailors. Two- and four-man timber huts, prefabricated in the South Island, were shipped north to cope with the demand of the thousands of Americans landing in New Zealand.

A Wellingtonian recalls, 'I was only a young schoolboy in the early days of the war, and I didn't understand what it was all about. I remember one day I was on the tram and a New Zealand soldier got on with his lemon-squeezer hat. I was amazed, I was only used to seeing American uniforms.'

As the Americans arrived with their dollars, schoolboys appeared on the streets. Down in Willis Street they sniffed the air for 'White Owl' cigar smoke, which would lead them to the entrance of the St George Hotel and the Marines. There on the pavement they set up their home-made shoeshine boxes and touted for trade. The Marines, some of whom no doubt had been streetwise kids themselves, were always generous to the boys and laughingly handed over chewing gum. After a shine they might hold out a handful of silver and invite the shiner to take a coin, a half-crown, perhaps even another one. It would have been an exotic sight for New Zealanders to see a slight barefooted Wellington schoolboy shining the shoes of some six-foot-plus black soldier. The boys collected Marine badges, engaged Marines in conversation hoping for a hand-out of gum (unavailable in New Zealand because of its sugar content), and poked round any American rubbish dump hoping to pick up some unconsidered trifle. Shoe cleaning may have been regarded as demeaning, but not by schoolboys when there was a chance of a silver dollar to roll around.

> Shoeshine boy, shine ma shoe,
> Have it done b' half pas' two.
> Shine 'em good and shine 'em black
> Else I'll take ma money back.

Pressing and drycleaning businesses also mushroomed to meet the demands of the Marines and their meticulous uniform standards.

The well-worn cliché about the Americans, that they were 'overpaid, oversexed and over here', was certainly true. Jeeps with officers and

Doing the 'Palais Glide' at a dance for US naval personnel in the Auckland Town Hall. *NZ Herald*

enlisted men drivers were everywhere, petrol rationing for them was unheard of. Every guest bar in reputable hotels, and some not so reputable, was crowded with officers naval, army and marine. And where there were the blue uniforms of the Navy, the dark greens of the Army or the olive drabs of the Marines, there were women; women starved of the company of their own men who were overseas. You only had to go to a cinema in a New Zealand country town to have evidence of that. There they were, row upon row of unescorted girls, and not a man in sight — unless of course the town was near an American camp. Then there was much to set the tongues wagging: who was there with whom, and she had no right to be there, with her husband away and all that, and that Robinson girl snuggling up to a Marine, and she engaged to that nice Jones boy who was away fighting in the Middle East . . .

It was certainly not men's company the Americans sought, not after being crammed into quarters thirty-two men to a hut, such as those up on the Auckland Domain. With so many unescorted women around, the visitors could take their pick. It was the women who married them, had children by them, entertained them; their mothers who cooked for them, were members of concert parties, who worked for them and in some cases nursed them. An Auckland nurse tells of her experiences with the Americans.

> We took all the infectious diseases at Ellerslie Racecourse. The existing Tea Kiosk you know today was for officers, and underneath the grandstand for enlisted men. We had a terrible lot of malaria cases and those with lung infections, also men with tinea. By tinea I mean dermatitis where men's legs right up to the knees were one ghastly suppurating mess. We had to use nose plugs, the smell was so frightful. Combat men had been in hot wet conditions for long periods in the jungle with no washing facilities and no sunlight on their limbs. We got them on the road to recovery, and then they were shipped out and back to the States. They were no good as combat men again. We worked very hard, and our patients were lovely men. One of them proposed to me formally once a week. As New Zealand nurses we were accustomed to doing all the work ourselves. Not so the American nurses, they delegated work to the patients. We got the message after a while too.

In the cities the wartime bureaucratic machine was 'manned' by young women directed to various offices by the manpower authorities. Up in the Auckland Domain were thousands of Marines, Navy, or Army men in their barracks; downtown in flats, hostels, boarding houses and private homes were the women. They met with an unbridled éclat on the dance floors, in the service clubs and in the streets. New Zealand men were not given to calling their girlfriends 'sugar' or 'honey' (it might well have been 'mate'), nor the women's mothers 'ma'am' (it might well have been 'the old woman').

Of the enlisted men, many were in their late teens or barely out of them, and some were patently homesick on arrival in New Zealand. To have $64 a month, to be clothed in the best, fed and bedded down for free was, for many, wealth beyond anything they had ever experienced. It would be no exaggeration to say that for some young boy from an Appalachian scratch farm, it would have been the first time he had had a decent pair of boots on his feet, if he had ever had them at all.

With their newly acquired wealth Marines, soldiers and sailors were eager to spend, and spend lavishly, most of all on women. On radio back in the States, they were singing of the men, *They're either too old or too grassy green*, but not in New Zealand. No lamentations rent the sky here. There was a *cri de coeur* from envious girls back home in the States about the girls in Australia and New Zealand. 'What have they got that we haven't?' 'Nothing, except that they've got it over here,' was the reply.

There might be a fracas in Manners Street, or a mugging in a toilet in Courtenay Place involving New Zealanders and Americans, but it was seldom over who got served first in some steak joint. Most often the cause was resentment at the popularity of the Americans with New Zealand women. The glamour of US men in their freshly laundered, starched and meticulously creased uniforms made a marked impact on women both young and old. The profile of the New Zealand soldier, with his 'bag-arsed' pants and tent-like great coat topped off with a lemon-squeezer hat, was not a pretty one in comparison. No wonder that when a bunch of red roses arrived at the front door, or a corsage to match their frock, women felt for the first time in their lives that they were being treated in a special way. New Zealand men felt out of it, unable to keep up.

Some might say that the few young New Zealand men around in

The Home Guard parades in Wellsford, North Auckland, 1942. Note the varying ages of the soldiers and the different types of rifles, probably privately owned.
Tudor Collins

those times had the appearance of 'loners', that there was a forlornness about them, that they were unable to fit comfortably into the scene. Young men graded medically unfit to serve could well be subjected to oblique or blunt comments like 'Why aren't you overseas with the boys?' Particularly critical of young men in civvies were married women whose husbands were overseas. Other men, forced to stay on farms where ageing or sick parents were unable to cope, found they just couldn't go into town on a Friday night. Some of those graded fit only for home service felt so out of it at dances and recreation huts frequented by the Americans that they ceased to go. In the face of the charisma and flair of the US Marines, hell-bent on romance and high adventure, the Kiwis did not stand a chance.

'Yanks, Yanks, don't talk to me about Yanks,' comments a New Zealand airman of those times. 'With their flash uniforms, the women were American mad. You couldn't buy any flowers, if you wanted a taxi the Marines and their almighty dollar were first priority, and you were just left waiting on the kerbside.'

Some of the biggest critics of the Americans, ironically enough, were the New Zealand troops who returned in 1943 after service in the Middle East and were discharged into civilian life. Many of them got jobs on the wharves and became part of that much denigrated group, 'the wharfies'. Some of these men resented the presence of the Americans because of their conduct towards New Zealand girls and wives while they were away. What the men failed to concede was that it takes two to tango, that the women were willing partners. And what was their own conduct like overseas? Had they never ventured down the red-light district in Cairo; had they always been pillars of rectitude?

It is common today to hear comments from young women born years after the Americans had left such as: 'My father couldn't stand the Yanks,' or, 'You want to hear my father on the subject of Yanks.' Middle-aged men of the time viewed the scene with mixed reactions. Some felt a kind of benevolent paternalism. Others, veterans of World War I who had seen it out in the porridge-like trenches on the Somme in France but were now too old to serve, had known it all before in the *estaminets* behind the lines of the Western Front. They knew that the glitter could not last forever, and that confrontation with the Japanese and all its sorry consequences was what the Americans were in for. So while some New Zealanders greeted the Americans with open arms, others were antagonistic or more reticent. But on what background were these varied reactions founded? What did they know about each other's countries?

Although the friendly invasion of New Zealand by US armed forces in 1942 was the first time this country had known foreign troops to camp on its soil, it was not the first American visit to these shores. One of the most exciting events for Aucklanders in 1908 was the arrival of the Great White Fleet, with Admiral Sperry in command in his flagship, the 12-inch-gun battleship USS *Connecticut* (16,000 tons). The fleet was called 'white' because of the colour of the hulls, which had gold scroll work on the bows and sterns as a concession to the styling of the ships of the past. Sixteen capital ships sailed into Waitemata Harbour on 9 August 1908 — 260,000 tons of United States naval might. All ships except the *Kearsage* bore the names of American states, such as the *Kansas, Minnesota, Nebraska, Missouri, Ohio, Wisconsin, Tennessee, Idaho, Kentucky, Vermont, Rhode Island, Louisiana, Virginia, Illinois* and *Georgia*. Colliers from Newport News, Virginia, had arrived ten days before to coal the ships. The flagship of the Royal Australian Navy, HMS *Powerful*, put in to port to welcome the fleet and liaise for the Australian visit. A local poet, W. Farmer Whyte, was moved to write:

> *Welcome! a hearty welcome. Hear*
> *The march of the tramping feet!*
> *We have come in our thousands from far and near*
> *To welcome the Great White Fleet!*
> *We have shouted you welcome and here's our hand,*
> *For the sake of the ties that bind!*
> *Though ye come to our shores from a distant land,*
> *Yet our hearts are intertwined.*

The fleet spent a week in Auckland during a 40,000-mile round-the-world tour to demonstrate the strength and mobility of America's growing naval power. Thousands of sailors, 15,000 in fact, swarmed ashore to taste the delights of New Zealand oysters, hot buckwheat, graham cakes, griddlecakes and soda biscuits, or to lean against the bars and order, not a pint or a half handle, but their Horses' Necks, Brain Dusters, Southerly Busters, or Bosom Caressers. There was deer and wallaby culling on Motutapu and Kawau Islands, and a ball at Government House. Admiral Sperry and a party of two hundred paid a visit to Rotorua. The united temperance societies arranged an evening in the Choral Hall of songs, recitations, weightlifting, and an address on the temptations of the Devil confronting the American sailors. About thirty arrived to get the message, but the local bars were a sell out. Two thousand Americans were introduced to rugby at Alexandra Park, and those who could tear themselves away from the girls and the bars, open in those years at night, could experience the doubtful merits of a drama at His Majesty's entitled *When Knights Were Bold*. The fleet left on 15 August for Sydney and then the Far East.

New Zealand was to wait until August 1925 for another such visit, when Admiral Robinson with his grey squadron of capital ships put

The USS *Connecticut*, flagship of the Great White Fleet which visited New Zealand in 1908. A junior officer in the fleet was Lieutenant W. F. Halsey, later in World War II to be Vice-Admiral W. F. ('Bull') Halsey.
Auckland Museum Library

down anchor in Auckland Harbour. This time they were modern battle-ships like the USS *Idaho* and *Missouri*, whose Old Glories fluttered at the stern of the quarter decks. Both hearts and Old Glories fluttered when the US sailors in their pork-pie hats stepped ashore. Again the USA was showing the flag, to remind New Zealand, Australia and the Far East (the Near East today) that it too had a coastline that bordered the Pacific Ocean.

Up until the late 1930s the American influence was imported with Hollywood films, pop songs and their purveyors like Bing Crosby and Frank Sinatra, jazz, and some radio soaps with Mr Watanabe or Gracie Allen and George Burns and other comics. The American luxury liners *Mariposa* and *Monterey*, sometimes the *Matsonia* or the *Lurline*, with their yellow and blue funnels and white hulls, were very familiar sights to Aucklanders because of their regular visits. Pan Am had just pioneered air routes down to the South Pacific. One of their planes went missing, and its pilot, Captain Edwin Musick, gave his name to Musick Point in the Waitemata Harbour. Most of the high-powered, roomy cars imported into this country, such as Ford, Chevrolet, Buick, Packard, Reo and Cadillac, were American.

Perhaps the most noted American visitor in the late twenties and early thirties was big-game fisherman Zane Grey. He was a writer of

11

soaps of the American Golden West, and his romances would have been read by thousands of New Zealanders. For many years he made an annual pilgrimage to the Bay of Islands or Whangaroa Harbour to catch the largest striped marlin ever, camping at what he called the 'Camp of Larks' at Otehei Bay on Urupukapuka Island. But most Americans seen in those days were from cruise ships and on safari to the main tourist areas of Rotorua and the Waitomo Caves.

For many New Zealanders in the early 1940s, America would have seemed a blend of myth, fable and fantasy land. The US might well have appeared as a land of residual frontier images, emanating from the days when the youth of this country would have read Zane Grey, Mark Twain, F. Scott Fitzgerald and Fenimore Cooper's books *The Last of the Mohicans*, *The Deerslayer* and *The Pathfinder*. Those stories of the American frontiersman saw him as soldier, woodsman, guide, friend of Indian braves and scourge of the Indian 'varmints'. Southern Americans came from a horse culture, where in colonial times the only military establishment was a rifle by the fireside. (There was even a cavalry unit on Bataan in the Philippines in 1942. Was there really a place for cavalry then? Said a colonel, 'They used 'em [horses] on Bataan, didn't they; they ate 'em.')

The songs of the day reflected the yearning of the American to get back to his roots, to be at one with nature. The lone star ranger — a repetitive character in New Zealand literature too — is depicted as the knight errant out on the prairie, vying with the baying of the coyotes. He appeared in songs like 'Home on the Range', 'I'm Headin' for the Last Round-Up', 'Wagon Wheels', 'There's a Bridle Hanging on the Wall', 'Deep in the Heart of Texas', and 'Don't Fence Me In'. Songs of regional nostalgia and the cool jazz of the forties reflected the sequence of folk experience in American history with the road gang songs, the cotton-picking songs, cowboy songs, trail and plantation songs, the hill-billies, the spiritual and the sinfuls, the blues of Billie Holliday and others, and the badman frontier songs like, 'Roll me over easy, roll me over slow, roll me over on my right side cause my left side hurts me so.'

Naturally, Americans and New Zealanders approached each other with certain preconceptions, some of which were based on history, and some perhaps on fiction. The difference in temperament between the two was not only evident in the relations between the sexes. What we knew about each other reflected in some sense the nature of each country's national identity and pride.

The average New Zealander's knowledge of his own country's history was, and frequently still is, so sparse as to be negligible. It is arguable that, in the 1940s, we knew more about American history than we did about our own; the average American's knowledge of New Zealand history, on the other hand, was nonexistent. New Zealanders could watch Hollywood Westerns, steeped in the names of Indian tribes like the Sioux, Cheyenne, Iroquois or Cree. The stories they told had much in common with New Zealand's history of the Maori wars, of Rangiriri, Ruapekapeka, of Te Kooti and Hone Heke. Yet little interest was shown by New Zealanders in their own pioneering past.

It was as if New Zealanders did not have a set of references, were not conscious of their heritage and so looked beyond their own frontier to another country for a set of values. Back in the 1920s schoolchildren saluted the flag once a week. (The flag may have been represented by two crossed Union Jacks on the painted tongue-and-groove classroom wall and not, it is noted, the New Zealand flag.) Even the name ANZAC had its shared connotation which tended to deny New Zealand a singular identity.

How many New Zealand boys and girls back in the twenties and thirties had to stand at their desks in the classroom and declaim that Whittier poem of the American Civil War, 'Barbara Frietchie', about the old girl who hung the Union flag from her window as General Stonewall Jackson rode by?

> *Up from the meadows rich with corn*
> *Clear in the cool September morn,*
> *The clustered spires of Frederick stand*
> *Green-walled by the hills of Maryland . . .*
> *Up the street came the rebel tread,*
> *Stonewall Jackson riding ahead . . .*
> *'Shoot if you must, this old gray head,*
> *But spare your country's flag,' she said . . .*
> *'Who touches a hair on yon gray head*
> *Dies like a dog! March on' he said.*

How incongruous the emphasis on foreign history, and the muted accent on our own. Who can blame the teachers if there were no balladeers or versifiers to tell about New Zealand's frontier days? American educationists, on the other hand, push American history from day one. Small wonder that US citizens are bursting with nationalistic pride, while New Zealanders, in part because of this appalling lack of historical knowledge, show little fervour.

Americans could dismiss New Zealand in a line. Many, if not most, had not heard of the country when arriving here in the early days of 1942. 'Orstralya', yes — 'Noo Zillund', no. Mind you, if you had some academic training it was far better to keep your head down, show yourself to be 'iggerant', rather than incur the ire of some 'topkick' of a sergeant who had spent time on the China Station and whose education had probably not advanced beyond grade school.

With the American War of Independence in mind, the idea that New Zealand was under the yoke of an England which took its taxes and exploited its resources died hard with some of the visitors. Those red splashes around the globe which indicated the influence of the British Crown could only indicate, in American eyes, a lack of independence. American servicemen were particularly derogatory about trade union practices in New Zealand, of men working to rule, declining to work in the rain, and spelling on the wharves, while conveniently forgetting that America had labour problems of its own at times.

New Zealanders and Americans have certain factors in common. Their beginnings were imbued with a colonial frontier spirit, their forebears were refugees from the Old World the 'Old Dart' to the New, many had British ancestry, their societies lacked a rigid class system, and their first generation was usually reared on the Bible. The germ of New Zealand's innate conservatism probably lay in the origins of its citizens. The majority of the first British migrants came from the dispossessed classes of a kingdom in which a tiny élite owned practically everything. They came here not with any crusading ideals, but because they saw a chance of grabbing a bigger share for themselves. This perhaps explains that free-enterprising streak in New Zealanders. A similar motivation could be attributed to the millions of migrants, who, economic castaways in their homelands, made their way to the New World of the United States near the turn of the century and later. New Zealanders need to remember that there are large parts of America where colonisation took place no earlier than it did in New Zealand. And the similarities are often surprising as one Auckland woman remembers when going to the pictures with a Marine in 1943. At the end, as was the custom, 'God Save the King' was played. Said the Marine, 'Why are they playing our anthem?' She explained the music was that of the national anthem of those times. The tune is the same as another favourite national song of the US, 'My country 'tis of thee, Sweet land of liberty, Of thee I sing'.

The New Zealand society that the American invaders of the 1940s found had latterly emerged from a depression, but the residual trammels of a pioneering society were still evident. At co-educational schools — and they would have been single sex if the economy could have afforded it — girls were forbidden to talk to the boys, to walk home with them or have conversations with them on street corners. The single-sex approach to human relationships in schools for adolescents led to unnatural attitudes for both boys and girls. There was a mystique about the opposite sex for pupils, which had still to be plumbed.

At country dances ('hops') the segregated situation of the schools could well be echoed, with all the 'sheilas' sitting down round the walls of the hall, and all the boys crowding together at the entrance. When the country 'combo' struck up for a foxtrot, the men moved like the surf coming in towards the girl of their choice. At a private party the men might well be out in the kitchen round a keg of beer, while the girls

14

made small talk in the lounge.

A very different sort of segregation occurred at times in Warkworth when the Marines were there. Una, a farmer's wife then, remembers: 'Married women on farms were desperate for music, for dancing, for some entertainment in their drab lives during those war years. When the Americans arrived it was an opportunity not to be monopolised by single girls, no sir. The Kiwi husbands, no great exponents of the light fantastic, tolerant, long suffering, or both, were prevailed upon to drive their wives in to the local dance, whereupon they would retire below stage to play cards with their mates and leave it to their wives to get on with it with the Yanks on the dance floor.' What the male conversation below stage was about, one might well imagine.

For some girls it would have been a new kind of wooing, for others their first and only. Girls aged sixteen at the beginning of the war suffered from an almost manless society. No wonder then, when thousands of Prince Charmings steamed over the horizon and into Auckland and Wellington harbours, the women could hardly believe their eyes. There would have been hundreds of girls whose first date was with an American.

This then was the New Zealand the Americans knew: dull (in part because of wartime conditions), egalitarian, an intimate society where one did not step out of line, and where most who left school early were defiantly anti-intellectual, where the values of friendliness and warmth were demonstrated in the small towns, which felt threatened by non-conformist ideas. It was a 'his' and 'hers' society, with Mum in her 'cardy' producing the hot buttered scones, and pipe-smoking Dad in the background in waistcoat and collarless shirt adding his grunts of communication. It could well be a place where the liveliest spot in town for the Americans was the YWCA, and in Auckland to dine à la carte was to patronise the Pie Cart down by the Ferry Buildings, where the house special was a couple of sausages floated on a cloud of mashed potatoes, surrounded by a moat of gravy and tinned peas. The boozy camaraderie of the pub ended at six o'clock and thereafter it was the movies or cruising the pavements. There were only non-representative rugby contests, and the issue of racism was not yet publicly acknowledged. Sex, judging by the printed media, with never a page-three nude, barely existed (but the Americans knew better). It was a land where farmers were called 'cockies' and the girls 'sheilas', 'hooray' meant goodbye, to be 'crook' was to be sick, 'roll-yer-owns' were the sign of a real Kiwi bloke, while 'tailormades' were a drawing-room affectation, where a habitual drunk was a 'piss-pot' and where the average New Zealander was 'a good bloke'.

The archetypal New Zealand male had evolved long before the onset of World War II. The role was, in large measure, a product of the pioneering times, when women were scarce, and it was reinforced by the macho status of rugby, where togetherness in a scrum bound one to one's mates. The steam rising on a cold winter's morning from a rugby scrum desperately cobbled together was a sign of masculinity denied to soccer and hockey players. Standing on the sidelines, divorced from the action, were the women.

Americans, encouraged in linguistic skills at school, tended to be more articulate than the average Kiwi joker. The silent 'Man Alone' New Zealand male, suspicious of language, talk and books, contrasted strongly with the fast-talking servicemen from bustling American cities.

Another element in the Americans' success was their deference to New Zealand women, a cultivated obeisance accompanied by flowers and a taxi at the door. Perhaps the American reverence for 'Mom' provides a clue to the origins of this behaviour. In big cities, suburbs and small towns the American father accepted diminished authority in order to devote time to making it outside the home. By default, 'Mom' became the head of the family and assumed the mantle of power. Since 'Mom' was the chief socialising agent, along with her son's usually female schoolteacher, the American boy could come to identify moral codes with women. Some were to find the transition from mother-sheltered families to the realities of an all-male army world too traumatic.

Love in America was charged with the power and violence of the acquisitive drive. The boy was expected to make advances, to boast of his prowess and exult in his conquests. The girl was expected to yield just enough to keep her partner interested, yet to withhold the final sexual favour. Such was the background of the men who hit Auckland and Wellington in the war years in search of women.

An American Marine Corps nurse in Wellington in the war years said, 'I am sure that half these cases of New Zealand girls being let down badly by our boys would never have happened if your girls had not been so credulous. They don't understand when an American man is ribbing or kidding them, just as British humour sometimes fools us. On such decisions I would say that the average American girl has a much keener intuition than your girls and has a come-back for every situation.' A New Zealand soldier in Italy asked a local girl in the profession what she thought of New Zealand men. 'Too shy when they're sober, too rough when they're drunk.'

'New Zealand girls are too sweet and not demanding enough of their menfolk,' said a Marine who, in peacetime, was on the staff of one of the large American daily papers. 'You give us the impression that you have no minds of your own. Our wives and girlfriends demand what they want, and I think that we respect them all the more for it. I do know that the average American woman does not work nearly as hard as you New Zealanders.'

It was the brashness, the hands-on approach (in more ways than one) that got up some New Zealand noses. It was a head-on collision between two cultures, the hang back wait-till-you're-introduced stuffiness of an English upbringing, and the couldn't-give-a-stuff approach of the Yanks. The transposition of English mores was more than even Lady Diana Duff-Cooper, that doyenne of the English aristocracy, could stomach when she visited New Zealand just before the outbreak of war. She wrote, 'Their patriotism was touching, their gentility painful, I suppose they were happy, but I couldn't bear it. Oh for a touch of honest vulgarity.' The American boys gave New Zealanders plenty of the latter. It was opulent vulgarity, when sometimes they would have been seen, in true soldier's slang, as 'pissed as a private on parade', and on other occasions echoing Ophelia's speech to Hamlet 'the glass of fashion and the mould of form, the observed of all the observers'. It was a dosage New Zealand deserved to jolt it out of its mediocrity.

Down in the Pacific the 3rd Division New Zealand Army boys met and worked with the Americans, unloaded their ships, moved their heavy 40-gallon drums of gas around, pinched their stores, wore their American-made uniforms, ate their Thanksgiving Day and Independence Day turkeys, enjoyed their outdoor movies, drank with them and swapped tales about New Zealand, listened to stories about easy New Zealand girls. The thieving by New Zealanders was reputedly chronic. Except beer — beer was sacrosanct. Pinch typewriters, jungle hammocks, clothes, boots; but beer was a no-no. There was little if any resentment towards the Americans from the New Zealand boys in the Pacific, only envy of the vast resources of Uncle Sam. The Americans were generous to a fault, and if the occasional New Zealand soldier received a 'Dear John' letter, that was only to be expected. New Zealand soldiers were known to stand in the queue at the Pink House brothel in Nouméa and sell their places to those Americans who had more urgent desires.

Here is how an American writer of the time described New Zealand men:

> The New Zealander was friendly, of good taste, and conservative in speech and manner. He enjoyed simple pleasures and preferred fine music to tasty food. The New Zealand soldiers were courteous, friendly lads, dressed in conservative woollen battledress with black shoes, humbly proud of their own fighting record in the war, and always accepting the Yank boasts with equanimity and patience.

The arrival of the American troops here in 1942 was in part a culture shock, but New Zealanders over the years had, through the shared fantasies of the Hollywood dream machine, been subjected to the incremental influence of the American way of life. The 'invaders' served

Hotel Cecil, Wellington, Headquarters for the American Red Cross. The Marines living it up and drinking it down at the milk bar. Present also, one New Zealand soldier, and one New Zealand airman. Note the prices! *Gordon Burt Collection, Alexander Turnbull Library*

to reinforce what New Zealanders had suspected. The ordinary house-holders stood agape at the size of the expedition; and they were always impressed by the generosity of the servicemen. It was stick chewing gum for the kids as they stood on the second rail of the farm gate waiting for the school bus, and cigarettes for the adults. New Zealanders living in an austere world of rationing saw that nothing was done on the cheap. New Zealand might order a gross, the US would order in the thousands. If it was a hospital, it would take hundreds of wounded; if it was stores, they would equip a division of 15,000 men. Cornwall Hospital (the 39th General) in Cornwall Park was as big as Auckland Hospital at the time, comprising 172 buildings, 350,000 square feet spread over eight acres. It made provision for 1500 patients. Out at Hobson Park, where steel fabrication was introduced to New Zealand, buildings equal to the floor area of the 39th General were constructed. It is estimated that warehouses to the equivalent of four million square feet were built to contain stores. Down on the wharves watersiders, assisted by 'seagulls', unloaded incredible quantities of supplies from Liberty ships. US Military Police on duty at the wharves had the occasional confrontations with watersiders accused of pilfering, but Jock Barnes, the watersiders' leader, was on hand to defuse the situation.

New Zealand must have felt dwarfed by the scale of operations, by the thousands of drums of petrol, the huge ammunition dumps, the constant grinding of heavy army vehicles carting stores day and night, the armadas of ships in Auckland and Wellington harbours, and the troops winding their way in single file, sometimes a couple of kilometres long, over the back country. How could the Allies lose the war, with the USA as an ally and its gargantuan resources? The status of the troops in the eyes of the public reflected the image of a very wealthy and powerful Uncle Sam.

New Zealanders grew used to the sight of Americans driving clapped-out cars, riding sit-up-and-beg bicycles, of the locals in American servicemen's clothing, of cars with their mudguards painted white so that they could be seen in the black-out, shop windows criss-crossed with sticky tape in case of air raids, jeeps galore (driven sometimes by New Zealand girls in American uniforms), and posters with cautionary messages such as 'Zip up your mouth'. Some Marines may have heard Dinah Shore singing 'You'd be so nice to come home to' in their adopted homes, but with the use of the family car and even breakfast in bed, they may have been forgiven for thinking they had already arrived in the promised land. In Wellington's Cecil Club, where countless romances blossomed, you could get real coffee, hamburgers and cheeseburgers, and breakfast on dry cereals unobtainable in New Zealand with the thickest yellowest cream in the land — all this for 25 cents American — and read the quaint newspapers with ads on the front page. 'It's probably raining now in Wellington, certainly the wind's blowing,' wrote back a Marine from the South Pacific, 'but I would give anything to be walking into the Cecil Club.'

CHAPTER TWO

Send in the Troops

A new generation of New Zealanders might well ask 'Why were the American troops here at all back in the 1940s?' For fifteen months after the declaration of war on 3 September 1939, Britain and her allies soldiered on alone in a defensive role against the Germans. American isolationists propounded the 'fortress' doctrine — arm and stay inside. A sympathetic President Franklin D. Roosevelt made fifty mothballed World War I destroyers available on a Lease-Lend arrangement, though he was not without his isolationist critics.

Then one catastrophic event changed the whole scene. The aerial bombing of Pearl Harbour, Hawaii, on Sunday 7 December 1941, and with it the destruction of a major portion of the US Pacific Fleet, brought an immediate declaration of war on Germany and Japan.

On the same day that the Japanese launched that attack from their aircraft carriers on an unsuspecting naval command in Hawaii, an equally surprised Malaya awoke to find the Japanese had landed on the Malayan Peninsula and were about to move south towards Singapore. Their possession of air bases in French Indo-China (Vietnam) gave them complete mastery of the air. On 10 December their torpedo bombers sank the 'unsinkable' British warships HMS *Prince of Wales* and *Repulse*, newly arrived from England. Churchill on receiving the news said, 'I never received a more direct shock.'

By Christmas Day, Hong Kong had fallen into Japanese hands. But more was in store for an already shocked British public, and also, this time, for an Australian and New Zealand public. Singapore, that much lauded impregnable bastion of imperial might, surrendered on 15 February to its Japanese invaders. Those massive guns which pointed out to sea had proved useless. Unexpectedly, the Japanese forces had chosen to move down through the apparently impenetrable jungles of the Malayan Peninsula, on foot and bicycles. To save unnecessary slaughter, the Allied Command marched across the causeway at Singapore to surrender to an exultant Japanese High Command. Lost was a pivotal stronghold of Allied power, along with many reputations, and discredited were the entrenched Whitehall theories of defence in depth. The Singapore guns remained mute. Ironically, at least one eight-inch gun was removed by the Japanese, and taken to Tarawa in the Gilbert Islands, where it was used to fire on the invading forces of the 2nd US Marine Division and the naval support fleet.

It was part of Japan's overall global strategy that Australia, when invaded and captured, was to become part of the Greater East Asia Prosperity Sphere, together with New Caledonia, Fiji, and Samoa. Should this come to pass, New Zealand could only be ripe for the plucking. General MacArthur was ordered by Washington to leave Bataan in the Philippines and make his headquarters in Australia. He arrived there on 18 March 1942. At that time in Canberra there was talk of withdrawing to the 'Brisbane Line' and abandoning the northern parts of Australia to the Japanese. The position was desperate. 'It was', MacArthur was to write later, 'my greatest shock and surprise of the whole war.' The Japanese, MacArthur said, had no word for defeat. On the offensive they were unstoppable, but on the defensive they were vulnerable. He compared their inflexibility to a fist which cannot loosen its grasp once it has seized something: 'A hand that closes never to open again is useless when the fighting turns to catch-as-catch-can wrestling.' But strategy for the average combat man did not mean a great deal. They were to be given an immediate objective, to land and destroy the enemy. If they knew nothing about New Guinea, New Ireland, the Solomons, the New Hebrides, Bougainville, New Britain or New Caledonia, New Zealanders knew very little more.

After the battle of Pearl Harbour came that of the Straits of Macassar, a naval defeat for the Allies. It gave the Japanese complete control of the Pacific for four months, during which time they conquered the greater part of the East Indies, the Philippines, and New Guinea, and kept the Allies guessing as to her next objective, whether it was to be Australia, India, or China.

Considerable political manoeuvring went on at that time in the upper echelons of the American Command in the Pacific, especially by that wily egocentric genius General MacArthur. He was extremely jealous of any commander encroaching on his territory, which was that sphere of operations west of the 159th meridian of longitude. This left the invasion of Japanese-held Guadalcanal to the US Navy under the overall command of Admiral Halsey, under whom came the Marine Corps. After that, every operation on land and sea west of Guadalcanal on the way to the Japanese homeland came under MacArthur's command.

The Australian Government, confronted with a possible Japanese invasion, decided to bring the two Middle East divisions home from North Africa. Whereas before it had been the sands of the deserts in their boots, now for the Aussies it was to be the mud and morass of the Kokoda Trail over the Owen Stanley Range in New Guinea. President Franklin D. Roosevelt approved of sending a Marine Corps division to New Zealand, provided the New Zealand Government agreed to leave its division in the Middle East. It was probably never envisaged that New Zealand would be a 'fall back' area and that fighting would actually take place on our shores. Given the mighty production

Tuneful tubas of the US Marine Corps Band (2nd Division) Sergeant Charles H. Flair (left) and Private First Class Claude Devers are the two Marines coaxing sweet music from their sousaphones. Wellington 1 May 1943. *Evening Post*

machine of the US, the transition from a passive to an active role did not take very long. Soon Henry J. Kaiser was rolling out thousands of his Liberty cargo ships of 7,176 tons from his Californian shipyards. It took 245 days to assemble the first ship's 30,000 components, but in one spectacular stunt, the USS *Robert E. Peary*, paint still wet, was launched four days and fifteen hours after keel laying. Thousands of Kaiser's female workers, Rosie the Riveters, as they were called, made this gigantic steel pre-fabrication production possible. Kaiser had known nothing about shipbuilding, and spoke of the 'front' and 'back' ends of the ship. 'I don't care what he calls 'em,' said Roosevelt, 'as long as he delivers.'

When, on 15 February 1942, the Japanese captured Singapore, into the bag went (among others) 13,000 Australians of the 8th Division. Four days later Darwin was attacked by Japanese high-level bombers. In forty minutes the town was almost destroyed. The hospital ship *Manunda* sustained a direct hit, the civilian hospital was all but demolished, the post office blown to bits. There were bodies in the bomb shelters, bodies blown into the mangrove swamps. Two hours later, fifty-four bombers came back and obliterated the RAAF aerodrome. There were 250 dead, 350 wounded.

Not only did Britain no longer rule the waves, but Australia had been blasted out of the skies. American pilots flying Kittyhawk fighters failed to achieve height quickly enough to combat the bombers. A stunned Australia reeled under the news, which the politicians deliberately played down. The two Australian infantry divisions were now home from the Middle East. Prime Minister John Curtin had refused Churchill's request to divert them to the Burma campaign. Australia's security came first, he said. By May 1942 there were 88,000 American troops in Australia, some of whom had originally been en route to the Philippines to reinforce MacArthur's beleaguered forces. The Japanese blockade, fortunately for them, prevented their passage north. Rockhampton and Townsville were taken over by the Americans for naval bases and R & R.

Then one Monday morning, 8 June 1942, some Sydneysiders got the shock of their lives. Six three-inch shells dropped out of the skies into the exclusive suburbs of Rose Bay and Bellevue Hill. The enthusiastic Commander Kiyoi Ageta of the Japanese submarine I-24 had had the impertinence to lay off the Sydney Heads and remind some affluent Sydney residents that they were at war. Naturally there was much toing and froing, not to say panic. But Sydney had already been reminded of the Japanese presence, because a week before, three Japanese midget submarines manned by suicide crews of two had breeched the boom defence in Sydney Harbour with varied results. One went through the magnetic loop indicator (cable loops laid on the sea bed to detect the presence, through disturbance of the magnetic field, of some foreign metal object), but then got entangled in a steel net. The crew self-

23

destructed the submarine and themselves. The second was damaged by depth charges, so much so that her two torpedoes became jammed in their tubes. The crew shot themselves. A diver went down and found the engine still running, the screw still turning. The third midget sub scored some success when its commander fired his torpedo at the heavy cruiser USS *Chicago*. It missed, but exploded beneath an Australian depot ship HMAS *Kuttabul*, killing 19 men. On the outward passage lucky Sub-Lieutenant Katsuhisa Ban again went through the magnetic loop indicator.

Within a week of these events, both Wellington and Auckland awoke to find some strangers within their gates — the Americans.

It is possible to identify in broad terms those particular American units which were in New Zealand and the areas in which they were camped. First it is necessary to be *au fait* with the military nomenclature of the Marine Corps. The structure and naming conventions of Marine Corps units changed several times during the war years (as they have done since). But at the time they were in New Zealand, a Marine division comprised three infantry regiments, one engineer regiment, one artillery regiment, and supporting special weapons and service battalions. Certain support services such as tanks or raider battalions could be attached for specific operations.

Infantry regiments (the New Zealand equivalent would be a brigade), commanded by a full colonel, comprised three battalions, each commanded by a lieutenant colonel. Artillery regiments were composed of three medium-gun battalions and one heavy-gun battalion, while engineer regiments comprised one engineer battalion, one pioneer battalion and one naval construction battalion. In those war years two battalions in the division were staffed by Navy personnel, and they were the medical battalions and the naval construction battalions or 'Seabees'. Sometimes the term 'triangular division' was used in reference to US units having three regiments, but the term was probably academic and used mostly in staff circles. Conversationally a Marine might identify himself as being in the '8th Marines', or 'One-eight' (meaning '1st Division 8th Regiment'), or '2nd MarDiv', or even '2nd Divvy'. It should be noted that the battalions and regiments within American Divisions (including the Marine Corps) do not follow in numerical order. The establishment of a typical US Army division is shown in the Appendix as for the 43rd Division.

There were six divisions of combat servicemen in New Zealand from 1942 to 1944. The only US land forces in Wellington were elements of 1 MarDiv (and then only briefly), and later the full complement of 2 MarDiv. Thus Wellingtonians knew only the Marines, not soldiers of the US Army divisions. In addition there was a constant stream of Navy

US Marine tanks parade down Lambton Quay, Wellington, 1943, as part of a
Liberty Loan procession. *John Pascoe Collection, Alexander Turnbull Library*

men in and out of the port. In the greater Auckland area were camped
the 37th US Army Division, 3 MarDiv, the 25th US Army Division and
the 43rd US Army Division.

Most of the 1st Marine Corps Division (under Major General A. Vandegrift) was in Wellington and the lower North Island area from 14
June until 22 July 1942. The regiments here were the 1st, 5th and 11th
(Artillery) but not the 7th, which was in Samoa. Camps included those
at McKay's Crossing, Camp Russell, Paekakariki, and many Marines
were at Hutt Park, home of the Wellington Trotting Club. This division
remained in Wellington only briefly, and having left New Zealand
shores, it never returned.

Certain units of the 2nd Marine Division (under Major General J.

Marston until 1 May 1943, thereafter under Major General Julian Smith) were in the Wellington area from November to December 1942, prior to going to the Guadalcanal campaign. They were the 6th Marines, 10th Marines (2nd Battalion only), 18th Marines (Companies C, E and F only), 2nd Medical Battalion (Company A only), 2nd Special Weapons Battalion (Battery C only) and the 2nd Tank Battalion (Company A only). Other regiments of this division did not come to New Zealand before being involved in the Guadalcanal fighting. The 2nd Marines sailed straight from San Diego to the Solomons via Fiji, as did the 8th Marines (with an additional stop at Samoa). The 6th Marines had been at McKay's Crossing in 1942. With the end of the fighting in Guadalcanal, all units of 2 MarDiv were in New Zealand by 1 March 1943.

The disposition of the Marines in 1943 was as follows: the 8th Marines (Infantry), Paekakariki; 2nd Marines (Infantry), Camp Russell; 6th Marines (Infantry), McKay's Crossing; Special Weapons Battalion, 2nd Tank Battalion, 2nd Parachute Battalion, and Scout Company, Titahi Bay. The 18th Engineers established Moonshine Camp in Judgeford Valley and the 10th Marines (Artillery) were at Pauatahanui, eighteen miles out of Wellington. In addition there was a multiplicity of service units scattered throughout Wellington city, with a receiving

Two US camps in the Auckland Domain, one in front of the Auckland Museum, the other near Carlton Gore Road. *P. W. Dept*

26

A typical US Army outpost with two- and four-men huts. State Highway 1 winds away to Wellsford and the North. *Tudor Collins*

camp at Central Park and hospitals at Anderson Park and Silverstream. There were recuperation and training camps at Solway Park and the Memorial Grounds in Masterton.

The 3rd Marine Corps Division (under Major General Charles D. Barrett) was officially activated on 16 September 1942 at Camp Elliott, San Diego, California, and was built round the 9th Marine Regiment, whose commanding officer, Colonel Lemuel C. Shepherd Jr, was later to become well known to Pukekohe residents. The division moved from San Diego to Auckland, and by early March 1943 most of the elements of the force, except for the 3rd Marine Regiment, were in their camps in the greater Auckland and Warkworth areas. Making up the division were three infantry regiments, the 3rd, 9th and 21st, an artillery regiment (the 12th) and an engineer regiment (the 19th). Special troops with the division were 3rd Headquarters Battalion, 3rd Parachute Battalion, 3rd Tank Battalion, 3rd Special Weapons Battalion, 3rd Service Battalion, 3rd Medical Battalion, and the 3rd Amphibian Tractor Battalion. The 9th Regiment (under Colonel L. Shepherd) and the 3rd Regiment (under Colonel O. R. Cauldwell) were in the Pukekohe and Auckland areas, and the 21st Regiment (under Colonel E. O.

Regimental Headquarters 169th Infantry, 43rd Division, Wilson Road, Warkworth, 1943. *Tudor Collins*

Ames) was in camps in the Warkworth area. The 19th Regiment (Engineers), commanded by Colonel R. M. Montague, was camped at Waikaraka Park, Auckland. The 19th Regiment was involved in the construction of Mob 6 Hospital, Cornwall Park, and also helped lay out the Cambria Park camp for the 3rd Marines. Elements of the 12th Artillery Regiment were in Warkworth, and so too was the 3rd Tank Battalion. The 3rd Amphibian Tractor Battalion was camped near the water at Whangateau, near Warkworth. In Whangarei, in camps previously occupied by New Zealand home defence troops, were further batteries of the 12th Marines Artillery Regiment. These camps were at Three Mile Bush and Maungatapere.

The 43rd Division US Army (under Major General Leonard Wing) arrived in Auckland on 22 October 1942. It camped in the greater Auckland area, with some units at Warkworth. The 192nd Field Artillery was at Hilldene, 152nd Field Artillery with the 103rd Infantry Regiment at Mangere Crossing, and the 169th Field Artillery Battalion and 169th Infantry Battalion at Warkworth. The 103rd Field Artillery was at Cambria Park, Puhinui. The division came to New Zealand twice: first in late October 1942, when it stayed only a few weeks in

Papakura Military Camp and surrounding areas, with some units in Warkworth, and again in March 1944, when it remained for around four months. The 152nd FA Battalion and the 103rd Infantry Regiment were in Warkworth for their second stay in New Zealand.

The 25th US Army Division (under Major General J. Lawton Collins) was camped in the greater Auckland area and Warkworth from 7 December 1943 to 24 February 1944. General Collins later became a corps commander in the war in Europe, followed by the appointment as chief of staff in the war in Korea. The division establishment comprised three regiments: the 27th Infantry Regiment (Wolfhound), the 35th Infantry (Cacti) and the 161st Infantry Regiment (National Guard). The first two were permanent units within the American forces. In the Auckland area the troops were mainly camped in the Papakura Military Camp, Cambria Camp, Puhinui, and the Pukekohe-Tuakau area. The 25th Division of 10,227 officers and men was reinforced by 5000 men by the end of February 1944. The establishment of the full division is shown in the Appendix.

The 145th Regiment of the 37th US Army Division, from Ohio, was the first US Army infantry unit to arrive in the South Pacific. These were also the first US Army men (as opposed to Marines) to come to New Zealand. There were several changes of plan, for initially the Advance Detachment of the Division set out for Melbourne on 20 April 1942. Then the commanding general, Major General Robert Beightler, was informed of a change of destination to the Fijian Islands. While the division was southbound for Fiji, ships carrying the 145th Regiment and auxiliary troops and their escorts received orders to divert to Auckland. Fiji was unable to accommodate the full division until such time as occupying New Zealand forces were repatriated to form the nucleus of the 3rd Division 2 NZEF.

The main body of the 37th, in the *President Coolidge* escorted by HMS *Leander* and two American destroyers, arrived at Suva on 10 June. (It was the *President Coolidge* that was to shuttle the Kiwis in Fiji back to New Zealand, and later return the Americans to man the sectors vacated by the New Zealanders.) The Advance Detachment had travelled from Melbourne to Auckland in late May. The convoy carrying the 145th passed down the Rangitoto Channel at twilight on 12 June 1942.

The 145th Infantry Regiment and division artillery command posts went into barracks at the Papakura Military Camp, the 1st Battalion 145th to Manurewa, the 2nd Battalion to Pukekohe racecourse, and the 3rd Battalion to Camp Karaka North. The 37th Signal Company settled in at Camp Orford, Manurewa, Companies B and C of the 117th Engineers Battalion went to Camp Hilldene, the 637th Tank Destroyer Battalion bivouacked at Camp Helvetia, and the 135th Field Artillery were at Camp Opaheke. For the 37th it was a very brief introduction

Uniform, summer style of a US Army man, 1943. It was the done thing for NZ girls to acquire and wear the green jackets. *Tudor Collins*

A Technical Sergeant of the US Army in his win uniform. Most young Americans were overseas. wonder American women complained that the remaining men 'were either too old or too grassy green'. *Tudor Collins*

to New Zealand, where (as one described it) they 'bulled, wined and dined'. The acquaintance was not to be renewed, except for those men sent back to hospitals in New Zealand. On 25 June 1942 the *President Coolidge* embarked 3199 officers and men and 60 nurses for Fiji. It returned on 31 July to take on board the last of the 37th Division.

If there is any dispute as to which was the first body of combat troops to come to New Zealand, it could be noted that the USS *Uruguay*, as part of a convoy from New York carrying over 13,000 American troops, bound first for Melbourne, ran short of water in the Pacific. Together with the USS *Santa Paula*, the *Uruguay* put into Auckland to take on water on 3 April 1942. The ships sailed next day, no troops being allowed ashore during docking.

Whether there were black American troops in New Zealand has been disputed in some quarters. There were no blacks in the 43rd Division and the 25th Division, but some did come in as reinforcements to Marine Corps units towards the end of the war. The 43rd Division in

Guadalcanal in January–February 1943 was relieved before coming to New Zealand by the 93rd US Army Division, whose officers (except for majors and above) and men were black. It is said that as fighting men, blacks had the reputation of being 'good in reverse'. This observation is not borne out by their heroism, as shown in Saipan. Bill, who was stationed in Wellington, recalls the attitudes of the Marines at the time.

Did we have negroes in the ranks? Yes, but for a start they were work troops used in the setting up of camps, driving trucks and that sort of duty. Later on, as in Saipan, they were back-up forces to the forward troops. They were not expected to fight, but if they were called upon to do so they sure got stuck in. Early on they were led by white officers. When news came to our outfit in Wellington that negroes had arrived as part of the Corps, a couple of Texans in our outfit blew their tops, reckoning they would hang them from the barn door. The Marine Corps was for the élite — no negroes. As northerners we could not have cared less, we were used to negroes, but not so the southerners. Today of course there are thousands of blacks in the Corps, many with officer status who command white troops, But back in those days they were usually on work details *and* segregated from the whites.

There would have been black patients in American hospitals in the Auckland and Wellington areas, but, 'I can't recall seeing negroes in the servicemen's clubs I attended,' says Joan, 'and that included the Catholic Servicemen's Club, the Catholic Seamen's Club and the Flying Angels Mission to Seamen. At the latter club we danced with them all, Indians, Lascars, all colours, and where they came from I would not know. It was an immutable rule of all servicemen's clubs, that if you were asked to dance, you did not decline. Another rule was you did not go home with a servicemen. As a war bride I was travelling by train across the States and a negro porter said to me, "You from Australia?" "No, New Zealand." "Negro troops were not allowed ashore in Australia," he replied.' There *were* black troops in Australia, however, and the story is told that a black serviceman was asked, 'What are you niggers doing in Australia?' He replied, 'Man, we're here to look after your White Australia Policy.'

An American officer on a bride ship going to America in 1944, engaged an Australian girl in conversation. 'You shouldn't be speaking to me you know.' 'Why is this?' said the American. 'I have been shunned by my so-called fellow Australian brides because I married an American negro serviceman.'

George related an anecdote which suggests that a similar approach may sometimes have been taken in New Zealand. 'Riding through Wellington one Sunday we came across literally thousands of black US Army men, one long column of them. They were from CB (Construction Battalion) outfits on transport in the harbour. Apparently the Marines had said there would be trouble if they let "the blacks" ashore

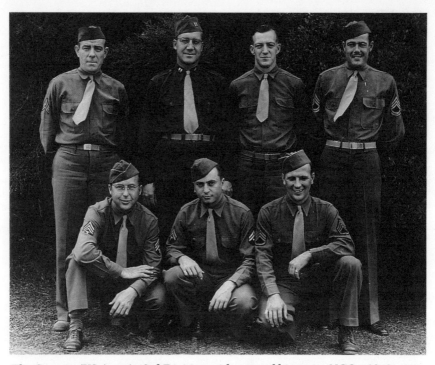

The Captain (US Army) 43rd Division with some of his senior NCOs, 1943.
Tudor Collins

on leave, so they took them on a route march instead.' George was one of Wellington's resident 'Marine-watchers', and none were more avid observers than the young and not so young women of the city.

There were very few American planes based at New Zealand airfields during the war. The 43rd US Army Division was given permission to operate Taylor Cub artillery co-op aircraft from Ardmore RNZAF Station in March 1944. The Americans called these planes 'Grass-hoppers', and Aucklanders may have seen them flying in formation in 1944–45.

'One-off' flights, or planes on special missions, passed through Whenuapai from 1942 onwards, together with heavy and medium transport aircraft (mostly C-47s and C-53s, although C-54 Skymasters came later). On at least one occasion a C-87 Liberator Express paid a visit, bringing Eleanor Roosevelt to Whenuapai on 27 August 1943. The heaviest USAAF aircraft to visit New Zealand during World War II, again on a special mission, was a Boeing B-29 Superfortress named 'Thumper', which landed on 10 July and was piloted by Captain J. C. Smith. Flying Fortresses (B-17E and F models) were regular visitors at

Whenuapai, some probably brand-new aircraft on delivery to Australia from the US.

Two USAAF planes based in New Zealand were a Howard DGA-15P and a twin-engined Beechcraft, operated by the American Legation in Wellington and used by the Air Attaché for ferrying VIPs and visiting officers.

The US Army Air Force had a small detachment of the 1551th Air Base Unit, Operation Location 4Y, working out of Whenuapai. Personnel comprised two to three officers and six enlisted men, whose shore duties were to handle administration, air passengers, fuelling and routine aircraft maintenance. VIPs passing through were detailed in the unit's reports, and in February 1945 ranking officers noted were Vice-Admiral John Newton (US Navy), Major General E. B. Gregory (Quartermaster), Major General N. T. Kirk (Surgeon General, US Army), Brigadier General J. F. Davis (Army of Information), Brigadier General J. S. Simmons (US Army) and Brigadier General J. M. Willis (Surgeon General, Pacific Ocean area). Before their departure they were entertained at a cocktail party in the Waverley Hotel, Auckland, by Colonel McCall, Army Island Commander.

The only US Navy aircraft based in New Zealand was a twin-engined Beechcraft (Beech SNB-2). Painted in olive-green camouflage and usually piloted by Lieutenant Petros, USMC, this plane was probably for the use of the Commander South Pacific Vice-Admiral Robert Ghormley, but as he was not here very long after his appointment, it may have gone with him. Vice-Admiral 'Bull' Halsey came on his personal aircraft, a PB4Y-1 (Liberator) called *Flying Sea Dog*, in May 1944, though he had been here before in January 1943.

No US battleship ever visited New Zealand during the war, nor did any large aircraft carriers, but cruisers coming here would have had a floatplane aboard. Naval transport aircraft were frequent visitors to Auckland; mostly RD4s at Whenuapai, and Coronados and Mariner flying-boats at Mechanics Bay. PBY-5A Catalinas were occasional visitors, usually on VIP or 'one-off' missions.

The only US Marine Corps aircraft to visit New Zealand were the twenty-seven Douglas SBD-3 or SBD-4 Dauntless Dive Bombers VMSB-141, which were stationed at Seagrove Aerodrome (near the Manukau Harbour) from May to July 1943. The Marines handed these aircraft over to the RNZAF for the use of the newly formed No. 25 (Dive Bomber) Squadron. 'V' indicated 'heavy than air', as opposed to airships, 'M' indicated 'Marines', 'S' indicated 'Scout', and 'B', 'Bomber'. The RNZAF flew these planes extensively until January 1944, and for a time they retained their original US markings. So, viewed from the ground, observers would have concluded the planes were being flown by US personnel.

The usual policy in the Marine Corps aviation command following the initial Guadalcanal campaign, and during the Bougainville occupation, was to keep an air squadron in the forward combat area for four to six weeks, then give the pilots and combat crews a week's leave in Sydney or Auckland. Following this brief respite from war, the squadron was usually eased back into combat via the South Pacific 'back area' — Espiritu Santo and Efate in the New Hebrides Group, where two to four weeks were spent in training and absorbing replacements. The USAAF and the US Navy had similar programmes for resting their aircrews. Thus New Zealanders would have seen many US aircrew, the officers more easily distinguishable with their 'wings up' on their uniforms.

The changing fortunes of war in the South Pacific altered air strategy affecting New Zealand. Had Fiji or Nouméa fallen to the Japanese, the air route for the US to Australia would have passed through Canton, Samoa (or Tonga) and Whenuapai, then over to Australia. Plans were developed to enlarge Whenuapai and Ohakea to take Flying Fortress bombers (all-up weight around 30 tons). Dispersal areas and revetments to protect aircraft were planned for a number of airfields, including those at Te Pirita, near Hororata in inland Canterbury, and summertime dispersal fields at Rotherham (Canterbury) and Galatea (near Taupo). These protective measures were detailed to circumvent Japanese aircraft attacks on New Zealand's airfields. In March 1942 work started on three 7000 feet stabilised grass runways at Te Pirita. The airfield was never used, although it is still recognisable today from the air.

As early as March 1942 the US Navy probed the possibility of establishing a main fleet base in the Auckland area, including provision for seventy-two flying-boat moorings and facilities for 320 ship-borne land planes. The 320 planes represented two carrier Air Groups, one aboard ship, one replacement group on land aerodromes. Ardmore near Papakura was chosen as a site for the new aerodrome, and two stabilised strips of 4580 feet were laid down. Seagrove, which was probably the proposed Navy carrier replacement airfield, was also put down, to be used first by the RNZAF, then by the Americans and finally the RNZAF again. As the danger of Japanese invasion receded with American successes in the South Pacific, plans for air bases were abandoned.

The presence of the US Navy ships in Auckland and Wellington was inescapable to harbour watchers, many of whom would have been girls trying to pick the profile of a returning warship with a special sailor on board. They could only guess, for no ship names were visible (although numbers could sometimes be seen), and there was never any mention in the press of the comings and goings through the harbour defence booms.

In the first eighteen months from June 1942, over 500 ships entered the port of Auckland. Repeat these sort of figures for the port of Wellington, and it is reasonable to assume that, all told, half a million American servicemen would have visited New Zealand, however transitory their stay. Auckland and Wellington residents, besides American and New Zealand troops, came to know the 'Unholy Three' — the *President Jackson* (under Captain Wertzel; 9255 tons), *President Adams* (under Captain Dean; 9500 tons) and the *President Hayes* (under Captain Benson; 9255 tons). Also in port at various times were the *President Monroe* (under Captain Hawkins; 9506 tons) and the *President Grant* (under Captain Synet; 9992 tons). All have gone to the breaker's yard, but not so the magnificent *President Coolidge* (25,967 tons), which used to dwarf the Auckland ferries and their goggle-eyed passengers as it lay alongside Princes Wharf. Today it lies on the sea-bed close to the shore in Vila Harbour, where skin divers go on voyages of discovery round its decks.

The UST *Uruguay* (under Captain Spaulding; 22,754 tons) was the first of the big transports carrying troops to come to Auckland, this in June 1942 with elements of the 37th US Army division. But there were many transports of similar size that came to New Zealand ports, such as the *Matsonia* (under Captain Guiness; 20,479 tons), *West Point* (under Captain Kelley; 26,545 tons), *Mount Vernon* (under Captain Powel; 24,289 tons) and *Lurline* (under Capt Berndtson; 23,940 tons).

Often in and out of Auckland and Wellington ports and well known to American (and New Zealand) troops were the USS *Talamanca* F15 (under Captain Bow; 6963 tons), USS *Hunter Liggett* (under Captain Patch; 15,000 tons), USS *Pinkney* (under Captain Hutson; 13,478 tons), UST *Crescent City* (under Captain Sullivan; 9000 tons) and USS *American Legion* (under Captain Keller; 13,736 tons). The *Nieuw Amsterdam* (under Captain Matherson; 36,287 tons) came to Auckland in January 1944. This ship had been in Wellington in July 1943 with the first furlough draft of New Zealand soldiers from the Middle East. The hospital ship USS *Solace* (under Captain Perlman; 8937 tons) came to Auckland with sick and wounded from the Guadalcanal area, first in September 1942, and thereafter almost on a monthly timetable. The *Solace* was the only hospital ship in Pearl Harbour the morning the Japanese struck.

The UST *Henry Knox* was the first of the Liberty ships to reach Auckland, in July 1942, and following this almost a hundred of this 7176-ton class came to bring and take away stores. Ships' names such as *Henry Longfellow*, *Andrew Carnegie*, *Alundra*, *James B. Hickok*, *Jas B. Otis*, *Geo M. Pullman*, *Oliver W. Holmes*, *Wilbur Wright*, *Cassiopeia*, *David Belasco* and *Cor-Caroli* would have been familiar to watersiders of the day.

One of the earliest US Navy ships to arrive in New Zealand was the repair ship *Rigel*, which came here from Honolulu on 16 May 1942 and remained tied up at the Hobson Wharf until 9 November, when it left for Nouméa. New Zealand men who went over this ship were amazed at the quantity and quality of the machinery available. For a very short time Vice-Admiral R. Ghormley was aboard, until he found suitable headquarters ashore. He was offered the Auckland War Memorial Museum building, but declined on the grounds that people back in the States would say, 'Old Ghormley's in a museum back in Owckland, Noo Zillun.' One of Ghormley's staff was Lieutenant Commander L. B. Johnson, a future President of the United States.

Lyndon Johnson was unknown in 1942, but another aide on the Admiral's staff to become familiar to some Aucklanders, particularly .the women, was Commander Gene Markey, the Public Relations Officer and Navy Censor. American wartime news had to pass through Markey's hands before being released to the press. Together with Commander Bushey, Markey led the courts martial in Auckland. He was a very genial and charming man, so charming in fact that he was to be the husband of three famous Hollywood film stars in succession: Hedy Lamarr, Joan Bennett and Myrna Loy. (Lamarr was famous — or infamous? — for a nude scene the film *Ecstasy*, while Myrna Loy starred in the *Third Man* series with William Powell, and Asta the dog.) Markey, who served on the lower deck in World War I, eventually attained the rank of rear admiral. After the war he became a film producer in Hollywood but then married again, this time to a rich Kentucky woman who bred thoroughbred horses.

The US Navy established barracks at Oriental Bay, Wellington, to service the amphibious craft to be used for the landing at Tarawa. Similarly, 'H'-type dormitories to accommodate a thousand Navy personnel were erected at Mechanics Bay, Auckland. Crews from ships that docked at the Devonport Naval Base for repairs stayed at Mechanics Bay. Private engineering firms in both Auckland and Wellington were under tremendous pressure doing maintenance work on American ships, this of course with a limited labour force. All work was on a 'charge-up' basis, with the instruction to 'never mind the cost, get on with it'.

New Zealand got to know these soldiers, sailors and airmen very rapidly. Most New Zealanders who had contact with the troops got to know the Marines. So what was the reality behind the stereotype? Thousands of the Marines were young, very young. The minimum age for enlistment was eighteen, but many sixteen- and seventeen-year-olds conned their mothers into signing them into the Marines. One twelve-year-old got as far as Guadalcanal before he was sent back home. 'I lived in Greymouth and I heard the Marines were coming on rest and recreation,' relates a New Zealander who was a boy at the time. 'I went down to the railway station to see them arrive. I was absolutely amazed, they were just like me, young, callow and immature. I could not believe it that youths so young would be pitted against the Japanese. I wondered why I was not going to the war. It was for me the most moving experience of the whole war, that boys so young could soon be heroes or dead.'

To be a Marine Corpsman during 1941–42 was to increase one's stature immeasurably in the eyes of the public. It would not be exaggerating to say that the men of the 1st, 2nd and 3rd Marine Divisions, the majority of whom came to New Zealand in 1942 and '43, were the flower of the youth of America, officered by graduates from Quantico, Virginia, trained to high professional standards. Marines, at least at the start of the war (until the draft came), were volunteers, so arguably the first troops were the best troops. Among those men was Bill, who was stationed in Wellington and is now permanently resident in New Zealand. He recalled what it was like to be a Marine.

We honestly didn't know about New Zealand. We didn't know where we were when we pulled in wharfside. But then we didn't know about Canada either. Most of us had never travelled, we only knew our own state if we knew that. Some would have known only their own scratch farm. Looking back our ignorance was so incredible as to be unbelievable. Our drill sergeants used to pound us round the streets of Wellington or Kaiwharawhara or Waterloo. We were driven very hard. If we were tough we had to be still tougher. We had to reach the traditional toughness of the regular Marines and have pride in the Corps. All Marines, at that time at any rate, were volunteers, and the standards of entry were very high. Your schooling had to be reasonable, but more than that, you had to be physically near perfect. One tooth missing and that was enough to keep you out of the Marines. You gave of your best, and they gave the best to you. Our equipment and clothing was the best that money could buy . . . The Marines had very high standards, they regarded themselves as the élite of the US defence forces. One time I was able to put a stripe on my arm, making me a 'private first class'. A China Marine came in and said, 'Hell, you've got a stripe up. Man, it took me ten years to get one of those!' Marines, regulars of course, who had been on the China station pre-war were called China Marines, or sometimes Pearl Harbour Marines.

Thank God we had some time in New Zealand. We loved the place, even if we were pounded around. We loved the people; hell, it was the only thing that saved us. Oh yes, there were fights in the streets of Wellington. We understood what it was all about. The New Zealanders resented our favouritism with their women. Our boys were done over in the Wellington lavatories, but I think we gave as good as got . . .

The general attitude in New Zealand was 'have fun, give it a go, hell we don't know where we'll be tomorrow . . .'

There was an expression in the thirties, 'Bud, you can tell that to the Marines,' meaning try it on them but not on me. There was another catch-cry too. 'Send in the Marines' was used when there was trouble in the world which came within the sphere of American influence. That aroused my interest in the Marines, indeed as a kid I always wanted to be one. When the Depression came along in the thirties, President Franklin Roosevelt got the Civilian Conservation Corps going. This enabled me, as a teenager and a city kid, to get out into the country areas on one of the irrigation or big drainage schemes. We lived in barracks and could earn a couple of stripes for efficiency. It took the pressure off families, and for many it was their saviour. We were not paid, but were fed and clothed, and saw the United States. It changed my life as a teenager, gave me pride, self-confidence and self-esteem. I spent six months in the Corps and then went back to school. When I joined the Marines, orders came naturally to me. I knew what to expect.

It was because of their aggression in taking on the Barbary pirates in the 1790s and patrolling and raiding the coasts of Mexico in the Mexico war that the Marines had captured the admiration of their fellow countrymen. Whenever trouble brewed in the Caribbean in the 1920s and '30s the cry from the politicians went up, 'Send in the Marines.'

A New Zealand soldier in the Pacific, Major John Marshall (later Sir John, Prime Minister of New Zealand), was seconded to the USMC Officers' School in Quantico in 1943 for a short time.

The training was tough, the morale high. The American Marine was a typical American. Because he had been picked for the job, he had to be better than the others. Though not regular soldiers, they were good, and they tried to live up to the tradition of the Marine Corps. The Marine officers were regulars and they were a pretty superior lot. Mind you, out in the boondocks, when it came to initiative I'd back the Kiwi soldier. I got on well with the Marines, officers and men. We spent most of our time in the classroom on tactics, laying down a scheme for the invasion of the Japanese naval station on the island of Truk, by-passed in any case. Eleanor Roosevelt, always a liberal, used her influence on her husband to allow negroes into the Marine Corps.

Harold, of the 43rd US Army division, confirms these impressions.

The Marines looked on themselves as the death-and-glory boys. The Army and the Navy might just as well have stayed at home. No one could get on with the Marines; they were a law unto themselves. I can remember one time in New Georgia in the Solomons when the Marines passed through our lines. We were digging foxholes and the Marines poked shit at us for wanting to take cover. Then the Jap bombs started to fall. What a scatteration, and were those Marine shovels flying! But then we all had our problems. The thing to do was to survive. I was one of the miracle ones. I did.

The Americans were cast in the role of crusading heroes, soldiering on a foreign soil, and about to move off to enemy territory. It is a peculiar trait of New Zealanders that they see glamour and an exotic aura about visiting troops but little about their own; it is part of the Kiwi clob-bering machine that our own are put down and the visitor exalted to the skies. People would present flowers to the Americans, even throw them at their feet, but this would have been a rare experience for New Zealand troops. It is only fair to comment, in case New Zealanders appear to be unduly denigrated, that by the end of 1942 New Zealand had been at war for three years, and the flower of her youth was overseas too. Unfortunately the fighter pilots, although awarded their medals for battling it out over Europe or the Pacific, were not on hand to heap praise on. Neither were the decorated sailors nor the men of the North African, Italian or Pacific campaigns. Some very young New Zealanders were serving overseas. It was possible to be a seaman boy of sixteen on a New Zealand naval vessel and be hunting German or Japanese raiders, to be eighteen and after a year's training become a sergeant pilot, navigator or tail gunner in the RAF. To serve overseas in the army, a recruit for the Second New Zealand Expeditionary Forces had to be twenty-one.

If the impact of the American troops' stay was apparently short and sharp, their influence here was not due to any innate superiority. It was not as if every GI had that air of sophistication the silver screen had suggested and the Marines liked to maintain. Certainly the overall standard of education was no higher, and arguably much lower than that of the average New Zealander. Recruiting stations throughout the United States became painfully aware of the low educational status of a large number of the recruits. It was this discovery that led, at the end of the war, to the GI Bill of Rights, entitling servicemen to continue their education on a paid basis, even to university level for those who wished it. Some, taking advantage of the favourable exchange rate, came to New Zealand universities to complete their courses.

The ignorance of the Americans about their own country may have appeared appalling to New Zealanders. New Zealand school children could look at a map of the world and trace the 'All Red Route' of the British Empire back to England. Back in the 1940s only a tiny propor-tion of the American armed forces had a college education. In addition, two out of every five draftees were rejected on the grounds of mal-nutrition. Then again, 'Momma' may have come through Ellis Island from Napoli and 'Poppa' from Roma, bringing all the background of Italian parentage and culture for their children to absorb. There were Poles in Chicago, Germans in Minnesota, Italians and Jews in New York; hardly surprising, then, that to a Texan, someone from Maine was like a visitor from outer space. A member of the 43rd Division recalls, 'I came from Maine but it took an Auckland girl to sing me *Riding down from Bangor, in an eastern train / After months of hunting in the woods of Maine* . . . I had never heard of it before.' It was as much as the average grade-school student could do to learn the history

All dressed up and somewhere to go. This US Army infantry captain poses for Tudor Collins. Tudor took hundreds of individual and group photos of the Americans which the boys were eager to send back to the States to wives and girlfriends. No less keen to acquire them were plenty of New Zealand women.
Tudor Collins

of his own state, let alone one of the forty-nine others. Down in the Pacific in the war years at the field picture shows, where the Americans built their seats in the trees and labelled them with their initials, Texas only needed to be mentioned on screen and there would be shrieks of delight puncturing the night air from Texans in the crowd.

Yet the ingenuousness (or ignorance) of the visitors did nothing in the eyes of many to negate their charm. There were plenty of New Zealand women who wanted to mother them, and they found a willing clientele. Young teenage girls and their even more knowing older sisters were not, in many cases, to be impressed by scholastic attainment, indeed, might well have been embarrassed by it. Of course, to suggest that the average GI, Marine or American sailor was the naive product of some Tennessee county settlement would be inaccurate. Thousands had been street kids to whom rural life was totally foreign, and who were inured to a highly competitive society where free enterprise, such as shining shoes or selling newspapers, demanded one stood or fell by one's own efforts. If Rifleman Joe, a Nebraskan cowhand who had previously never been further than the county fair, was to survive among buddies from the back streets of the big cities, he had to learn fast.

What servicemen may have lacked in general knowledge, they made up for in appearance. Only the very best in materials went into the uniforms of service personnel. One woman remembers a comment made by her mother, who had a contingent of Americans camped at the bottom of the garden. 'I've been very busy ironing the American boys' shirts, and they are so fussy, the creases have to be just so.' Not only were the servicemen and women well dressed, they were clothed with the aura of the greatest nation on earth. The Marines had standards of personal cleanliness and appearance second to none. They were impeccably groomed and had a charisma about them which New Zealanders found exciting and, for many women, irresistible. In a word, they had style. But if they had style, they had to have courage too, for they were to be committed to some of the bloodiest battles in the war, notably Iwo Jima and Okinawa, where the Americans suffered horrendous losses. Understandably some servicemen and units did not measure up to the demands set upon them in jungle warfare.

It has to be said that the American divisions were a cross-section of the polyglot population of the States, where tastes and mores were hopelessly intermingled. The nuclei of the 25th Division may have come from Hawaii, and the 43rds from the New England states, but with time and the draft, reinforcements to the divisions could have come from anywhere. The Marines may have been recruited from any part of the States, but the Corps had always drawn on a disproportionate number of men from the Deep South, where the military traditions of the American Civil War still lingered on. The Navy and the Air Force drew on the universities for their officer recruits, but examined all comers for enlisted rank. The Army formed its divisions from geographical areas, but only at the beginning.

Southern blacks, used to being down and therefore having a low level of expectation, survived the war better than those from the North or white soldiers. Because of their authoritarian norms and rural orientation, the Southern states played a disproportionate role in supplying soldiers beyond the demand of their populations. It was the well-educated men from the urban and industrial enclave for whom service life became an ordeal. The soldier who fared best, and remained free from psychological trauma, was likely to be a boy with little education, coming from a farm or a small town. As citizen soldiers, however, many had been plucked from the sidewalks of Los Angeles, Chicago or Dallas, and thrown into an alien environment, facing a foe imbued with religious fervour and prepared to die if necessary for his Emperor. Death for the Japanese was to be preferred to disgrace, and disgrace was to be defeated or taken prisoner.

No such consuming passion for Uncle Sam was evident in the ranks of the GIs. Americans went to war, like most New Zealanders, to maintain the status quo. There were those, mostly politicians, who declaimed about the high moral purpose of the war, but jingoism went down like a failed sponge cake with the troops. 'Get your ass over here,' or 'Give us some real beer, not the horse piss of the PX,' could well have been their reaction. But there was a gut feeling for one's buddies. Never leave your mate to do what you yourself should be doing. Mateship led to the literal decimation of some rifle battalions on Okinawa amid indescribable scenes of carnage, where the blood of Americans and Japanese ran together.

As with most soldiers, the GIs' aim was to survive, and the best way to survive was to go forward. Men returning from the trauma of Guadalcanal to R & R in New Zealand were reluctant to speak of their experiences. 'It was hell,' they said. 'When you only have a hole in the ground to catnap in, life is reduced to the basics.' Which may explain the extensive use of anal metaphorical expressions by American soldiers. It was 'shit-house luck', 'crap-house buzz', or 'stop pissing in your pants'; everything was 'crap, piss and corruption' or 'horseshit on a platter'; 'you couldn't stack shit with a shovel', or 'get your ass in a sling' or 'things were colder than a welldigger's ass'. One of the very last imprecations hurled at the troops before going in to fight was 'Keep your assholes tight'. Loose bowels could well attack every man under the horrific conditions on Iwo Jima and Okinawa. There, life was not metaphorical but gut-wrenching and direct, and a soldier's mental alertness and physical fitness helped him to survive.

From the time a 'ductee' (one who had been inducted into a branch of the armed services) entered 'boot camp', he was aurally assaulted with anal and sexual rhetoric. Whereas a New Zealand sergeant might wake his boys with 'Wakey wakey, feet on the floor', an American drill sergeant would say to his 'boots', 'OK, shitheads, hands off cocks, on with the socks.' A New Zealand officer eating in an American officers' mess very quickly became aware of the competitive sexual abuse that officers hurled around the mess-room, particularly at breakfast time, when the sexual exploits of the bedroom raiders of the night before were related.

There is a story about one recruit wishing to join the Marines who was told that, in order to conform to certain health standards, he would have to have himself circumcised. 'Circumcised? Circumcised?' cried the astounded young man, 'Why, what the hell do you think I am going to do to the enemy?'

Homosexuality within the services, if proven, was treated with all the philistine rancour of reactionary 'straights'. Sexual deviation, even if merely suspected among the troops, was pursued with a Gestapo-like thoroughness. The punishments handed down could be extraordinary, such as a sentence of eighty-five years in the Portsmouth Naval Gaol. Yet some young boots would have been completely unaware that homosexuality existed.

Every branch of the US forces had its jargon. Because there were more Marines here, and for longer periods than other branches of the forces, New Zealanders became familiar with some of their expressions. 'Shootin' the breeze' or 'shootin' the shit' was gossip, a 'snow job' was a deception, and Navy men were always 'swabbies' (those who swabbed down the decks). A Marine never went on leave but was 'granted liberty', say 'a seventy-two' or 'forty-eight' (hour leave). An officer from the ranks was a 'mustang', a company commander, 'skipper'. Every Marine was 'Mac' to every other Marine, while every US soldier was a 'doggie' or 'dogface', and was barked at. 'Lad' was a generic term for any subordinate. To be absent without leave was to be 'over the hill'; to be 'under hack' was to be under arrest; and 'working one's bolt' was manipulating people. A hotel bar was a 'slopchute', a latrine was 'a head', swamps were 'boondocks', and field boots, 'boondockers'. Battledress was 'dungarees', underwear 'skivvies', 'scuttlebutt' rumours, dufflebags 'seabags', and to straighten up was 'to square away' whether one's person or one's belongings.

That the conduct of the American servicemen in New Zealand was, for the overwhelming majority, beyond reproach, may have been because of the harsh punishments handed down to offenders. George Washington, first president of the United States, employed a Prussian general to organise the American armed forces. The Prussians were not known for their leniency towards offenders and recalcitrants in the ranks, nor in the officer caste. Those oppressive methods are still evident in the US Forces today; for example, at the West Point Academy for officer training, 'hazing' (deliberate provocation) is practised to test candidates for officer rank almost to breaking point.

All of the servicemen who came to New Zealand in the war years grew up in the period of Prohibition (1920–1933). This coincided with the Depression of the late 1920s and early '30s, with its soup-kitchen lines and scenes of degradation unknown since the days of the American Civil War. 'We have nothing to fear but fear itself,' said Franklin D. Roosevelt, as he dragged his country up and out of its recession with his New Deal. When Roosevelt took office in 1933 there were at least thirteen million unemployed, thousands of banks in the country had closed their doors, and people were eating dandelions to stay alive. Roosevelt rescued America not once but twice, first from a depression and then a war. He not only rescued America but changed it forever. Roosevelt found the country completely dominated by WASPS. He gave Catholics and other non-WASPS their due share of the action, and began the process by which blacks were eventually to claim theirs. A boy who was thirteen in 1933 would have been twenty-one and ready to be inducted into the armed forces at the outbreak of war. For some of these young men, the translation from the ranks of the unemployed to the uniform of Uncle Sam might well have been like raising Lazarus from the dead.

If these servicemen brought politics with them, their polemics would have had been of little interest to New Zealanders, the majority of whom knew little or nothing of Republican or Democratic Party philosophies. Nor would the Americans have shown much interest in New Zealand politics, which in wartime was not the adversarial scene we know today. Some Southerners brought their racial prejudices, but these were no bar to crossing the picket line of colour in order to indulge in a little sexual dalliance. Some also retained the attitude born of the slave days, that people in menial positions should know their station in life, and that was at the bottom of the heap.

Not all the Americans were drinkers, and the gratuitous use of four-letter words, though common to most, was not normal practice among those from the Bible Belt. Service chaplains included Roman Catholic fathers, Jewish rabbis, Lutherans, Episcopalians, Baptists, Methodists, Mormons and representatives of those pentecostal fringe religions endemic in the United States. Many of the servicemen attended services or social events at the local churches. There were also a number of tearaways who had no intention of attending a church service, except perhaps before their unit moved up to the front line.

Any involvement in cultural activities could only be sporadic, given the reason for the Americans' presence in New Zealand. Perhaps an exception could be made in the case of the 2nd Marine Corps Division, which was stationed in Wellington and to the north for ten months, the longest stay of any American combat unit present as a division and not fragmented. 'Our second home,' the veterans of that division call New Zealand, and they have held reunions here. The prolonged stay of the 2nd Division made Wellingtonians and those living north to Masterton conscious of the same faces, the same platoons and their 'sound-offs' as they crunched their way around towns and villages. In addition, one small group of American troops was here for two years at a stretch. These were the servicemen who were in charge of stores, unloading ships, servicing motor transport and naval ships, manning the hospitals, baking the bread, policing the streets. Because of the longevity and continuity of their stay, many of these men married or became engaged to New Zealand girls.

Viv was a schoolboy during the war, and talked about how the experiences of those years modified his preconceptions.

> I was at school when war was on, and when the Japs came in I wasn't frightened at all. I was only hoping it would last so that I could join up. Of course in those days we all believed that the Japs ate carrots in order to see at nights, and everything they made was cheap and nasty and copied, that they were little men and they couldn't fight. How wrong we all were. I got a shock when the Yanks arrived round here. I thought they all lived in New York, wore two-tone black and white shoes and smoked cigars. I was shocked to see how young they were . . . I became very conscious of the colour thing too. I didn't realise how vehement some

44

were about negroes. If there were Yanks visiting our farm and we were going down to the chicken house they might say, 'Ain't no niggers there, is there?', the inference being there could be 'niggers' hiding from the military police or robbing the chicken run. They all had to have knives and they were forever sharpening them. I assumed they were for close fighting in the jungle. Well, knives weren't new to New Zealanders. Have a look at old-time photos and you will see New Zealand youths with sheath knives, even at the beach, on the back of their belts. One Marine used to come round to pick up Aunty for Red Cross duty. He was pretty dark, Hispanic I would say, and he not only smoked cigars but he chewed them. He was an old sweat probably. If others couldn't hack it, he was there to lean on. No, the Yanks were a great bunch of boys, they made a big impression on me as a schoolboy. There was always yards of chewing gum, and because I had red hair they used to say, 'Say, kid, you gotta big sister?' I always thought their chances of getting through the war unscathed were pretty slim.'

Another New Zealander who was young at the time recalled his impression of the troops.

There were all sorts all right. When the Marines were in camp on our property I loved being with them. I was only nine at the time, an impressionable age. They all looked so young to me and took such pride in their uniform — man, they were smart. I used to eat in the chow line with them. There was always bags of ice cream and great big tins of preserved fruit. But when the Marines left and the Army came in, that was a different story. There were all sorts and they were an older group. There were American Indians, negroes, men whose accents I couldn't understand. I was frightened. I didn't go down into the camp then. Looking back, though I didn't understand it at the time, I think one or two had designs on me.

New Zealanders may have approached the visitors with both fear and fascination. There was one thing, however, that they could be assured of: there would never be a dull moment when the troops were in town.

CHAPTER THREE

Culture Shock and
Wartime Entertainments

Truth, it is said, is the first casualty of war, but there is another that runs it close — liquor. Finding space for hard liquor in ships traversing U-boat-infested waters was a low priority. Hence the black market trading in that commodity, and in military camps the brewing of any concoctions which produced fire-water calculated to scorch the back of the throat. Servicemen everywhere went to extraordinary lengths to acquire alcohol. Down in the Pacific, when Japanese landing craft were captured, it was not unknown for soldiers to steal the compass in order to get the alcohol on which the card floated.

A combat correspondent with the Marines here in New Zealand wrote the following description of local drinking conditions for his Washington newspaper.

> Most New Zealand towns serve hard liquor to the general public (service-men included) between five and six in the afternoon, with nothing available at other times but a very bitter Australian beer. After six, a thirsty man with a craving for Scotch can get results only if he's a guest at a hotel. The public bars are rationed a certain small allotment of Scotch and brandy (rye or bourbon are unheard of). There's a prefabricated drink which goes under the name of Manhattan, but any resemblance to the Stateside cocktail of the same name is purely coincidental. The larger of these public bars breaks out two bottles of Scotch and two of brandy promptly at five o'clock, and will refuse to serve more than one drink at a time to a customer or to serve doubles. It should not be necessary to describe a public bar at 5 p.m. I have tried mightily, but have never succeeded in drinking more than one Scotch and soda (without ice of course) before being told 'Sorry, but Scotch is all gone.'
>
> On occasion I've been lucky enough to sneak in a quick gulp of brandy before that too is all gone. There's nothing left then but to switch to rum, a local version of West Indian rum and when that runs out, to the bitter beer. The whole system is not conducive to quiet relaxed drinking, and by 5.15–5.30 at the latest, I'm on the street again feeling as though I'd just come out of a football scrimmage or a dress sale for women and junior misses.

In banks, barber shops, pubs and cafes, prices were marked in both dollars and pounds, shillings and pence. And what sort of prices were the troops confronted with? Unbelievably cheap. A phone call cost a penny, a tram ride twopence, and a bottle of beer one shilling and sixpence. There were stares of disbelief when steak complete with French fries, tea and loads of bread and butter was charged at no more than half a crown. Tea was something most Americans initially avoided but grudgingly accepted after tasting the alternative. Coffee New Zealand-style was cheap enough at threepence a cup, but it was stewed in an urn for hours. Even the New Zealand troops declined to stomach it. Bourbon was in short supply in New Zealand bars, but cream-heavy milk, with flavours added, was a favourite non-alcoholic drink of the Americans.

Not only was liquor rationed, but clothing also, and women in the war years struggled to dress well. It was a time of make-do and improvise, but no form of improvisation could compensate for the lack of silk stockings. The ration was one pair every six months, and then one outing and a ladder could negate months of waiting. There were of course other aids to glamour, but lisle and rayon did nothing for a shapely leg in the eyes of the wearer, or the beholder. Teenagers settled for bobby socks. Those women who had menfolk in Egypt could hope for a supplement in silk stockings, but American servicemen were an alternative source of supply. Even back in the States, silk stockings were in short supply, but a new synthetic marvel was about to surface — nylons.

But it was food rationing which reminded New Zealanders daily there was a war on. Sugar, butter, eggs, cream, tea and pork were rationed. Tobacco, potatoes and rice were in short supply. One commodity opened all doors — cigarettes. Those families who had servicemen in the Pacific combat zone could receive cartons of cigarettes bought at the American PX (Post Exchange) stores. Lucky Strike, Camels, Philip Morris, Pall Mall, Kool, Chesterfield or Chelsea — any brand was acceptable. A carton of cigarettes, and the shopkeeper would reach below the counter for all those rationed commodities that housewives wanted. Naturally American servicemen were generous with their gifts of tobacco to friends and acquaintances. If it came to a choice between currency or cigarettes, the locals would opt for the latter, though they were not averse to garnering American dollars, which legally had to be paid into a bank.

The first commodity to be rationed, in 1939, was petrol. After the attack on Pearl Harbour, petrol was further rationed, so that a small car was allotted six gallons for two months, and a large car twelve gallons. Coupons could not be hoarded, as they had to be used in the specified time. Gas producers of all kinds and shapes made their appearances on running boards or back bumpers. Coal gas and charcoal burners were popular, while kerosene and mineral turps were added to petrol to augment the supply. The importation of cars in any form was banned in 1940, and for five years mechanics and owners patched and improvised to keep old motors on the road. Bicycles too were in short supply and, as with motor cars, so were the rubber tyres that went with them. With the fall of Malaya and Singapore, the Allies had recourse to synthetic rubber to equip their vehicles. Although public transport, including trains, was well patronised, travel beyond a hundred miles at certain times during the war years required a permit. 'Is your journey really necessary?' was the catch-cry.

American servicemen could easily tote round the much-in-demand Chesterfield cigarettes ('There's many a girl ruined on a Chesterfield'), but petrol was hardly a convenient form of currency. Nonetheless, a great deal of American petrol found its way into the tanks of New Zealand motorists. Petrol was coloured in those days, and woe betide the motorist who was caught with the wrong colour in his tank.

Upon their arrival American troops received plenty of advice from their superiors on how to conduct themselves in New Zealand society. One such booklet was called *The Pocket Guide to New Zealand 1943*, which attempted to prepare the troops for the ineviatble culture shock.

WHAT YOU WON'T FIND

For instance, you will not find central heating in private houses. There are few hotels of the luxury class and few night clubs. You will quickly run into what the New Zealanders themselves call the *Blue Laws*, which

'Milko' — a Wellington milkman selling his wares to Marines down on the wharves. The Americans' love of milk astounded New Zealanders. *USA National Archives*

close bars, dance halls, movies and theaters on Sunday, except for certain movies which are allowed open for members of the Armed Forces. These you can visit in uniform and you can take two civilians with you (that is to enable you to take her mother along as well). Frankly, organised entertainment is pretty scarce in New Zealand. No hotdogs or hamburgers. And except in camp you won't get the kind of coffee you're used to. So what? People come from all over the world to enjoy the good things that New Zealand possesses and not to compare it with their home town.

MEET THE PEOPLE

They tend to be more reserved than ourselves. Actually they're a pioneering crowd, extremely democratic and without class distinction. Nobody is very poor and nobody is very rich. Only 1% have taxable incomes of $10,000 or over. They will probably call you Yanks or Yankees, whether you come from the North or from the South, and will say you have a Yankee accent even if you speak with a South Carolina drawl. Women will be pleased, but will think it a little strange when you say 'yes, ma'am', though men will not think it strange to hear 'yes, sir'.

One Marine remembers his time in Wellington.

In the chow line it was maple syrup on flapjacks for breakfast, and later the usual chili con carne, spam, and Vienna sausages out of a tin. We ate plenty of New Zealand mutton, but mostly beef, because our cooks knew more about cooking beef. But it was the same old thing, and the thought of a juicy steak straight off the hotplate downtown in Wellington brought tears to the eyes of the strongest Marine.

Phyllis recalls her memories of the Marines and their reactions to food.

But the Marines were hungry for home life and just someone to open up to. When they were out on manoeuvres some would come in at night for a bit of home cooking. How they loved it and how they could eat! We baked a lot in those days, not like now.

Ina, who was fourteen when the Americans arrived, remembers,

Our family had a caravan on the Whangateau Domain, we were one of three there. The Americans took the Domain over but let us stay there. So there we were surrounded by all these young Marines. They used to bring us our breakfast of pancakes and maple syrup. Can you imagine it, breakfast in bed served by a Marine. I remember the cook's name was Pignatelli. He used to cook in his funny little cookhouse and the Marines would eat in the Hall. The Hall is still there of course . . . My mother kept one cow and I think she only milked it in order to supply the Marines with milk.

Various units coming to New Zealand printed their own information in booklet form, and a certain amount of sermonising was done about the local folks. In 'Notes on the People of New Zealand', the 3rd Marine

While 'Pohutu' plays, US naval personnel are snapped at Rotorua. *NZ Herald*

Division Intelligence branch has this to say:

> The first impression that one forms of the people of New Zealand is that they are a reserved, sober, and industrious people. Subsequent contacts confirm these early impressions. New Zealanders, being of English stock, are rather stoical and unenthusiastic in manner to the outsider. However, although they appear unenthusiastic they are not basically so for they enjoy life and living as much as any other people; they just do not make a display of their emotions. Although reserved towards strangers they are by no means unsociable and will do all they can to be agreeable to acquaintances. Marines who have preceded us to the Islands [New Zealand] invariably state that they have been most cordially treated by the inhabitants.
>
> The wants and amusements of the people have always been extremely simple according to our standards. This can be understood better when it is known that the average income per person in peacetime has always

been just under $1000 a year. Few people are very rich and none are very poor. The standard of living is more nearly the same for all people in New Zealand than is the case in any other country and this holds true in both urban and rural districts.

In view of the relatively low income compared to our standards, the people have learned to be extremely economical and frugal. Likewise their standards in the way of amusements are much simpler than ours. The average working man has his neighbourhood pub where he congregates with his friends and neighbors over a glass of 'stout' or ale. The atmosphere of these pubs is usually one of simple quiet; boisterousness such as is often encountered in our tap rooms is almost entirely lacking, and when it does occur it is resented very deeply. As in England each pub has its dart board and the men are almost always expert at the game. Strangers should not barge in on dart games uninvited for two reasons. One is that they will invariably be outclassed and the other is that the men play darts to see who in a particular group will pay for a round of drinks, just the same as we shake dice for drinks in our country.

US sailors do the sights of Whakarewarewa, Rotorua. *NZ Herald*

American tourists do the Rotorua sights. 1943.

Speaking of women, it is taken for granted that you will be discreet in your dealings with New Zealand girls. Many of them are engaged or married to men who are fighting overseas. Do not take advantage of their loneliness. Remember New Zealand is a small country with a small population. Any sort of scandal travels very quickly. Regard yourself not only as an ambassador for Uncle Sam but as a soldier and a gentleman.

Your recently increased pay will go a long way in New Zealand, where prices are comparatively low, and where the rate of exchange is in your favor. So you may find yourself with more spending money than most New Zealand men, whether soldiers or civilians. Don't toss it around. It won't make you popular and can very easily make for hard feelings.

FOOD AND DRINK — AND TEA

Are you fond of lamb? That's good — because you're going to get lots of it. New Zealanders eat fabulous quantities of lamb and mutton, and also a good deal of beef, but little pork or veal. Try mutton as they serve it, roasted with mint sauce and roast potatoes . . . Although there are no hot dog or hamburger stands as such, you will find a New Zealand institution called the Pie Cart. This is a stand which is set up at night in one of the main squares of the town and where you can sit down and get a good cheap meal of sausages, potatoes, eggs and other such food. But even there

'Chow-time'. A sergeants' mess of a Marine unit of the 2nd Marine Division, Wellington area, 1943. *John Pascoe Collection, Alexander Turnbull Library*

you won't find the kind of coffee you are used to. In fact you won't get it anywhere except in camp, because one of the characteristics which the New Zealanders share with the British is a complete inability to make coffee.

And now we come to the all-important subject of 'teas', not simply the stuff you used to have at home. In fact it may be more than a beverage. It may be a whole meal! So you'd better learn a little something about it . . . If you are invited to 'tea' perhaps the safest thing to do is to ask your host to name the hour . . .

For the Americans in New Zealand, nothing was too good in quality. If it was water, even the purest, it had to be treated, meat had to be inspected by American veterinarians, milk always had to be pasteurised.

In fact, feeding the Americans was a monumental task. The sale of pork was banned to encourage farmers to carry their pigs on to greater baconer weights. Only hospitals, foreign forces and ship suppliers were allowed to deal in pork. The result was inevitable, a black market in porkers. Traffic officers were asked to be on the look-out for black marketeers trucking dodgy pork into Auckland and Wellington. Not only was New Zealand feeding Americans in camp, the country was also helping to feed Americans in the Pacific. American supply ships, the well-known Liberty ships built by Kaiser, would dock in Wellington on Monday night, and in a week they would be loaded to the gunwales with food. A typical order would be 500,000 lb of bacon and 250,000 lb of pork. Watties Canneries in Hawke's Bay would supply 25,000 lb of tomatoes, for twopence a pound, cases extra.

The Americans were super-sensitive on food hygiene and, on one occasion, a random check revealed fur and droppings were found in a can of rabbit meat. The whole consignment was condemned and a Wellington shipper found himself with an unwanted ton of canned rabbit. (An unsuspecting British Government later took the order.) One Marine now living in New Zealand has in his possession a can of water sent from Boston for use by the Marines in the Pacific. The shipping space demanded by canned water must have been tremendous. One of the Americans' first requests was for a chicken farm. This was built in the Hutt Valley at a cost of £6000. The day-old chicks were bought at one shilling a time and the chickens were supplied to American hospitals. There were times when the Marines were fed on meat, butter and fruit that, because of the shortage of shipping, was sitting in cool stores instead of being sent to a beleaguered Britain.

As stated before, frugality has always been a virtue with New Zealanders and even in normal times they seldom permitted themselves to buy more than they actually needed in the way of the necessities of life. Since the outbreak of war they have been making sacrifices to an extent unknown to us as yet. They have been depriving themselves so that their troops and those of their allies may be properly supplied. Spending money simply for the sake of spending it is going to deprive these people of things they need and will result in unnecessary hardship to them and consequent resentment on their part. American forces are paid more than the average working man in New Zealand, and a wanton display and spending of money will naturally be an annoyance to them. Let us be careful on this score. We are their guests; let us not tax their hospitality too much.

The appearance of the people of New Zealand is attractive and healthy, perhaps because of their racial stock, climate and general interest in outdoor life and sports. When understood they are found to be a quiet, cheerful, good-humoured people but they are also full of determination to prevent disturbing their way of life . . . A quiet courteous conduct toward a courteous quiet people is expected of all hands.

Senior citizens today may say that, with a few qualifications, is a fair summation of New Zealanders in the war years. The present generation might well greet it with a great big horse laugh. Others might simply reply that other times have other manners.

One anonymous serviceman recorded his reaction to New Zealand in verse.

DOWN UNDER (AS AN AMERICAN SEES IT)

This land they call Down Under
In the south Pacific sea,
And what on earth can be its worth
Sure beats the likes of me.

People call the bar-rooms pubs,
They close at six each night.
Ask a person here a question
And he calmly says 'Too right'.

A sidewalk is a footpath,
A buggy is a pram,
And above all things a street car
They call a blinking tram.

They call you 'Yank', or 'joker',
Frankly I don't get the jest,
And if you act American
You're a 'queer bloke' at the best.

If you're tired you're 'all knocked up',
And when you're sick you're crook.
There's no defining words like these
In any blinking book.

The movies here are called 'the flicks',
Old wine is ten days brewed,

It costs a chap a quid a quart
(Paid only when you're screwed).

One thing about this country though
It rains but once a year,
And to prove that what I say is true
It hasn't stopped since I've been here.

Lest you want to be a pauper, boys,
Take heed to what I say,
Don't try to save your money
For New Zealand's rainy day.

Is there anything unique about the way Americans saw New Zealand? Not at all. An American corporal with the US Forces in Australia wrote his impressions of the 'Ockers' in terms that sound very familiar.

I think it was the trip to town that convinced us. Whatever it was, we woke one morning and opened our eyes, and there it was staring us right in the face, the realisation that 'this country is at war'. It wasn't the same war we'd known back in the States during those last months of 1942. There weren't any posters, and what there were, were faded beyond recognition. There weren't any celebrities out selling bonds. The celebrities were all in England flying Spitfires. Nobody went round audibly horrified at the possible effects of gas-rationing. In short, unlike our country, nobody visibly burst any blood vessels remembering Pearl Harbour or anything else. They didn't have to. Here in Australia the '— — war' was old stuff. And did they go to a dance they didn't stand round staring at the national colours in crepe paper or talking to a hat-check girl disguised as the Goddess of Liberty and thinking 'My, how patriotic we are'. They went to a dance because they wanted to dance and forget 'the — — war' for a couple of hours. There weren't any snappy civilians receiving, as they were in the States, all the best attention and all the best service to the exclusion of the poor soldiering. Did we meet any Aussie civilians at all, we knew almost to a certainty that they were 4F, mentally deficient, or working twelve hours a day in a war-plant and chiefly interested in getting home to bed.

We were something new. Glamorous characters from America. The America our friends knew all about from seeing 'the pictures'. Some of us, the shallow ones, did our best to live up to this advance publicity, some of us did our best to tear it down. Whether or not we succeeded I can't say. We were the first Yanks to land at this particular port of debarkation, and for that reason horribly new and appreciated. Some of us took this adoration as only our due. A few of us were embarrassed by it, all of us soaked it up.

Others resented this adoration. They were the AIF [Australian Imperial Forces] returned. Returned from the Middle East, after Greece, Syria, Crete and the Western Desert. They were understandably burned up to find the female population gone 'Yank crazy'. But what could they do?

Fish such as you have never seen. Snapper caught in the Kaipara Harbour. The boys enjoy a day out. *Tudor Collins*

Fish, sacks of it, enough to feed the multitude or at least the battalion. Note the net in the background and foreground, 1943. *Tudor Collins*

Not only fish but fowl too! Let's hope it was in the shooting season, 1943.
Tudor Collins

The rest of the population resented highly any slurring remarks about 'the saviours of dear Old Aussie'. So the AIF returned suffered more or less in silence, got falling-down drunk with that 'devil damn the rest of the world' philosophy that is picked up in the front lines, and tried to even the score by consistently bumming us for all the cigarettes we were fool enough to offer. Now and then they would ask us, 'I s'y Yank d'ya reckon if we went to the Stites the —— sheilas 'ud go for us like they go for you chaps 'ere?' We told them, 'They sure would, Dig.' And probably they would at that, women being what they are.

Our uniform, too, outclassed anything the AIF could climb into. Compared with those veterans we looked like so many little cadets just out of the local academy and steeped in the tradition that shiny brass buttons make a soldier. The AIF ran to sweaters and baggy trousers held up with suspenders, something unheard of in our army. Undeniably they looked a rough tough bunch of boys, which they were. They joined the army of their own free will for the '——- hell of it' and gone overseas, while the smart lads considered the AIF a rough lot, stayed at home and played the ponies and waited for the Government to call 'em up.

Towards the end of the war, a slice of American culture was imported for the homesick troops. One morning in mid-April 1944, Aucklanders turning the radio dial would have heard an unfamiliar voice — 'Good morning, GIs, Bluejackets and Leathernecks, this is Station 1ZM Auckland, your American Expeditionary Station in New Zealand, bringing you by courtesy of the Government of New Zealand, your favourite programmes from back home. And this is Private Frank Gaunt introducing the announcing and operating staff: Sergeant Larry Dysart, known to us as Simon Legree, the man with the whip, programme supervisor; Corporal Karl Jean, announcer and operator; and Private Gene Twombly, announcer and operator . . .'

There will be many Aucklanders today who will remember with affection the American announcers, who, if they were not exactly the 'voices that breathed o'er Eden', brought a new dimension into the stereotyped radio of the day. Aucklanders were not used to being greeted with 'Hello, all you lovely people out there', not from a New Zealand radio station, where announcers were expected to suppress any projection of personality and stick strictly to the script on hand. From the first week the station generated a tremendous amount of mail, most of it enthusiastic. The announcers' relaxed and outgoing style was the antithesis of official radio edicts in this country at the time, so it was no surprise that the younger generation fell over themselves in the praise of the station.

1ZM was at that time the home station of Mr W. W. Rogers, its founder. Strained relations surfaced between Rogers and the then Labour Government, so that the Ministry of broadcasting was pleased to offer the station to the American Radio Service, which solved its own political problem and earned the thanks of the Americans. Programmes put on then that will arouse memories were *Duffy's Tavern, It Pays to be Ignorant, Make-Believe Ballroom Time, Music America Loves Best, Turn-Tune-Time* with Gene Twombly, *Classical Corner* (Karl Jean), *American College Songs* (Larry Dysart) and *Thirty-Minute Dramas* (Frank Gaunt).

Those who received the signal (and it was often heard as far south as Wellington) could only have been impressed by the very recent million-dollar programmes straight from the States, with the commercials deleted. The programme did the rounds of the AEAFRS (American Expeditionary Armed Forces Radio Services) circuit, from Nouméa, to Munda and Guadalcanal in the Solomons, and Bougainville.

Ex-Sergeant Larry Dysart, back in Auckland with his New Zealand wife on a regular trip, told the story of an Anzac Day memorial service, during which the band of the 43rd Division US Army played 'God Defend New Zealand', and in answer to that supplication, though the inference was not intentional, followed with 'The Yanks Are Coming'.

Larry gave this account of his time at 1ZM back in 1944.

When my buddy and I stepped ashore at Auckland the first person we met was a bobby [policeman]. 'Where can we get a milk shake and a hamburger?' 'You must be Americans,' he said. I enjoyed my stay in New Zealand. After all, I courted and married a New Zealand girl. Indeed I conducted part of my courtship over the air by playing certain Bing Crosby records. That by the way was one of our most popular programmes, a three-hour session of Bing's records, which we had to repeat because of so many requests. I wrote and told Bing and he very kindly replied. We also played request records for the American patients in the 39th General Hospital in Cornwall Park. They didn't have station ratings in those days, but as our programmes were tops back in the States, and appealed to a broad spectrum of society there, we assumed that broadly speaking that was the case here. The large amount of fan mail we received confirms this. The American accents of the announcers distinguished the station on the dial, and made us easily identifiable. We broadcast from the basement of the 1YA building at the top of Shortland Street and we had excellent relations with the 1YA people. Those were the days in New Zealand radio of Scrim and Aunt Daisy. We did the news, which was cleared, security-wise, by Lieutenant Commander Brookes-Gifford, USN. . . .

Yes, New Zealanders were searching for good entertainment, and I think we were able to give it to them. What pleased the forces, pleased Aucklanders. We found New Zealanders friendly, considerate and conservative. Overall I think we created goodwill and we were put to the test by the way we conducted ourselves. Unfortunately a small body of Marines would go ocassionally haywire, which did nothing for our good name. Some of our customs I know Aucklanders found very funny. When the armoured car drew alongside the kerb at the Bank of New Zealand in Queen Street to collect the pay for the troops, we had an armoured guard on both sides of the entrance with their pistols pointing to the skies. Well, it was funny then but not unrealistic forty years later.

By the end of 1944 the war in the Pacific was getting closer to the mainland of Japan, and the number of American personnel in Auckland diminished. In December of that year the station was handed back to the Minister of Broadcasting and the familiar voices of Dysart, Twombly, Grant and Jean were heard no more. They moved on to Nouméa to continue radio work for the forces there. Did the ten-month session here influence local broadcasting? This is how a local radio official saw the situation.

In those days we broadcast by the seat of our pants. There were no such things as listener polls, and we had absolutely no knowledge whether 1ZM was stealing our audience or we were stealing theirs. I know this, they had all the privileges and fewer responsibilities. They ignored copyright and we did it at our peril. They could, as an armed services network, the Mosquito network, get away with murder. At times the station manager and the Americans were uneasy bed-fellows. They had no commercial breaks, relied entirely on canned material from the States and had no recourse to studio material. But then they had very few on their staff. I regarded them as pirates in a way, 'fly-by-the nighters'.

[The Mosquito network referred to the radio station at Nouméa, New Caledonia, and the stations on Munda (New Georgia), Guadalcanal, and Bougainville in the Solomons. Mosquitoes in all these places were a serviceman's never-ending enemy.]

That may have been the reaction from the entrenched radio people of those times, but it was not the response from many of the young people of Auckland in 1944.

Bill, who was a Marine stationed in Wellington, recalls another radio station.

We used to listen to Tokyo Rose, the Japanese propagandist broadcasting from Tokyo. God she was clever. She would say — 'Yes Mary Jane Muller back in Santa Ana in California, your husband Joe is missing in New Guinea,' or 'Buddy Schmidt, 2nd Marine Division in Wellington, who's with your wife Jane tonight back in Chattanooga, Tennessee?' She knew which units were on which island in the Pacific. I can tell you the boys did not like her. Her propaganda script was a first class job. She played all the nostalgic records, like 'Home on the Range', 'Don't Get Around Much Anymore' or 'Who's Lonesome Tonight'. The Japanese troops, by the way, were supplied with Japanese women. It was certainly the case on Saipan where I saw these classy looking Jap dames and on Okinawa where the Jap officers had their own supply of women.

Throughout the war, there were some swinging times in Auckland. The Grand Hotel in Princes Street had been taken over for the use of American officers, likewise the Waverley Hotel in Customs Street East. Hotel Auckland was the American Red Cross Centre for enlisted men. Every night up at the Peter Pan Cabaret in Upper Queen Street it was 'Take the A-Train', 'You'll Never Know' or choo-chooing somebody home with 'Chattanooga Choo-choo'. The Wintergarden Cabaret beneath the Civic, with its ascending Wurlitzer organ and stars twinkling in a midnight sky, was reserved for officers to entertain their befurred, gin-and-Chevrolet women friends. The orchestra played in a golden barge, and the lions with sparkling eyes looked on. Visiting American ships would take over the facilities for the night. Partners for the visiting officers were always available from the Navy League organisation and the American Red Cross, which had a list of 'respectable' girls. Regina, a ballet mistress at the time, had a chorus line of girls, called the Lucky Lovelies, who put on a nightly floor show for the Americans, and she remembers those days well.

How could I ever forget them? They were the golden hours of the forties and that's for sure. It was glamour such as we had never known; the officers' uniforms, the long evening frocks of the girls set a scene which Auckland had seldom known. We did gypsy numbers, Can-Can, South American and Russian, the Americans loved them all. We had special

The Navy whoops it up at the Majestic Cabaret Wellington, 1943. *Allerdice Collection, Alexander Turnbull Library*

nights for Independence Day, Thanksgiving Day, and the Americans were always appreciative. There were flowers for the girls and always attention. Of course my girls were generally enraptured, they were looking at a different breed, such manners, such courtesy, and sometimes the nylons. It was no knockabout scene there. Drink, as everywhere, had to be discreetly hidden, brought in within the folds of the women's evening frocks, though fur coats were a favourite hiding place. The police were never known to visit the Civic, anyhow the Americans had their own MPs on patrol nearby. After the show my girls would go home in taxis; there was never any mixing with the guests, that was a strict rule of the management, and the girls had to be home at reasonable hours in order to attend to their wartime jobs.

Pop songs told the story of the times. Before America came into the war there was a procession of English songs, either schmaltzy and outrageously nostalgic like 'We'll Meet Again', 'White Cliffs of Dover', 'When They Sound the Last All Clear', 'It's a Lovely Day Tomorrow', sung with a sob in every line by Vera Lynn, the sweetheart of the forces, or the near-national anthem 'There'll Always be an England', sung with unabashed fervour by New Zealanders, most of whom had never been there, but probably had British ancestry.

'We're going to hang out the washing on the Siegfried Line' died a sudden death when the Germans had no need to defend it, but marched forward and over the French Maginot Line too. 'Kiss me goodnight, sergeant-major, tuck me in my little wooden bed' was okay to sing in 1940–41 but would be highly suspect these days. Less emotive and more episodic was 'The Quartermaster's Store', with beer you couldn't get near. One song common to all Allied troops, whether American, British, Australian, Canadian or New Zealanders, was 'Bless 'em All', with its unprintable verses. On one occasion in Fiji New Zealand soldiers were belting out their version of 'F—- 'em All' under the showers after their weekly route march, when the colonel came in, swagger stick and all, and tried to put a stop to it. The boys pretended they couldn't see him in the clouds of steam. Down in the wet canteens, amid the slopped 'horse piss', the troops were always ready to 'Roll out the Barrel'. There were not the blatant recruiting songs of the Boer War like 'Soldiers of the Queen' or 'We don't want to lose you, but we think you ought to go' of World War I. But if World War I had its 'Take me back to dear Old Blighty', and 'Hello, hello, who's your lady friend', America now provided a spate of nostalgic songs, which were played in every dance hall in New Zealand and plugged on the radio. There was the repetitive theme of men thinking of their girls back home as in 'You'd Be So Nice to Come Home to', 'I've got a Girl in Kalamazoo', 'Embraceable You', 'Sweetheart of Sigma Chi', 'I'll be Home for Christmas', 'You'll Never Know How Much I Love You', 'Dolores', 'Amapola', 'Marie Elena', 'Tangerine', 'You Can Roll a Silver Dollar', 'Sweet Georgia Brown', 'Blueberry Hill' and 'I'll Be Seeing You'. Back home in the States the girls were singing about their men overseas in 'Don't Get Around Much Anymore', 'They're Either Too Old or Too Grassy Green', 'Someone to Watch Over Me', 'Who's Lonesome Tonight' and 'I'm Getting Sentimental Over You'.

The big bands of Harry James, Glen Miller, Tommy Dorsey and Artie Shaw ushered in swing with 'In the Mood', 'String of Pearls', 'Take the 'A' Train', 'Adios', 'Chattanooga Choo Choo'. Their tunes were also played by the regimental bands, smooth music with a preponderance of saxo-phones, which New Zealanders enjoyed for the first time.

The Andrews Sisters belted out 'The Boogie Woogie Bugle Boy of Company B', a favourite song for the jitterbuggers up at the Peter Pan. 'Hold that Tiger' and 'Strip-Tease Polka' had their adherents, but in the huts up at Camp Hale in the Auckland Domain or Camp Bunn out at Tamaki there would be the unashamed sentimental tunes with mouth organ backing, like 'Moonlight Bay', 'Dixie', 'The Wabash Cannonball', 'Birmingham Jail', 'Red River Valley', 'You Are My Sunshine', and 'Red Sails in the Sunset'. Irving Berlin's 'White Christmas' came out at the end of 1942 and was sung with maudlin nostalgia in the steaming camps of the South Pacific by the troops, many of whom had never

A halloween party for Marines and sailors at the 39th General Hospital, Auckland, 15 December 1943. *NZ Herald*

known a white Christmas (or a 'white mistress', in the version they often used to sing). Around this time too, George M. Cohan's film *Yankee Doodle Dandy* was screened, with a revival of the World War I song 'The Yanks Are Coming'. For lame-duck planes returning to base there was 'Coming in on a Wing and a Prayer', with 'Praise the Lord and Pass the Ammunition' for the gunners.

The sedate cheek-to-cheek foxtrots of the ballroom made way for the razzle-dazzle gee-whiz jitterbugging. This hyped-up style of unbridled dancing, which the young women took to like born-again chorus girls, was a further indication of the smashing down of some of the old taboos. On the wall at the Peter Pan Cabaret was a sign that read 'No full skirts when jitterbugging'.

Ann Powell's hotel, the New Criterion in Albert Street, was a favourite drinking spot for the Americans. The Downtown Club in Customs Street, run by the YWCA for Allied troops, was generally monopolised by US servicemen. The ballroom of Government House in Princes Street was used for Saturday night dances when various organisations sponsored the evenings. For less elegant surroundings there were the Orange Hall, the Druids Hall, Masonic Hall and the Crystal Palace out in Mt Eden Road. But for those who liked beer, T-bone steaks and swing music and had a fat wallet, there was El Rey out in the western suburbs. You were moving in fast company if you were able to say you had spent the night at El Rey. For the Americans it must have been redolent of the Prohibition days of the early thirties. Smoke hung in the large room, with its magnificent low bay window providing a view out on to the Manukau. Women were there in long evening frocks, men probably in the officer's uniform of some branch of the US Forces. Snow, who blew trumpet in the band, recalls those times.

> Hillsborough was (and still is) a dry area but that didn't matter to the El Rey patrons. There used to be loads of grog there, and it was very blatant. The customers used to shout us but we had our own grog planted out in the wash-house among all the laundry and the mangles. The band played all the Glenn Miller hits of the day, tunes like 'It's Been a Long, Long Time', 'You'll Never Know', 'I Don't Want to Set the World on Fire', and 'Dream'. On occasion, particularly after midnight, 'musos' from town would come out with their wives. They used to be able to get in provided they played a tune of course.

Reg played sax in the band, and remembers the generosity of El Rey's American patrons.

> A Yank would come up and he would want us to play a request. 'It'll cost you — 10 quid,' we'd say, and the Yank would pull out a roll of dollar notes, they didn't know the value of a dollar, they were hill-billies some of them, didn't know what to do with the money, just rolling in money. Another time there was a woman there, no names no pack drill. She knew one of the boys in the band. This night she was with a Yankee major, helluva nice chap. She said, 'This major of mine is from Texas. Would you play 'Deep in the Heart of Texas'? From then on, whenever he was there with a woman we played 'Deep in the Heart' and there was a bottle of whisky for us.

Del, piano player and band leader, has his share of anecdotes.

> A lot of Americans used to go there along with the élite of Auckland. All the girls were there of course. Liquor out in Hillsborough was illegal but the police turned a blind eye. Some of the regulars were brass hats, like Admiral Richard E. Byrd. He was no snob, this bloke. We had a little drinking room out the back and he used to give us a dozen beer. The admiral made hush-hush trips. We know that now, we didn't then; they were totally secret. But we know that he used to go down to the Antarctic, something about setting up a US base down there. The club also attracted the Americans who reckoned they could play. We used to get all sorts of Yanks — Navy blokes, Army blokes, Marines and the bull-shitters who'd say they used to play with Tommy Dorsey or whoever, and you'd sit them up there with a trumpet or a sax and they were hopeless. But some of those Yanks were really great players, they had it.

Today the El Rey night club is the St David's Church Hall.

The YWCA's Downtown Club attracted more servicemen than any other club, and in 1943 they would have been mostly American.

Because it was an adjunct of the YWCA, no alcohol was allowed on the premises, and consequently it welcomed the less flamboyant servicemen. There was no hanky panky at the Downtown Club. It was all dignity and decorum and long evening dresses at the Saturday night dance. Tearaway American boys, more or less inebriated, sought out the smoke-laden and murky interiors of Auckland jitterbugging dives rather than brave the baleful stares of the Downtown chaperones. Dances closed at 11 p.m. to enable the girls to get home on public transport. No girl would fall by the wayside, not if the YWCA had anything to do with it. And so the Americans whiled away the hours with maxinas, valetas, foxtrots and jitterbugging. Photos of afternoon tea assignations with Americans reveal a staid and sedate atmosphere, with girls in hats, their gloves alongside their handbags. Anxious mothers could be assured that their daughters were in safe hands. But some daughters didn't want to be in safe hands. In that case they were probably not at the Downtown Club. 'I remember,' said Joan, 'one American officer arriving at the club and saying, "Introduce me to a nice girl, will you. I've been accosted about twenty-five times since moving up here from the wharf."' There was nothing new about the behaviour of women down on the Auckland wharves, where it was not unknown for sexual dalliance to go on through the iron railings which kept the public off the wharves. Says a young girl of those times, 'It only needed a naval ship to arrive in the Waitemata Harbour and these girls would emerge. I would see them in the doorways of shops in Queen Street dressed in tight black skirts, a red jacket, upswept hair-do, a white shoulder-bag and high heels. Where they came from I never could fathom.' Some girls would crawl under the barbed wire around Victoria Park to get into the camp.

In a wage-controlled economy, where the only shop open on a Sunday was the milk bar, the Americans spent thousands of dollars on flowers, taxis, restaurants, jewellers and purchases in the camp PX stores to repay New Zealand families for their hospitality. To dine out in wartime Auckland was to be taken to the Silver Grill, the Empire, the City Grill, Cook's, Blake's, the Regent, the Burlington, or Farmers, and if you wanted damask dinner napkins, starched white tablecloths and shiny silver, Milne and Choyce was the scene.

For hard-drinking men in Auckland there was the Royal in Victoria Street, where the Americans requisitioned a floor or more of the accommodation. Vic, a wartime licensee of the Royal, recalled the pub's social life.

Civvies kept to themselves. They didn't hit it off with the services. The Americans always drank in groups, Marines, Army, Navy, and seldom seemed to mix. The women came in droves looking for company and, man, there was plenty of it. Women didn't drink in the main bars in those days, only the lounge bars. There were fights and skirmishes, but by and large the Yanks were very well behaved. But the penalties were so severe. The American MPs, who hunted in packs, were men to be feared. I was never ever guilty of ringing for MPs. The boys could only drink beer. We got twelve assorted bottles of spirits a week. Over the road from us was the Victoria, this was the New Zealand Navy boys' doss-house. Americans didn't drink there. Then there was the Thistle, Derby, Central, Metropolitan, City Club, Auckland, Waverley, Imperial, Empire, Carpenter's Arms, Queen's Head and the United Service, all gone, or their names have'.

By early 1943 the authorities had permitted the American presence to be publicised in the press without identifying particular units, referring to divisions by names, or mentioning their movements. The social pages of the newspapers were announcing engagements of New Zealand girls to the Americans and publishing photos of international marriages.

A Wellington jeweller commented: 'They come in with their pockets full of dollars and are eager to buy anything they fancy. They buy rings for their girlfriends and rings like knuckledusters for themselves. Watches disappear as soon as we put them out, so too do greenstone and black opals.' Orchids were also swooped on as soon as they appeared in florists' windows. 'Sailors love roses and sweetpeas, being at sea for long

'Not even a mention'. Marines study a Wellington newspaper. Troop movements were strictly censored. 2 December 1942. *Evening Post*

periods they have to have something that reminds them of home,' said a florist. Twelve-year-old schoolboys were on the streets selling corsages from home-made trays slung around their necks. For a ball put on by the Americans at the Peter Pan, Auckland, florists would receive orders for hundreds of corsages, one presented at the door to every girl.

In January 1943 Admiral 'Bull' Halsey, Commander South Pacific, was in New Zealand. So too in that year was Commander Gene Tunney, former heavyweight boxing champion of the world, and comedian Joe E. Brown, who was later to dance a famous *pas de deux* in Marilyn Monroe's *Some Like It Hot*. The troops amused themselves at the Glide Skating Rink in Wellington, and officers were photographed on the lawn at the Trentham Races accompanied by American Marine Corps nurses. Up in Auckland the Americans volunteered to help pick the vegetables grown by the Department of Agriculture on 500 acres at Mangere. When the 7.30 a.m. commuter train from Upper Hutt to Wellington was derailed and three passengers were killed, American medical teams were on the spot.

President Roosevelt sent his wife Eleanor as an envoy to cheer the troops, tour the convalescent wards, attend dances, rallies, games of American gridiron football, and exude her renowned charm. She arrived in a Liberator C-87 and was greeted by the Governor-General, Sir Cyril Newall, and Prime Minister Peter Fraser. She visited the US naval hospital at Silverstream, was taken round Rotorua by Guide Rangi, visited the Cecil Club and pinned her name on Washington, DC, on the giant mural map there of the States, to join hundreds of Marine names. In a speech she said, 'Many of the women at home would like to send a message to the women of New Zealand. They would like to say "thank you" for the kindness you have shown to our American boys.' General MacArthur during the war saw President Roosevelt and said in parting, 'Give my regards to your wife Mr President.' The President replied, 'Should you see my wife, give her *my* regards will you!'

Some movie houses remained open on Sundays as a concession to uniformed Americans and their friends. An occasional USO concert party turned up to entertain the troops, while the 6th Marines in Wellington produced a show of their own, the 'Fourragère Follies'. The 'fourragère' (literally 'fodder') was a military distinction earned by the 6th Marines during World War I at Belleau Wood in France, and conferred on the unit by the French. It consisted of a green braid worn round the left shoulder. The Marine divisional band of seventy or more players under the baton of M/G Olagnez became well known to Wellingtonians and the lower North Island. The sousaphone, which wound around the player like a giant boa constrictor, was something new to Wellington. Clarinettest Artie Shaw and his hot 'licorice stick' was another drawcard for the troops. He and his Navy band helped to entertain a thousand returning New Zealand servicemen and their friends in the RNZAF hall at Rongotai.

Coffee places and milk bars with exotic names like Hot Dog, Florida, California and Sunshine sprang up along Willis Street and Lambton Quay. The American Red Cross in Hotel Cecil supplied restaurant facilities, dance floor, gymnasium, lunch counter, hobby rooms and showers. But it was the chow — ham and eggs, doughnuts and real American coffee — that was the crowd pleaser with American and Allied troops alike. Webby's Club, founded by Gwen Webb for servicemen in 1940, hosted hundreds of visiting servicemen in the old converted grain store in Lower Cuba Street. Every hotel in Wellington packed the Marines in, until that archaic shout at six o'clock of 'Time, gentlemen, please' pitchforked befuddled troops onto the streets. But gone now are the Cecil, the Midland, and the Grand Hotel, where Mr Coltman was a friendly host to so many. No longer will a returning American find the French Maid coffee shop in Lambton Quay, where a paternal Mr Singleton kept an eye on proceedings. But he will find an up-market Green Parrot restaurant in Taranaki Street, open all night in the war years for the after-movie Marine crowds and their 'styke and aigs' orders.

Leo, a waiter at the Green Parrot during the war years, reminisces about his customers then.

The streets were blacked out, and one winter's night in 1942 strange soldiers came into the restaurant. It took me a while to see they were Marines because no one ever heard of them coming. I got on well with the Marines. We had regular ones there every day, many of them met their future wives there . . . At the Green Parrot they knew they were never overcharged. We were getting that friendly with them, even tips were out of the question. They would never offer, neither would we take. The Marines were amazed they were getting a steak for two bob. The milk was free, it was never charged. We never gave anyone tickets, we memorised every order. Their favourite order? Steak, raw tomatoes and a glass of milk. We didn't have waitresses, other restaurants did and the Marines always got preferential treatment from the girls. When the midnight earthquake [experienced in Wellington and up as far as Masterton in June 1942] was there, the only customers we had were Marines. I heard one say, 'Say, bud, this is worse than god-damn Pearl Harbour' . . .

We had lots of officers come in, including a Hollywood movie actor, Louis Hayward, who went under the name of Captain Richards to avoid the rush of the ladies. The MPs — not politicians (though they came too) but military police — were regulars, dropping in for a cup of tea any time of the night. An American serviceman could not be on the streets after midnight. The MPs used to shut their eyes, or at least some of them did, some of them didn't. You only had to dial the MPs' number and they would be on the spot in a minute.

We had regular Marine boys, and before they went away they would come and say goodbye, leaving messages for their girlfriends and that. The Army never liked to come round when the Marines were there. The Marines called the Army men 'doggies' or 'dogface'. If an Army man walked into the restaurant the young Marines would start barking like dogs. You met all nationalities and heard all languages, Italian, Jugoslav, Greek, Irish. If they spoke Italian they were Italian, but also good Americans. They still recognised their own background. Very few coloured men came into the restaurant. That could have caused a riot . . . Few New Zealand troops came into the restaurant, they recognised the Green Parrot as Marine territory. Liquor was hard to come by. Whisky (not Scotch) was $20 on the black market, it came from the South Island somewhere. The Green Parrot was open seven nights a week from 5 p.m. to 2 a.m. We had all sorts; in a night restaurant you get the lot, from the top to the bottom. The air-raid shelter was in front of the restaurant, mad of logs and standing on the ground. I was a sort of air-raid warden.

Life was a cabaret old chum for the Americans at the Majestic Cabaret in downtown Wellington. 'Before the war,' said Doreen, 'there was always a good band and very good supper for the all-inclusive price of 2s 6d (25 cents). It was a great pick-up place, if you were so inclined.' Tassie, too, remembers the Majestic well. She belonged to the Spinsters Club, founded by a group of women who banded together to offer hospitality to the servicemen. During the Masterton earthquake in June 1942 their Manners Street premises were badly damaged and they sought alternative premises. 'We went along to see Freddie Carr at the Majestic, expecting to be thrown out. Instead he told us we could use the Majestic free of charge every Sunday for as long as we wished. He said his staff was at our disposal, we couldn't believe our ears. Meals and afternoons teas were provided for any soldier, sailor, airman or merchant seamen. The girls saved coupons, pooled resources and raided their mothers' larders. We baked and baked and made millions of sandwiches. Although we couldn't make fruit cakes we used our ingenuity to come up with all sorts of good food.'

During the week nights Navy men and Marines crowded the dance floor, bringing their liquor, in what was supposed to be a dry area, in lemonade bottles. This might well have been pure alcohol acquired from some American dispensary and was used to lace fruit drinks. After the war the subterfuges of hiding liquor in the women's furs or up the pseudo-stone fireplace chimneys of the cabaret were resorted to. During the war liquor, when available, was openly consumed and provided the decorum of the ballroom was not blatantly disturbed, the police stayed away. Photos of those cabaret days in the Alexander Turnbull Library show that behaviour was unrestrained.

In the meantime, vast quantities of stubbies of beer with brand

70

names like Budweiser, Schlitz, and Lucky were consumed in the camps. If whisky was available it was Australian Corio. The 'gyrenes' called it jump whisky — one drink would make you jump like a kangaroo. Naturally the boys were not above brewing up hellfire concoctions of their own. One popular mixed drink, called 'Shell-shock', was one-third port wine and two-thirds stout.

Bert, a Marine in camp near Wellington and now living in New Zealand, described a typical night out.

After we had squared away in camp, we came in on the rattler from Paekakariki on Friday nights and headed for the Midland. The officers used to hang out in the Grand; we made the Midland our headquarters. We aimed to be there at five o'clock when Scotch whisky was available for one hour. We got loaded on Scotch and, being young, we could drink a lot. I drank for effect; it was the thing to do. We would sit there at

A night out with the Marines in the Majestic Cabaret, Wellington, 1943.

the tables with their white tablecloths for two or three hours with the glasses stacked in the middle. We couldn't buy after six, but we didn't have to leave. When we did, we went up to the St Francis Hall in the Terrace area, where the American Red Cross ladies looked after us. As seventeen- and eighteen-year-olds we loved milk and ice-cream and we loved the steak. It wasn't the best steak, it wasn't T-bone but I liked it. New Zealand seemed like it was a little behind the times, but it had what we wanted: good food, liquor and girls.

When women in the various government offices heard the concerted tramp of feet outside they knew the Marines had hit town. They would fly to the windows to look for familiar faces. Not only would the switch-boards light up, but up would go the haircurlers for the evening's date. Deep in the heart of the urban jungles, girls flaunted the favours of their American boyfriends, wearing *Semper Fidelis* Marine Corps badges, and it was considered the in-thing to get around in American green fatigue jackets, producing Camel, Philip Morris or Chesterfield cigarettes at will. One schoolgirl remembers how the American sailors used to throw money from the Wellington trams:

> I was too proud to pick it up, but I used to put my foot on a coin. Two bob was two bob in those days. The Marines had heavy signet rings with all sorts of signs on them, and their chunky gold-faced identification bracelets were not exactly as worn by the short-back-and-sides Kiwis. I was told that this jewellery was not to be worn in the jungle, where the light could catch it and make you a target for the Japs. [Officers did not wear distinguishing badges of rank in the jungle, which would attract the special attention of Japanese snipers, nor did enlisted men wear their stripes.]

An Auckland newspaper recently invited letters from its readers on reminiscences of the Americans' stay in the war years. Here is a selection of their bitter-sweet memories.

> When I was a child of about eight in 1942 I remember quite clearly when the US Marines were in New Zealand. My mother had sent me down the road to buy some goods. In those years all we heard about was the war, the Germans and the Japanese, and of course we had siren warnings at nights, when we had to pull down the blinds. I had only gone about a hundred yards down the road when suddenly around the corner came a long line of jeeps with soldiers in their camouflage uniforms sitting inside. What a shock I got. I took off back home at high speed shouting out to my mother to 'Get inside quick. The Germans are coming.' What a relief when it was explained to me that these men weren't Germans but Americans who were over here in New Zealand protecting our land. What I do recall is their friendliness and hospitality as they stopped their jeeps and got out at our front gate and gave us biscuits and sweets and had a friendly chat to my parents on the Wairoa–Gisborne main road on their way up north.

Janet, who was also surprised at the American presence, related the following incident.

One day as my mother drove her two-door Ford Prefect towards the railway line at McKay's Crossing near Paekakariki I noticed that the ground beneath the grove of gum trees there was covered with sleeping and exhausted Americans. It was not until I read *War Cry* by Leon Uris about fifteen years later that I realised that the men I had seen that day had just completed a forced march from their camp to Foxton and back. Their next stop was Guadalcanal.

Many readers who wrote, and most of them were women, wished to remain anonymous. Yesterday's love affairs were not something they wanted bruited around the dinner table. Rose was one of those who had an American friend during the war.

He was at the hospital in Rosebank Road, Avondale. He was a bulldozer driver making air-strips somewhere in the Pacific Islands. He had been blown up and landed twenty feet away from where he had been working. To look at him you wouldn't have known he was sick, but some of the other boys thought he wouldn't live long enough to go home. He was 'the answer to a maiden's prayer', tall, dark and handsome. I had no boyfriend at the time and he visited our home and we went to the pictures in Auckland. He came from Roby in Texas and never said anything my mother could have disapproved of. I did have a photo of him but destroyed it when I got married. My American left Auckland after about three months. I never found out what happened to him, the boys wouldn't tell me. I'm afraid he may have died.

Liz must have sent her contribution with a nostalgic tear.

Auckland, 1943 — yes I can still see all those good-looking tall Americans marching up Queen Street and hear the band playing the 'Marines Hymn', 'Over There', and 'Yankee Doodle'. I was only about fourteen at the time but my heart missed a beat. My hair was long and I always wore a red rose in it, and gold ear-rings. There was candy and flowers and dancing nearly every night at the Peter Pan. There was also the sadness of hearing the news that George or Tim wouldn't be coming back. Killed at Guadalcanal. But still the dances went on. Glenn Miller-style music — 'American Patrol' or 'I've Got a Girl in Kalamazoo'. My war daddy wrote to me from the Islands nearly every day. He was one of the lucky ones who made it back to the States and married the girl back home. My two children are grown up now and I think New Zealand is a great place. Happily married as I am, I'll always remember my war daddy. Forty-three years have gone by but those letters still come, like they did from the Islands during the war, and his good wife often tells him 'Someday we'll get a train from West Virginia and then one of them big planes in California and you can show me that beautiful country you talk so much about with your war buddies.' My war daddy takes his grandchildren to Myrtle Beach every summer; but he always remembers to draw a heart on the sand: 'Send it to New Zealand,' he says to the waves on the outgoing tide, 'to the girl who was my sweetheart in 1943.'

A young Auckland girl at business college also told her story.

I was sixteen in 1944, a shy, self-conscious, quiet girl living in a sheltered world that was filled with romantic hopes and dreams on the one hand and the harsh realities of a country at war on the other. My father and brother were in the New Zealand Air Force, and Auckland city was teeming with American servicemen intent on enjoying themselves every last minute before facing the horrors of Pacific warfare. They were different and exciting with their smart uniforms, smooth accents, and they definitely had a winning way with the women. Business college had finished early that summer's day and I stood in the queue for the 1 p.m. bus at the city terminal. Two American sailors joined the small group of passengers. Their swagger was fascinating. Their Navy outfits added to their glamour. My eyes were drawn repeatedly to one in particular who had wavy black hair, tanned skin, blue eyes and a big gold ring in one ear (something quite uncommon in my world). He was Errol Flynn, Tyrone Power and every other pirate hero in real life. I sat in the facing seats near the back of the bus and was amazed and apprehensive when he left his friend and sat beside me. To my horror he leaned close, put his arm round my shoulders, asked what colour my eyes were and crooned *You'd be so nice to come home to / You'd be so nice by the fire*. I squirmed in embarrassment. Neighbours and friends of my mother boarded the bus and stared and looked away. It was not the thing in our little moral world to be seen with American servicemen, let alone be cuddled up in public at 2 p.m. I only wished I could crawl away under the seat. Instead I dug out my shorthand book and tried to study but could not see a word before me. Eventually he gave me up and shifted back to his friend. A New Zealand airman promptly slipped into the vacant seat. I murmured a quiet 'thank you' but a quick smile was the only answer. How young and naive we were in those days. Now, forty years later, I can only laugh at the fool I was, and hope they all fared well in the war.

This mixture of nervousness and romantic attraction was probably a typical reaction among young New Zealand women to the strangers in their midst, the Marines, soldiers and sailors who represented the military might of Uncle Sam. For many, the attraction proved strong enough to end in marriage.

CHAPTER FOUR

War Brides, War Effort

Nearly 1400 New Zealand women married American servicemen and went to the States as war brides. Some obviously hoped that they would find themselves transported to a life in the happy-ever-after-land of an affluent American suburb, but there was often a considerable gap between the fantasy and the reality. Some of these marriages were disasters, when the glamour of the uniform vanished and only the harsh reality of impoverished surroundings in an alien world remained. Many other marriages have survived to this day, and couples, sometimes with their families, make regular pilgrimages back to New Zealand today.

Some New Zealand girls might well have married Americans just to get to the States, where they jettisoned their husbands to cast round for other conquests. Marriages did not automatically confer American citizenship nor was marriage to an American serviceman in New Zealand a straightforward exercise. A girl's background was researched by an American chaplain before official permission was granted to a serviceman to marry. Girls were subject to the indignity of an examination for possible venereal disease, and also for pregnancy.

An order of the day signed by Major General John Marston, commander of 2 MarDiv at the time, instructed the investigating officer to 'determine the moral and social status of the woman concerned'. It further stated that 'Officers and enlisted men who marry without authority will be disobeying an order of the Secretary of Navy and will be subject to severe disciplinary measures.'

'You will notice,' said a war bride now resident in the Wellington area with her ex-Marine husband, 'that the edict says nothing about the "moral status" of the Marine. That apparently was assumed always to be beyond reproach.' In spite of that order there must have been secret marriages. One American donned a New Zealand uniform and was smuggled back from the Solomons on the ship *Talamanca* by a New Zealand sergeant (the American's future brother-in-law). He married his Papakura fiancée and he and his wife are still happily married in the States, where he is one of America's most successful coin dealers.

The division did not make it easy for a Marine to marry a New Zealand girl. He had to provide $200 in ready cash for his bride's passage to the States, and he also had to submit evidence that he would be gainfully employed after the war. His application for permission to marry had to be approved by a chaplain, his commanding officer and the divisional personnel office. His military record was examined and

Carroll Phillips, 169th Field Artillery, US Army 43rd Division and Lois (née Dill) of Kaipara Flats, leave the Church of England, Warkworth on the occasion of their marriage, May 1944.

the findings submitted to the girl's family. A Marine officer visited the girl's family home to judge whether she would be worthy of American citizenship.

Once the serviceman had returned to the States, he had to request in writing that his wife join him there. Without this documentation a war bride was unable to gain entry to America. There were isolated cases of men who, on returning home, had second thoughts about the marriage they had contracted in New Zealand; there was nothing the bride could do if no request was forthcoming.

Beneath the facade of hedonism, of boozing, of jitterbugging, of the helter-skelter pursuit of a good time, lay the agonising of many New Zealand girls and sorrowing parents. There were girls whose New Zealand husbands had been killed fighting overseas, some with a child born after the father's departure, girls whose fiancés had been killed, girls with fiancés or husbands posted missing or confirmed prisoners of war. Single girls who entered relationships with Americans often found themselves in the same circumstances. But then the lines of demarcation became blurred when separated wives, war widows or fiancées took up with the Americans. Some childless war widows, consumed with sorrow at the loss of their New Zealand husband of but a week, month or year, could never bring themselves to marry again. They could never pick up the pieces, their brief memories of married love they could only take to the grave. Others with the unbridled passion that wartime generates threw all caution to the wind, played the field and took on all crew-cut comers.

Many girls became pregnant to American servicemen, some married their lovers, some did not. Some were unable to marry because their American lovers were already married. Others found themselves pregnant with the American father overseas. If the father admitted paternity he may have felt constrained to do something about it. He could wait until he was a time-expired man, then hitch-hike back to New Zealand and marry the girl with or without official permission. Or he may have decided to do nothing. American servicemen in New Zealand were continually exhorted by their superiors to behave or take the consequences. Servicemen court-martialled and found guilty of some offence could, as part of their punishment, be dispatched to the forward fighting areas in the South Pacific at a moment's notice. Left tormented was a pregnant girl, facing the prospect of back-street abortionists and the ever-present danger of septicaemia. Brittle happiness there may have been in New Zealand society, but sadness reached into hundreds of extended families in those war years, with women usually the losers.

The figures for illegitimate births in New Zealand show that there were 1120 in 1939; by 1944 the total had risen to 1999. The latter figure would include women who, having farewelled servicemen lovers either American or New Zealand, subsequently found themselves pregnant with no man on hand to legitimise the birth. Viewed with scepticism must be the well-worn stories of apparently white American servicemen who, when married to New Zealand girls, fathered children with negroid features and dark skins. Of equally doubtful authenticity are tales of American servicemen found guilty of rape who were taken outside to international waters and there shot.

One Auckland woman concerned for the fate of unmarried pregnant girls offered a refuge for them in their trouble. May Harvey, wealthy in her own right, compassionate and caring, began the Motherhood of Man organisation. She arranged hostel accommodation, rural employment with sympathetic people for girls during their pregnancy, and attended if necessary to adoption procedures. The fund and property she established then still exists, the income allocated by trustees to various charitable organisations. May did not apportion blame, and certainly not to the Americans; she was concerned only with the end result.

Even the women who became engaged or married to Americans were not always highly regarded. Elizabeth was one woman who resented the label of 'war bride'.

Among some locals the term carried a certain amount of innuendo that you were taking a risk, that you would probably never see your husband again, that he would have, on getting to the States, changed his mind. There were those cynics who enjoyed putting you down and resented the fact that you were leaving dull New Zealand for the glamorous United States. Well, any international marriage is a risk, but those of the war years contracted in unusual times carried an extra risk. I went on holiday and when I came back I found my Marine husband-to-be had been shipped back to the States. I didn't see him for three years, during which time he served on Okinawa. I flew to America in a Constellation plane, island-hopping all the way, with people being put off and petrol being put on. We war-brides-to-be managed to hold on to our seats. Before we were allowed to land we had to have our return fare and post a bond of $500. I arrived in San Francisco to be greeted with a dozen roses and my fiancé in his Studebaker coupé. I have never regretted marrying an American. We lived in the States for twenty years and came back to New Zealand in 1965 to live in the Wellington area, where I first met my husband.

In Wellington, girls engaged or married to Americans started up the Young Eagles Club, an organisation whose aims were to learn about each other, where their future homes in America were likely to be, when they were going, on which ship, and to lend each other moral support. American Red Cross officials gave lectures on life in America and the sort of problems that could confront an immigrant wife, and where to go for assistance.

The YWCA in Auckland sponsored the formation of the American Kiwi Club, a similar organisation. Over 600 girls, many already wives and mothers, attended talks at the club to learn about life in America, and to meet other girls who would be going to the same state. As the New Zealand girls moved out, Canadian war brides, wives of New Zealand airmen who had trained in Canada, moved in. As for the small number of American women in this country, the US Navy nurses in the

78

wards of the American hospitals in Auckland and Wellington, if any married New Zealand men it must have been a rare occurrence.

Jean, an Auckland girl who became a war bride, was the product of a strictly conforming Catholic family, whose teachings she had never questioned. In February 1945 she travelled to America.

Looking back, I was so incredibly innocent that it was only when I got on the boat for America and saw the conduct of some war brides that the scales fell away from my eyes. I had heard about the behaviour of girls down at the Auckland wharves at night, but no respectable girl spent time down there so how should I have known what went on? I was a rare New Zealand girl in that I was not yet married to a US serviceman, but I was allowed to get a passage on a ship to the US in order to marry. I had to undergo a medical exam and had I known what it was all about, I don't think I would have gone. It was pretty bloody awful and entailed an internal examination by an American doctor who was rude and vulgar.

'We went over to the States in the *General Mitchell*, which, beside carrying war brides, had troops on board returning from the Burma campaign, some American nurses who had served there, and some Chinese who were going to be trained as aircrew. We were booked to go on the *Talamanca* some months before, but the ship was diverted for troop transportation, so we had a second lot of goodbyes to go through. In addition New Zealand brides had had their pay allocation revoked because this would be paid in the States. Consequently, many got on the *Mitchell* with precious little money.

When we got on board the captain gave us a lecture. He said his ship was not equipped to carry women. Strict hygiene would have to be observed, as he did not want disease breaking out on the ship. I was in a cabin with twelve women and eight babies. Because I was single I was on two meals a day; mothers were on three. I was detailed to look after babies, mind you, my husband-to-be had paid for my passage, but that counted for nought. There was an inspection every day of the cabin but many of the mothers could not have cared less. For the first time I realised that when New Zealanders said that some girls would do anything to get to the States, that there was truth in it. All I can say is that the conduct of some war brides on that ship left a great deal to be desired. One American nurse said to me, 'I wish I could find the mother of that baby; it's been crying all day.' When the nurse finally found the mother she was told, 'I don't give a damn about the baby.'

We were given use of half of the officers' lounge. Officers were not allowed on our side but girls could go over to the officers' side. May I say that one half of that lounge looked as if it was seldom used. I can only marvel at my own naivety and innocence. [Jean's husband chimed in here with, 'She was innocent and I kept her that way.']

We went to the States non-stop in twelve days to land at Los Angeles. We were not expected and were taken to a hotel where there were no beds left. The city was absolutely swarming with US servicemen who would have found good use for the hotel beds. After all, San Diego, the

'USA here we come!' War brides on board ship leaving New Zealand for America, 1945.

main US Navy base was close by. The management said they would put up cots for us in the dining room. 'No way,' said my girlfriend. 'We'll sweat it out in a lounge chair.' As it was, we looked after a couple of babies whose mothers had hived off with servicemen. Then the management said we could have the bell-hop's room, so we did get a bed.

I found American people lovely — warm and friendly. My husband was in the Army and we were sent to Kansas. We didn't live in barracks, my husband would not contemplate it and when I asked why he said, 'You've just got no idea of what goes on in barracks.' 'Such as?' 'Such as parties where names are thrown into a hat for a little wife swapping.' Honestly I was so incredibly naive — I had lived a sheltered life in a middle-class Mt Eden home, belonged to a private tennis club, attended mass each Sunday. I was so squeaky clean, so to speak, that by today's standards it is unbelievable.

I was very lonely, but through the USO I got a job at the Kansas State Agriculture College. People were very kind to me. One time there was a morning tea and I asked, 'Are we going to have a shout?' This was greeted uproariously. 'Shout,' they cried. 'What does that mean?' Some English girls I met at the English Speaking Union in New York found it very difficult to settle down in the US. Some could not take being teased about their accent. New Zealand girls fitted in much more easily.

Americans in those war years in New Zealand put women on a pedestal. They respected them, they were good to them, they knew how to treat women. After all, America is a matriarchal society where 'momma' rules all. An American, you felt, considered himself lucky to be taking you out. No, I don't think New Zealand men of the time were 'loners', but they were certainly chauvinists. By 1943 most of them were overseas, especially the 'macho' ones who saw war as a great big adventure. Left behind were the married men, the unfit singles and those in essential industry. There was a vacuum left that the Americans were only too happy to fill — it was as simple as that. After all they had plenty of money and plenty of leisure.

Jean's husband interrupted to say, 'When I arrived here as a member of the 25th Division I had a year's pay to spend, well over a $1000. In the first month I spent $80 on flowers . . . . £1 New Zealand was worth $3.24. As a Tech Sergeant I was paid $150 a month. A private got $64 in his hand. We all carried insurance on our lives of $10,000, whether we liked it or not.' Jean continued:

When I went before the judge for my naturalisation papers in the US I had already prepared myself by swotting up on the Amendments to the American Constitution and thought I was prepared mentally for any question. And then the judge asked me, 'July 4 — what do we commemorate in the United States on that date?' My mind went blank. In the embarrassing silence my counsel weighed in with, 'Your honour, you must forgive her, where she comes from they wear grass skirts and have bare feet.' By this time I was able to come up with, 'Independence Day, your honour.'

If you did marry an American, lived in the States and the marriage ended in divorce, you could be told to leave the country if you had not taken out American citizenship papers. The question that might well occur to New Zealanders is, why do some American ex-servicemen prefer to live in New Zealand rather than the United States? When the last hurrah sounded, and it was back into civvy street, most New Zealand–American couples did live in the States. But many wives soon felt the call to be with ageing or ill parents. Some of the men with no strong family ties did not find it a difficult decision to settle for life in New Zealand. Many of them make an almost annual pilgrimage back to the States. Most of those who settled here have retained their American citizenship, and so have those wives who took out papers. The children of some couples, born in America and therefore American citizens, have elected to stay in the States. They do not have dual citizenship. Children born in New Zealand to an American father may have dual citizenship under certain circumstances, but certainly not if a person has sworn allegiance to the United States.

Annette met her husband at a dance in the American camp in Victoria Park, Auckland. She, too, travelled on a bride ship to America, stopping first at Sydney to pick up Australian war brides. Her experience on the journey was similar to Jean's.

Those brides without babies were quartered below the waterline. It was considered that we could easily get on deck for fresh air. In San Francisco the train came right onto the wharf. For those going to New York, it was four days and four nights on the train. I was bound for Fairbairn, Nebraska, via Cheyenne, Wyoming. The train stopped at every little station all through the night, letting one girl off here, two there. Sometimes we could see there was no one to meet them. I was as frightened as could be. Hell, I thought, is this going to happen to me? But my husband was there. I had never seen him in civvy clothes. It was two years since we had met. I stepped down with my New Zealand rug and suitcase. I had sent him a photo of what I would be wearing. He was there with his car with the rumble seat.

I was dreadfully lonely for a start. I was a city girl and we were on the outskirts of a small town. I couldn't drive so I shut myself up in my room and read until another New Zealand bride in the town contacted me. I lived with my Polish in-laws, who only spoke Polish and had come to America through Ellis Island. I felt like an outsider. I didn't learn Polish, only the swear words. My husband didn't want me to work, so that put the kibosh on that. He had three jobs in order to get enough money together for a house. The baby came along but I was desperately unhappy. When I went to have my hair done, I was told that they were too busy. I didn't realise I was being boycotted because I had taken this Polish boy when there were so many eligible Polish girls in the district. It was hard to adjust, everything was so different; you had to watch stepping off the kerb, even the butter was different. I was so unhappy that my mother sent me a return ticket home to New Zealand. So baby and I went back home, and when we returned to America we had a house and everything worked out fine.

It's something I'm proud of, being a war bride, being a New Zealander. I call America home now, but even though I'm a naturalised American I still think of myself as a New Zealander.

Another Auckland woman related how she met her Marine husband. It might not have been love at first sight, but it was fairly close to that; and wartime romance, at least in this case, had more glamour than its peacetime equivalent.

One night I was coming out of the Peter Pan with a girlfriend (we had had just a little too much of jitterbugging, which the tearaway US Navy boys had brought to Auckland) when a couple of Marine officers passed us going in. 'Just a minute,' I said to my friend. 'I've just seen the man I'm going to marry.' So we went back in and sat down, and this particular Marine came up and asked my girlfriend for a dance. Then he asked her for a second dance, but my girlfriend, aware of my earlier remark, said she was 'too knocked up', and so he asked me. 'What did she mean, "too knocked up"?' he asked me. So I explained, and added it didn't have its American connotation.

Well, we got married and the colonel lent us a jeep and gave us the gas for our honeymoon in Rotorua. We stopped at a hotel on the way, a sludgy old place where the proprietor wanted proof we were married. We pushed on to Rotorua and got in at an old boarding house . . .

Because I hadn't had a twenty-first birthday party my husband gave me a party in the Grand Hotel in Auckland, which had been taken over for American officers. All the top brass were there, including Major General 'Howlin' Mad' Smith, who held my hand and took me to a show later at the St James. We partied our lives away in those days at the top of the Farmers, Peter Pan, El Rey, and the Civic Wintergarden, which the Americans had taken over for their guests. After the pictures the boat in the middle of the stage came up, and the Wurlitzer organ on the left ascended from its pit.

They were heady days, I can tell you. We danced to all the Glenn Miller music, and did the Lambeth Walk. The Americans were lavish with their gifts; with $300 a month, junior officers could afford to be. We were spoilt all right. The officers used to bring in their 'alky' — pure alcohol which had been pinched from their hospitals — and mix it with grapefruit. I'm afraid when the New Zealand troops came home they had to pick up the pieces.

I went to America on a bride ship with English evacuees returning home, and a hotchpotch of troops. We were down in 'D' deck in a dormitory used for transporting troops; 200 war brides, mostly New Zealanders, plus forty-three babies aged five months to two years. I had a top bunk. I was lucky to get on the ship. I was six months pregnant and they didn't want to take me. There was only one ship's doctor for us all. We weren't allowed to move round the ship — there were too many sex-starved men on board. For life-boat drill I was placed in a group of men because my Christian name is Georgea and they assumed when scanning the lists I was a man. I wanted to leave and go with the women, but the men wouldn't let me. Then I went down with diarrhoea and they put me on arrowroot, or what they called China clay. We changed ship at Panama, and at least we had a cabin then, even if the toilets were unisex. I think the men enjoyed putting on displays at the urinals.

We set out on the train from the Gulf and moved through Arizona into what looked like to me an arid wilderness. It was a frightening experience. We let girls off here and there, where there just seemed to be Red Indians, cowboys, horses and buggies. [This account is not necessarily typical. Another war bride who made a similar journey reported that her train was met by the Red Cross at every station, and felt that it was very well organised.]

But I loved America; New Zealanders were very popular and my mother-in-law took me to her heart. My husband would never talk of his war experiences. He was at Iwo Jima, and when two years ago I saw a TV documentary on the landing there, and heard from the veterans about the ghastly carnage on that island, I began to understand. He died of cancer in his late forties from injuries caused in a wartime accident when he was crushed between ship and lighter.

If there was romance for some during wartime, then there was also a great deal of hard work. Many civilians were required to keep the country running and to assist the Americans. The 'Manpower Authorities' were responsible for directing labour to essential industries. Mavis was one of many women who worked at the ammunition plant at Ford Motors in Lower Hutt during the war.

I was there because I had to be there. Like all the others, 500 odd of us, I was manpowered to the job. We lived in a hostel and were bussed to and from the works. Naturally there were plenty of Marines round the hostel. They were not permitted any further than the reception room. If you were caught with a man in your room all hell would break loose, not from the girls but from the dragons who ran the place. Even in the ammunition factory one lunch room was for girls only, with the men in their own, and never the twain shall meet. Mrs Roosevelt came through the plant one day, and Admiral Halsey was another of the hordes of visitors we had. It was all a publicity exercise in those days to show how everyone was contributing to the war effort. We stuck lolly papers on the back of his uniform.

Our work was all highly secret and we were sworn to secrecy (of course the girls reckoned they had a spy in their midst). If we stayed away from work without due cause we had to go before the manpower officer and he could fine us for absenteeism. We went on strike once. We were using a certain red paint on a component of the shells we were making and it was making us sick. Also there were no curtains on the window and the sun was shining on our backs. So we went on strike. We lay down on the factory floor for three or four hours until we won our case.

We didn't actually fill the 25-pounder shells with explosive, we only made the components. The parts were then sent to India for the completion of the shell. We were paid 2s 3d an hour (22 cents) with 30 shillings ($3) deducted for our board and lodgings. When the landing was made in Europe in June 1944 we got an urgent message to step up production. Field-Marshal Rundstedt was holding up the Allied advance, and so we were put on shift. It was terrible trying to sleep during the day.

The Americans invited us to all their dances. There were no lemon-squeezer hats round in those days, only the forage caps of the Marines. Then suddenly the American boys disappeared overnight; gone, we were to learn later, to Tarawa, and for some, to death. We carried on right to the end. We were at Gracefield, but down the Petone road were the girls in the W. D. & H. O. Wills factory making cigarettes, manpowered into their jobs, and like us living in hostels.

Girls were manpowered from all over New Zealand to work in centres far from home. Invercargill girls and those from Whangarei worked in

Picking the peas at Patumahoe. US Army men assist NZ land girls to harvest the crops near Auckland, 22 December 1943. *NZ Herald*

the Ford munitions plant at Lower Hutt. Photos of those working in the plant are remarkable for one thing: the lack of Maori women. According to several women who were in their twenties during the war Maori women were manpowered and were encouraged by their elders to work in industries which contributed to the war effort. The number of Maori people in the cities in the war years is estimated at less than ten per cent. For Islanders, the percentage was negligible. When conscription into the armed forces was introduced in 1940 Maori men were exempted, but many did volunteer and served overseas and at home. Pakeha girls from the age of eighteen, unless in essential work, could be directed into industry. If you were a clothing machinist you would certainly be making soldiers' battledress. Some, to avoid being shunted into the fish factory or somewhere equally unpleasant, joined the services. (Another means of escape was to get pregnant.)

Lorna, a member of the New Zealand Women's Auxiliary Army Corps, told her story.

I was seventeen when I started driving for the New Zealand Army. The Americans were very short of their own men, and when New Zealand civilian men drivers were employed it was alleged there were occasions when truck-loads of goods went missing. We girls were asked if we wished to drive for the Americans, and thirty of us joined up with the US Marine Corps as truck drivers.

Our headquarters for a start was in the Northern Automobile Company's premises, now Auckland's Aotea Square. We drove our loads out to Camp Bunn, the Marine Corps 3rd Base Depot in Tamaki. It was later the 3rd Field Ammunition Depot. Whether it was the biggest ammo depot in New Zealand I don't know, but there were acres and acres of ammunition in what is now Winstone's Quarry. It was so big the sentries used horses to guard the place. I remember one American Indian on a piebald horse riding the boundary.

We worked sometimes a ninety-hour week and I felt very nervous at

'Women only!' Munition workers of the Ford Motor Company at their Christmas party in their hostel, Woburn, Lower Hutt, 1944. Even at the works the sexes were separated at lunch-time. Munitions were made from 1941 through to 1945.

times. I can tell you that if the enemy had bombed that area of shells and machine-gun ammunition, half of Auckland would have gone up with it.

Camp Bunn, named for a Marine Corps officer, was built by the 43rd Division engineers, though there were New Zealand tradesmen on the job. The Americans fell over themselves when they saw the New Zealanders knocking off for morning and afternoon tea. It was unheard of in the States, and particularly in wartime. Something else the Americans latched on to was the term 'joker', referring to a New Zealand man. They found this hilarious, and every local was then a 'joker' to the Yanks, and we girls were called 'jokerettes'.

Camp Bunn sometimes housed thousands of Marines, some of whom had come back from the combat areas for rest and recreation. There were some very young boys among them who had put their ages up in order to get in the Corps. There were those who were near suicidal, and we used to have them in the driving cab with us in order to take their mind off Guadalcanal, New Georgia and other campaigns. My mother felt terribly sorry for the boys out at Camp Bunn. There was only the grotty old Panmure pub for local entertainment, so she got dances going for them in the Panmure School. After the war the long dormitory huts became transit housing for civilians, and the recreation hut became the Oakley Picture Theatre.

People talk about the Battle of Queen Street as if it was another Battle of Manners Street [For an account of this so-called 'battle', see chapter seven.] But if there was a fracas in Queen Street there were usually no Kiwis involved. They were all away. No, it was American versus American, Marine versus the Army, the 'dogfaces' as the Marines called them. Feelings ran high in those times as to who took the brunt of the fighting down in the Pacific. The Marines considered themselves the élite of the fighting forces, and others came in at the end . . . I remember one time there was a strike on and I was detailed to pick up dehydrated potatoes in Pukekohe. Near Wesley College I came upon an American Army boy hitch-hiking, so I gave him a lift. I was punished for that; no one wearing the Marine Corps uniform gave a 'dogface' a ride. I was put on to loading out frozen meat from the freezing chambers down on the Quay Street wharf. No one liked that job.

The colour bar didn't show up much in Auckland, but that's because there weren't too many Southerners in those particular outfits. I saw little if any discrimination against negroes. But for all ranks, crime, even minor misdemeanours, earned terribly severe punishment. It only needed people to complain about a Marine's conduct and he was pulled in by the shore patrol. They shaved all his hair off and literally threw him into the 'brig'. All round the brig were rocks, prisoners had to whitewash with tooth-brushs. If it was a major crime, say black marketing in military goods, he was shipped back home and, if found guilty, could lose all his civilian rights.

As the result of lead poisoning, I was taken off heavy trucks for a while and went on to jeeps and stationwagons. One time I was driving in the jeep and I gave a New Zealand airman a lift. I was in my normal US Marine Corps uniform, tailored locally by Jaffe's by the way, and he was

'ra-ing' on about how American women were much nicer than New
Zealand girls. I let him go on and then just before he got out he said,
'Where do you come from?' and I replied in a good ol' Kiwi twang,
'Auckland, dear boy.'

Aucklanders reacted pretty well to us in our American uniforms until
the troopships started to come back from the Middle East. Then we saw
all those same girls who had been down at the docks crying when their
American boyfriends sailed away, now crying as their boyfriends and
husbands came back from overseas. You have no idea at the abuse we
stopped at times. One time I drove on in my big heavy ten-wheeler International and the boyos were playing throwing pennies at a stick. 'There's
a war on, you know,' I called out. Some, only some, gave us a hard time.
Backing those ten-wheelers between the pillars in the wharf sheds was
very hard work for a girl, and it wasn't helped at times when the goods
were in difficult places. We used to pick up an Alsatian dog to ride in our
cabs when we moved round Auckland. If any stray hands came into the
cab, the Alsatian knew what it was all about and acted accordingly.

One time an American admiral came to Auckland, and I drove him
round. He called me 'Uncle Bill', don't ask me why. He was very
impressed with the Auckland Museum building, and as he looked down
harbour he said to me, 'Thank God we stopped them at the Coral Sea,
otherwise they would have been here.'

According to Jock Barnes, president of the Watersiders' Union during
the war years, there was trouble with the Americans right from the
start.

Auckland was the main base for vast amounts of supplies brought here
by the Liberty ships. By God, some of the Yanks were an arrogant
bunch. There they were down in the holds with their pistols at the ready,
treating us like criminals. 'We've shot longshoremen overseas and we'll
shoot you if necessary,' they said. Well, we were not just going to have
trigger-happy Yanks standing over us. We were working long hours,
twenty-four hours a day, seven days a week. It was reaching the stage
that you only got home at Christmas and the kids would say, 'Who's that
man?'

In time we did establish a reasonable working relationship with the
Americans, and this was because the officer-in-charge, Colonel
Chianese, was a reasonable man, a good guy. The men at the top were
okay, but down below they were bloody arrogant. One of the officers
said to me, referring to some Americans, 'I haven't got a high opinion
of this mob anyway, many of them have been let out of jails to come
here.'

One or two of the Americans were running a Mafia-type racket,
hijacking truck-loads of supplies; not just petty pillaging, but 'tea leafing'
[thieving] on a grand scale. Truck-loads of petrol would disappear, don't
ask me where it went. Then they tried to divert suspicion onto us. One
time gloves for officers were found in the wharfies' bags. Well, we had
no place to put our gear, the boys would just dump their lunch bags

88

anywhere. Anybody could have put stuff in their bags, unbeknown to them. The American MPs said they were going to present charges against six of our men and took 'em up into their office. I was president of the union and I said to the Yank officer in charge, 'I've got a thousand men out there, drop all charges, let 'em go or else.' I can tell you the Yanks had the shits that time. The situation was defused and with time we established a comfortable working relationship. In the end they saw it was better to leave the job of unloading ships to us. There was little you could take off the wharf anyway, your bags were likely to be searched at the gates.

Commodore Jupp, the American boss in Auckland, wrote to us and congratulated us later on our war effort. We were working colossal hours and we wanted more men in the work force. When the Kiwi boys came home from the Middle East on furlough, there was this fracas over not going back to the war. Those who refused to return were given dis-honourable discharges. They were supposed to work where directed by the manpower authorities. We took many of them, including some from the Maori Battalion, into the union when we increased our membership by 600.

The Yanks were amazed at the low rates of pay we got, 3s 10d [35 cents] an hour, and offered us another two shillings [20 cents] an hour, but Fraser, Prime Minister at the time (and my remarks about him are unprintable), stepped in and refused to allow it. We could only have a shilling [10 cent] rise. The Yanks still thought this was a pathetic rate of pay. We got time-and-a-half overtime and double time for Sundays. If we have been accused of not working in the wet, that's all bullshit. Actually the Yanks negotiated a much more liberal wet-weather clause than our own crowd.

As I say, we had a lot of Maoris in our ranks, and the American army of occupation had an ambivalent attitude to them. The Americans from the Deep South wanted to treat them like shit. There weren't going to be any lynching parties from Alabama as far as we were concerned. It was as if the army of occupation was two countries, the North and the South . . .

'In the meantime the Yanks were living the life of Riley. They were never strapped for dollars, could eat in the steak joints without having to surrender coupons for meat like we had to. The women were down on the wharves in their droves, at least as far as the gates — civilians were not allowed on the wharves in wartime. The pinnaces from the Navy ships brought their liberty men ashore to the Admiralty Steps. The Yanks had taken over the whole of Princes Wharf for the duration . . . Let's face it, the bedroom commandos had it all their own way with Auckland women, but they were no different from any other bunch of troops overseas who would have reacted in exactly the same way. There were the society girls decked out in their finery, photographed on the lawn at the Ellerslie Races with their Yank officers, and there were the girls who dispensed their favours through the iron railings to the wharves with 'uprighters' and 'hang onto the bars, love'.

There certainly was preferential treatment handed out to the Yanks, but that reaction was inevitable. I know they were shacked up with New

Sorting it all out on Aotea Quay, Wellington, 1942. Ships had to be unloaded and then re-loaded in order of priority for combat purposes.
USA National Archives

Zealand women, but then so they were in Australia and England and I'm not moralising about that lot . . . The Yanks, by the way, brought over fork lifts with them, the first time we had seen them. But their equipment and uniforms were so good, it made our boys look as if they were decked out in stuff from the rag bag. And yes, if there were New Zealand girls getting round in American uniforms they were lumped in with the Yanks.

There is one myth concerning the Americans which has persisted over the years, that somewhere in the greater Auckland area there is a cache or caches of American arms buried in unidentified dumps. American ex-servicemen living here react to such suggestions with shouts of deri-

90

sion. 'Impossible,' they say. 'Never heard of it,' say others. And yet I am told that there are people who know people who have dug up machine-guns in boxes, still in their greaseproof paper. Caches of American arms will remain a myth until time should prove otherwise.

It is true of course that large quantities of American equipment were dumped just before units moved out of their camps for an overseas destination, including clothes, cans of food, tea, coffee, sugar, tobacco, chewing tobacco, snuff, empty beer bottles and worn-out equipment such as camp stretchers. Naturally some items due to be discarded found their way onto the black market. Servicemen smuggled out supplies and loaded up their friends with items about to be dumped. In addition, every member of the forces received at regular intervals a free supply of toothpaste, shaving cream (Barbasol), sweets, and cigarettes or pipe tobacco such as Prince Albert, Edgeworth or Bull Durham roll-your-own tobacco in a little string bag. Servicemen accumulated an embarrassing supply of such items and were pleased to be able to give it away. There were American clothing stores where servicemen could readily purchase such items as lumber jackets at give-away prices, shirts, trousers, men's khaki balloon-seated underpants at twenty cents a time, and large khaki handkerchiefs at a dollar a dozen. It is no surprise that many New Zealand civilians in those times were walking round in American service clothing.

That there was a 'Mafia' operating within the services hijacking truck-loads of supplies to move on to the black market was always the opinion of some watersiders. Says Jock Barnes, 'There were two — can't name 'em, they might still be alive. They didn't do just a little bit of tea-leafing, it was by the truck-load out of Sylvia Park. When those two left, they owned farms and racehorses.' Black marketing, if proven, earned severe jail sentences for service personnel back Stateside. It was not a risk to be undertaken lightly.

Captain John Wann was seconded to the cargo department of the US Joint Purchasing Board during 1943. The organisation took over Princes Wharf and spread to the other wharves as required.

Our job was to load and unload the Liberty ships which came into Auckland. They were 445 feet long, 7176 tons displacement. For a start they had trouble with them. Some broke up forward of the bridge, sepa-rated into two parts. They were welded ships and lacked the flexibility of hulls constructed by the time-tested riveted method. Before the war I had served on the Queen Mary, and it had two joints in its length which you could actually see and hear moving. But Kaiser solved this weakness in his ships very quickly — he had to.

We had to load the ships so that when they called at the different war ports in the South Pacific, stores could be unloaded quickly. It was no use putting all the flour or the sugar at the bottom of the hold. We had to build pillars of provisions according to the plan handed to us by the

Americans. The wharfies had to load the cargo so that it wouldn't shift in heavy seas.

The orders would go out to the Americans' bulk store at Sylvia Park, Mt Wellington, or to the Chelsea Sugar Refinery or the Northern Roller Mills. The trucks, sometimes driven by New Zealand girls, would come into the wharf sheds to their allocated bays and to this day you can see the chalked writing on Princes Wharf: 'Corned Beef', 'Carrots', 'Peas Can', and 'Candy' (but no 'Kilroy was here').

The wharfies were all right. They got stuck in. At times they didn't know whether they were coming or going. They got on with the Americans okay, as far as I could see. I can't remember any strikes. Shifts went on all through the night with a hot meal at 1 a.m. I didn't see any thieving going on. But what happened when the loaded trucks drove off the wharves for Sylvia Park, I wouldn't know. There were police on the gates and the Americans had security people.

No names identified the Liberty ships, only numbers. Moored off the Rangitoto beacon was the *Duchess*, the inspection vessel. All incoming ships had to report to her. A searchlight lit up the area at night. The Liberty ships came here unescorted. The chances of enemy submarine action in 1943 were not great. They were too far away from their home base to be serviced. Ship raiders did more damage than submarines. One Liberty ship was tied up at the Hobson Wharf for months. The UST *William Williams* was hit by a torpedo which came out the other side of the ship. After the war the Liberty ships were acquired by various nations including the Greeks, who used them for ages. Their oil-fired steam boilers pushed them along at eleven or twelve knots. It is doubtful if any are afloat now.

Keith, a Warkworth man, had something to do with the establishment of the camps in his area and had first-hand experience of dumping. Part of his job was to onload the trains at Kaipara Flats.

Stuff came from all over the North Island, and we had to direct the drivers to the camp sites. At times we weren't sure of the locations, and the drivers certainly weren't. We just used to dump the stuff where we thought it should go and that was that. Cement we would dump on the ground. I can remember tons of it in jute bags being out in the open for months on end.

When the government decided to step up farm production I was ordered back to the farm. I had a great big Buick in those days, and on the road to Waiwera we would come on the Americans strung out in single file hitch-hiking a ride. I stopped to pick up a couple one day and they said, 'We'll get in if you give our buddies along the road a lift.' They used to split up into pairs, there was more chance of a lift. We took them home for tea and they wanted to see the cows being milked, and of course drink the milk. 'Come down to the camp and get some of the bread we heave out every day,' they said. So I used to go down twice a week and get the chucked-out bread and feed it to the pigs.

One day one of the Yanks said to me, 'I've got an idea we're moving on. Come down for a party.' I went down in the Buick and as soon as I got out of the car it disappeared and then a little later reappeared. 'Better go home now,' one of them said to me, which was rather a strange remark I thought at the time. Well, when I went to get into the car I could hardly make it for Lucky Lager beer, Prince Albert tobacco and cartons of this and that. 'I can't go out with this, you'll get me shot,' I said. 'We'll ride on the running board with you past the sentry,' they replied.

The stuff that was dumped by the Americans was fantastic. Tobacco in tins, sides of mutton (no one would eat it, it wasn't even stored but simply dumped off the truck when it arrived), blankets, radios. When a unit moved on to a battle area, that was the big dumping time.

Frank Cometti worked with the Lend-Lease Organisation in Washington from 1943 on behalf of New Zealand. He was 'on loan' from General Motors, and his story suggests that the New Zealand Government was not as quick to take advantage of American generosity as civilians were.

We processed the requisitions from New Zealand for trucks and parts in order to keep the economy ticking over here. We got a grant of £3,000,000 but then we had to compete against Britain, Canada, Australia and South Africa for our share of the cake. Towards the end of the war we got notification that we had been granted a quota of 1000 three-ton trucks for New Zealand. Of course I was elated and sent off a cable to New Zealand. Back came a personal cable from Prime Minister Peter Fraser to say that, while appreciating the offer of trucks, Cabinet felt it must decline the offer and hope that the trucks were made available to more deserving countries. The other countries were totally incredulous that such an offer had been turned down. Then of course the fight started as to who was going to get the trucks. In the end South Africa got them. Fraser was too honest, too sincere.

They were exciting times in Washington for Frank Cometti. For some they were more than exciting, he said, for there were a dozen women to every man. When American servicemen went away they left behind a wife looking for a job and Washington needed thousands and thousands of women to process the paper war. 'After the war,' said Frank Cometti regretfully, 'all debts under Lend-Lease were forgotten, so bang went 1000 very cheap three-ton trucks.'

CHAPTER FIVE

From Guadalcanal to Bougainville

The first six months of 1942 were desperate times for the Allies in the South Pacific, times that called for incredible demands. Major General Alexander Archer Vandegrift, USMC, a Virginian in his mid-fifties, was ordered to establish a full complement of the 1st Marine Division, and be ready to go on the offensive in the South Pacific. 'Cobble together' may have been a more appropriate description, for Vandegrift, though readily conceding the necessity, was dismayed to find that he had to shed many of his experienced men, who were required for the training of new units. 'Colonel Edson's levy against our division coming at such a critical time annoyed the devil out of me, but there wasn't one earthly thing I could do about it,' Vandegrift was to write later.

The 1st Marine Regiment (there were four regiments to the division) had been in Culebra, Puerto Rico; the 5th Marines were once employed in Nicaragua in holding down a rebellion there; the 7th Marines had known service in Cuba; and the 11th Marines (Artillery) were active at Guantanamo Bay, Cuba, in 1941. Vandegrift's division was a mishmash. There were 'Old China' hands, inveterate gamblers all, who chewed tobacco, dipped snuff, drank hair tonic in preference to the 'horse piss' of the Post Exchange, and knew the bar girls in every dive from Shanghai, to Manila, to Tientsin and Peking. And then there were the recruits or 'grunts', some with down on their cheeks, fresh out of boot camp on Parris Island, South Carolina. These then were the first Marines Wellington was to know, albeit briefly, in June–July 1942. It was the first time a division of the Marine Corps had sailed on combat duty from the United States.

It was in Tent City (Camp Lejeune), North Carolina, that the Firsts did their training, and it was here that Vandegrift received his orders in April 1942. A plan, codenamed Lone Wolf, instructed him to move with his troops to Wellington at the earliest possible moment. Vandegrift was told his division would not be expected to go into action before January 1943.

Two officers, dispatched to Wellington to search out suitable camp sites, decided that areas close to the Tararua Ranges, with their jungle-like terrain, met their requirements. 'The matter of the buildings was not easily solved. Lumber and labour were both short in New Zealand,' wrote one American later. He added, 'The camp was finally built with green lumber by New Zealand women.'

The advance echelon of the division boarded trains at New Run

(Camp Lejeune) on 1 May 1942, bound for Norfolk, Virginia. The average age of the personnel was estimated to be below twenty years, with ninety per cent of the men enlisted since Pearl Harbour. The convoy, with Vandegrift by tradition the last to go aboard the USS *Wakefield*, sailed together with the USS *de Brazil* on 20 May for the Panama Canal en route for Wellington. Vandegrift's second echelon, under Brigadier General W. H. Rupertus, entrained for the West Coast of the US, there to go on board the MV *John Ericsson*. The troops were fed on rancid butter, rotten eggs and little fresh food. Hundreds went down with dysentery. Rupertus was due to arrive in Wellington on 11 July. The ships that brought the equipment for the Division were the *Electra*, *Lipscombe Lykes*, *Alcyone*, *Libra*, *Alchiba*, *Mizar*, *Elliott* and *Barnett*. The USS *Wakefield*, crammed to the gunwales with Marines, nosed its way into harbour on the morning of 14 June 1942.

Hardly 42nd Street, but home on the range for units of the 1st Division US Marines, Paekakariki, June 1942. *Evening Post*

On 26 June General Vandegrift was called to a conference in Auckland at the headquarters of Vice-Admiral Robert L. Ghormley, commander of the Pacific Area, and the General's immediate superior in the field. 'I'm afraid I have bad news for you,' said Ghormley, and handed him an envelope. An astounded Vandegrift was to read: 'Occupy and defend Tulagi and adjacent positions (Guadalcanal and Florida Island and the Santa Cruz Islands) in order to deny those areas to the enemy and to provide United States bases, in preparation for further offensive action.' 'D-Day' was 1 August — little more than a month away. Later Vandegrift was given a slight respite; D-Day was postponed until 7 August. Vandegrift was to make a landing on Guadalcanal and he had only a little over five weeks to get there. The General had to move fast on what was nicknamed Operation Shoestring. One third of his division was in Wellington, one third in Samoa and one third on the water. The majority of his men had been in uniform for barely six months.

There was a frantic search for maps and intelligence about the island. Lieutenant Colonel Goettge, Division Intelligence Officer, flew to Australia to seek out men who had run plantations in the Solomons, missionaries, traders, itinerant ship traders, anybody who could add to the sum total of intelligence. Some men were commissioned or made petty officers in the Australian armed forces so that they could accompany the Firsts. In what appeared to be an inoperable time scale, Vandegrift was scheduled to fight his way ashore at Guadalcanal less than a month after Rupertus arrived in Wellington with his echelon. Stores needed to be broken down, sorted and combat-loaded. Aotea Quay with the rains became, in the words of one Marine, 'A fucked-up swamp of cornflakes, cigarettes, broken food cases, Hershey bars and rain-soaked inadequate cardboard boxes.' Then the Wellington wharfies went on strike. The Marines had to turn to and do their own unloading and loading. Graffiti appeared on Wellington lavatory walls proclaiming that 'All wharfies is bastards'. The telescoped time scale left little opportunity for socialising. Orders were given to reduce equipment and supplies to the absolute bare minimum, to take only those items actually required to live and fight.

When the ships carrying the 1st Marine Division crept out of harbour at dawn on 22 July, it was the last Wellington ever saw of these Marines as a unit. Many of those fit young men who sailed away were to come back as patients, mainly malaria cases, to American and New Zealand hospitals in Wellington and Auckland. In charge of the convoy was Rear Admiral Richmond Kelly Turner, flying his flag on the USS *McCawley* (also known as the 'Wacky Mac', after a Brigadier General of the Marine Corps in the 1920s). Out of Wellington the 'Wacky Mac' hoisted a signal, the convoy was bound for Guadalcanal. No one had ever heard of it, where was it? The first stage of Operation Watch-tower, the invasion of Guadalcanal, was under way.

Marines off the transport ships prepare to settle in at Paekakariki, but not for long. Within six weeks they will be landing on Guadalcanal in the Solomons. June 1942. *Evening Post*

On 24 July the Wellington combat force rendezvoused at Koro Island in the Fiji group with the rest of the invasion fleet from Nouméa, Pearl Harbour and San Diego, for conferences and landing practices, which one senior officer described by saying, 'If we were praising them, a balls-up would have been an exaggeration.' Included now in the landing forces was the main body of the 2nd Marine Division, which had come down from San Diego via Hawaii in the 'Unholy Three' — the USS *President Jackson, President Adams, and the President Hayes.*

If Wellington was not to know 1 MarDiv again, it was subsequently to become a second home to 2 MarDiv, a fighting force which virtually sailed into the battle zone when it joined up with the invasion troops off Koro Island. The flotilla of twenty-three ships moved towards Tulagi and Guadalcanal on 31 July, with 19,000 Marines ready to storm ashore. The ships involved in that landing, many of which were to become well known to Wellingtonians and Aucklanders, were the *Fuller, American Legion, Bellatrix, McCawley, Barnett, Elliott, Libra,*

Fall out time on a route march, Oriental Bay, Wellington, 1942. The first Marines to arrive had some age on them, many of them being in the permanent Marine forces. *Free Lance Collection, Alexander Turnbull Library*

Hunter Liggett, Alchiba, Formalhaut, Betelgeuse, Crescent City, President Hayes, President Adams, President Jackson, Alhena, Neville, Zeilin, Heywood, and the destroyers *Colhoun, Gregory, Little* and *McKean.* The USS *Quincy* ushered in the first American land offensive of World War II with an eight-inch salvo at 0613 hours on 7 August.

Incongruous as it may seem now, the strategy of this battle was initially directed from Dilworth Buildings, Queen Street, Auckland. Vice-Admiral Ghormley had set up his command post aboard the USS *Rigel* in Waitemata Harbour in mid-May 1942, but moved ashore into the Dilworth Buildings on 10 June. The timid Ghormley, who was not completely sold on the wisdom of the Guadalcanal campaign, was to be given the 'heave-ho' and replaced by the pugnacious Vice-Admiral William F. ('Bull') Halsey at the end of September 1942. On being given the top job, Halsey reacted with 'Jesus Christ and General Jackson! This is the hottest potato they ever handed me.' By this time headquarters had been moved to Nouméa. Lasting six months, Guadalcanal was the longest campaign in the Pacific, and at the end of two months it was touch and go whether the Americans could hang on. It was a battle the Allies could not afford to lose, for Australia could well have been the next Japanese objective.

Four days after the landing Colonel Goettge was dead. A captured Japanese soldier told the intelligence people that there were other Japanese ready to surrender. Goettge took a selected detachment of twenty-five men, many from the intelligence section, to investigate. They landed at night on the beach. The Japanese were ready for them, and only three men lived to tell the tale. One who got back was half American Indian. Near dawn he had slid into the sea to swim to safety and had looked back to see 'swords flashing in the sun'. No trace of the bodies of the Marines was ever found. From that day on the catch-cry was, 'The only good Jap is a dead Jap.'

The Amerindians, incidentally, were much admired by the Marines and Army for their woodcraft and their ability to move through the jungle at night undetected. Many of them were to be found in the ranks

Ships being combat loaded at Aotea Quay for the war in the Solomons. With the ammunition in the foreground an air raid on Wellington wharves would have been disastrous. July 1942. *USA National Archives*

of the raider battalions of the Marine Corps. Navajo Indians were used to send messages over phones during land battles. (It was assumed the Japanese did not speak Navajo.)

Bill was in Lieutenant Colonel Merritt A. Edson's 1st Marine Raider Battalion, attached to 1 MarDiv. He describes the experience of many Marines confronted with their first active service.

Of course everybody wanted to go where the action was. You had to volunteer for the Raider Battalion and you had to be super-fit to get in . . . We were in Wellington Harbour at Lambton Quay for six weeks, living aboard ship. We had liberty every day, playing tennis, hanging out in the bars, wheeling round the women like seagulls round the town dump. Then we took off, we didn't know where to, but eventually it was Tulagi off the island of Guadalcanal, and then Guadalcanal itself with 1 MarDiv and the onslaught on Bloody Ridge. One of the ridges is known in Marine history as Edson's Ridge. Edson had to be where the shit was flying. Some of us, who had wished to be where the action was, wished we'd volunteered for legation duty in some South American republic. Edson, later promoted to Brigadier, was also at the Tarawa landing with 2 MarDiv. The man who won the Medal of Honor for his courage on Guadalcanal, Lieutenant Colonel Edson, was to die by his own hand in New Hampshire in 1955. I was invalided back to Auckland after Guadalcanal, and was in hospital in what is today the Remuera Ladies Bowling Club.

Tim, who was with 2 MarDiv in Guadalcanal and later married and settled in New Zealand, tells how it was in the early days.

It was five months of misery, of patrols, of a scrap here and a scrap there, disease, malaria, gastro-enteritis, dysentery, dengue fever and yellow jaundice. You had to be young for that kind of soldiering, you were too old at thirty. One of the boys in my platoon was of Mexican extraction and had experience knifing alligators in the Everglades in Florida. He used to go out on his own at night and get himself a pair of Japanese ears. He scared the shit out of me. When I was on sentry duty at night he would creep up on me and touch me on the shoulder. Christ, I didn't even know he was there. On patrol we had to look out for Jap snipers. They used to put them up in a tree, strap them in so to speak, and feed them water and crackers. In the end we would get 'em, and they would hang there from the trees half starved and dead.

After weeks of fighting in Guadalcanal, the Marines looked to the Army to relieve them, but they waited in vain. To the tune of 'Bless 'em All' the song went

But Douglas MacArthur said, 'No'.
He said, 'There's a reason, it isn't the season,
Besides there is no USO.'

100

Artillery pieces (105mm Howitzers) awaiting loading, Aotea Quay, July 1942.
USA National Archives

It was a war of attrition for some time, with grievous losses on both sides, but the victory over the Japanese seven months later signalled the beginning of the end for the enemy. If it was not the turning point of the war it was very close to it. During the campaign both sides had their successes and disasters. On 8 August the 'Tokyo Express' (Japanese warships which came down the Slot at night looking for US Navy craft) came boiling down from the north and in the Battle of Savo Island, the American and Australian navies lost four ships and 1023 men in 44 minutes. The USS *Vincennes*, *Quincy* and *Astoria* and the HMAS *Canberra* became the first of many ships to settle on what came to be known as 'Ironbound Sound'. In addition, the USS *Chicago* lost part of her bow but avoided sinking.

The Battle of Savo Island was the worst defeat at sea inflicted on the US Navy. The sea and the night belonged to the Tokyo Express for a while. During August the Japanese Navy prowled 'The Slot' with impunity, even bombarding the Marines ashore. ('The Slot' was a channel

101

of about fifty nautical miles between the two rows of large islands that form the Solomons.) The Americans had to wait until November for their revenge. During that month the Japanese mounted a large naval force to escort thousands of fresh ground troops to Guadalcanal in order to deal the Americans a death blow. On the night of 12 November, Japanese escorts covering the transport of troops collided with American escorts protecting the movement of American troops. In the battle that ensued, the US lost one battleship and two destroyers. It was that night that the battleship USS *Washington*, with 16-inch guns aboard, steamed up 'The Slot' and met the Tokyo Express head on. It was one of those rare occasions in World War II when battleship met battleship. That night the Emperor of Japan's 14-inch-gun battleship the *Kirishima* joined the iron graveyard. But twenty-four hours later Marine and Navy aircraft hit the jackpot when they spotted eleven enemy transports steaming down 'The Slot' towards Guadalcanal with 10,000 troops. Only 4000 landed, and the Japanese that night lost another battleship and two heavy cruisers, which joined the graveyard

A Marine loading party comes off duty for 'chow', Aotea Quay. Two things the Marines did not appreciate, the Wellington winter, and the fact the wharfies (longshoremen) went on strike. July 1942. *USA National Archives*

at the bottom of the Ironbound Sound. Those three days of naval engagement really sealed the fate of the Japanese on Guadalcanal. About this time, too, cryptographers back in the States broke the Japanese code. The magic box that did so was christened MAGIC, but so secret was MAGIC that only certain commanders were privy to its revelations.

It was a bloody battle on the ground, where flame-throwers were used for the first time by the Americans. Both sides took a severe mauling, with the Marines under Vandegrift taking the brunt of it as far as the Americans were concerned. The 1st Marine Division was taken out of the line for rest and recreation in Australia and was replaced by the 8th Marines from Samoan training grounds, the US Army Americal Division from New Caledonia, and the 25th US Army Division from Hawaii. To relieve other troops came the 43rd US Army Division from Auckland. The Battle of Guadalcanal was all over by the end of January 1943, and on 9 February the island was declared secure. The 8th Marines of 2 MarDiv sailed for Wellington, arriving there on 16 February 1943 and then moving to their camp at Paekakariki.

The 3rd Marine Division came on to New Zealand via Hawaii. En route troops were given jungle training in Guadalcanal and Samoa. By 12 March 1943 the entire division was in its various camps in the Pukekohe and Warkworth areas, where it was to stay for five months. New Zealand in the first half of 1943 had two full Marine Corps divisions in camps: the 2nd in Wellington training for an objective up near the Equator in the Gilbert Islands, the 3rd for a limited objective assault on Bougainville in the Solomon Islands 1300 miles to the south-west of the Gilberts. The 1st Marine Division (much reinforced), after a rest period in Melbourne following the Guadalcanal campaign, was in training for an assault on Cape Gloucester in New Britain, to the north of New Guinea.

Amphibious exercises for the 3rd Marines were laid on soon after their arrival in New Zealand. On 15 March some local farmers and their families at Martin's Bay near Warkworth got a surprise. George, a young farmer at the time, remembers the occasion.

Suddenly one day without warning three large American transports appeared off Martin's Beach. First of all the troops practised scrambling down the nets into the landing craft, and then later the boys stormed ashore in their full battle kit. Not only did the Marines come ashore but also 3000 tons of arms, goods and equipment, which were transported over the inadequate Rodney roads of the time and taken to Kaipara Flats railway station, there to be railed back to Auckland to be used for further exercises. In the meantime the Leathernecks were engaged in sham fighting in the bay area. We were working away one day getting firewood

Getting it all together and sorting it out for the Guadalcanal campaign, Aotea
Quay, Wellington, 1943. *Alexander Turnbull Library*

out of the bush and *wham*, bullets started to ricochet round us. We got
to hell out of it smartly. You can still see some of the fox holes they dug
in those days.

The Marines must have been very careless with their gear, for we
picked up bayonets and drinking canteens for years after. If a New
Zealand soldier lost a bayonet there would almost have been a court of
enquiry. Not so the Yanks; apparently there were plenty more where they
came from.

The Marines simulated fighting their way overland through fences and
farms all the way to camps in the Warkworth area. You couldn't walk
without tripping over the signal boys' wires . . . The RNZAF co-operated
by dive-bombing the troops from their Kittyhawks. Prime Minister Peter
Fraser was an interested spectator and also a target, I understand, for
their flour bombs. There were Hudsons and Harvards there too, acting as
bombers. The locals were amazed at the antics of the Air Force boys with
their hedge-hopping, and clipping the tops of the trees with their low run-
ins. Across the road one of the American tanks went across a wooden
bridge but its weight was too much on the return trip. The bridge col-
lapsed, the tank did a somersault. Two of the crew had their heads out
of the tank and were killed. It took two bulldozers to pull the tank,
covered in raupo and mud, out of the creek. The Americans built another

bridge out of rimu, but although it was a great job, the timber was unsuitable for outside work and the bridge didn't last.

The three transports out in the bay were the *President Jackson*, *Adams* and *Hayes*, the 'Unholy Three', well known to New Zealand troops in the Pacific. The first exercise involved the 9th Marines from Pukekohe. Later in the month the 21st Marines, camped in Warkworth, had their turn. This time the landing was opposed by other troops from the Warkworth area. There was also a one-day exercise on the Takatu Peninsula at Christian Bay, which is but a nautical mile from Kawau Island. It was an amphibious landing from the 'Unholy Three' opposed by Kittyhawk fighters. Said a local farmer who was there that day, 'The fighters came in so low from the land they nearly knocked the Yanks out of their landing craft. It sure was exciting stuff. A Marine said to me afterwards, "Your Kiwi boys sure are dare-devils."'

A pre-requisite for any soldier on an amphibious exercise was his ability to scramble over the ship's side with all the required equipment, go down the nets perhaps twenty feet or more and land in the waiting landing craft on a rising wave. It was the helmsman's job to keep his craft close to the ship's side, not easy in a heavy sea, and the soldier's job not to drop his rifle on some unsuspecting buddy below, nor to fall fully laden between the craft and the ship's side, where his chances of surviving were not good.

The field uniform for a combat man might consist of steel helmet (mosquito head-net tucked up inside), shirt, trousers (definitely no shorts because of the anopheles mosquito, whose bite bore the germ of malaria), leggings, 'shoes' (boots to New Zealanders), underclothing, coat according to season; a haversack carrying his mess kit, canteen and a cup in a carrier, first-aid kit on his belt, pack containing blanket, shelter tent, poles, pins, toilet articles, gas mask, entrenching tool, and reserve ration. In addition, the infantryman carried rifle and bayonet, 136 rounds of ammunition and a hand grenade, an all-up load of 64 lb. Some of these items would be deleted from the kits of troops going ashore in the early waves onto unknown territory, particularly in tropical climates.

In Wellington Harbour in May 1943 were some US Navy personnel carriers, the *American Legion*, *Neville*, *Fuller*, *Hunter Liggett* and the *McCawley*. It was envisaged that these ships would be used for amphibious landings, but time, the tides and the weather were unfavourable, so exercises were confined to combat loadings and net practice. The young mums of Petone were amazed to see Marines come over the sea wall in those early days of training. There was no place in a shopping area to consolidate their positions, a far cry from the Guadalcanal they were to know, with its Lever's coconut plantations along the foreshore.

Warships and transports anchored in Wellington Harbour in July 1942 ready to
load and escort Marines of the 1st Division for the onslaught on Guadalcanal.
Evening Post

Both Americans and New Zealanders have vivid memories of 3rd
Marine Division's time in New Zealand. Bertram A. Yaffe from Provi-
dence, Rhode Island, is a Marine who has made the pilgrimage back.
In 1988 he returned to Warkworth with his wife Sybil.

> I was in the 3rd Tank Battalion of the 3rd Division, attached to the 21st
> Marines. One company of our tanks was attached to each regiment. We
> had light tanks; we got medium tanks when we went into Guam, but that
> was after Bougainville. There were the 9th Marines, 21st Marines and the
> 12th Marines who trained at Tapora and were an artillery regiment. One
> of our regiments, the 3rd, was in Samoa and came to New Zealand later.
> Marines in Warkworth who said they had been in action would have been
> members the 1st or 2nd Marines who had been transferred to the 3rd
> Marines.
>
> We were here for six months. In many ways it was a land I never
> forgot. The people were so friendly I was determined I would come back.
> I was twenty-two years old and an officer. The oldest man I can

remember in our outfit was twenty-nine. I censored the mail for the company. The thing that came through was the interplay of youth, Marine versus Marine. I wrote a play called *The Chrysalis Sleep*, a two-act work. The theme was a maturing youth being influenced by a more mature Marine with a young New Zealand mother in the background.

The war was the good war, as far as any war is a good war. We were proud to be part of it. It was the thing to do. It was all tremendously heroic. Of course different Marines responded differently. We were amazed at the knowledge of New Zealanders about us. We officers used to sit round the fire and discuss this astounding information that the locals had about the US. But my abiding impression was of the people and the topography, the mountains and the terrain. I fell in love with the hills. I felt I just had to come back and feel it all again, and I have not been disappointed.

Max was mayor of Pukekohe during the war years, when sometimes as many as 30,000 troops were camped in and around the town. On his office wall is a photo of an American officer, Colonel Lemuel Shepherd, 9th Marine Corps, who later became a three-star general and commander of the whole of that élite corps. Shepherd was in Pukekohe with his corpsmen back in 1943, together with other regiments of 3 MarDiv, and Max helped him co-ordinate the activities of the troops with the needs of the town.

I drew up a roster of what the town wanted and gave the colonel in charge a map of those places we wanted guarded. We had to find places for grog, flour, and we had thousands of 40-gallon drums of high-octane petrol, bound for the Pacific, out in the middle of the racecourse, piled as high as haystacks and surrounded by barbed wire. The drill hall was packed to the ceiling with hand grenades. For a year my house was never out of the sound of heavy American Army trucks grinding their way, day and night, to and from the Auckland wharves. Headquarters for the Marines was down at the Franklin racecourse, where the stewards' building became their administration centre. We built a huge stone fireplace to keep the building warm. One of our first edicts was to put the Pukekohe Hill out of bounds to the troops. But of course that didn't keep the high, wide, and handsome boyos away from the girls.

I had an arrangement with the colonel in charge that no more than 5000 troops would be given leave at night at a time. Their military police were on duty at every pub in the district, consequently the conduct of the troops was exemplary. If it wasn't, the MPs did not hesitate for one moment to use their long batons. If new stock appeared in the shops, it disappeared over night. When a detachment left you would find push-bikes in the hedges all round the town, abandoned by the Marines who had used them for getting around. Their colonel came to me and said he wanted to set up a prophylactic station in the town. I suggested a side street, but no, he wanted it slap in the middle of the road in the middle of the town. And that's where the 'blue light' went, slap bang in Massey Street.

The older women in the town were absolutely tremendous; they worked like beavers to entertain and extend hospitality to the Yanks. As for the young girls, they had stars in their eyes, but then the Americans were pretty damned appealing. Naturally there were many international marriages.

One time there I made a bad blue; in retrospect it was a very silly idea. The New Zealand troops had come home on furlough from the Middle East, and they were moving up the Main Trunk Line with whistle stops at big and small stations. I suggested to the American officer in charge that it would be a nice gesture if an American Army band played them into the Pukekohe station. I was there with the town clerk to give an official welcome home to the boys. But when the Kiwis saw the Americans it was like a red rag to a bull. It was not my most inspired idea.

But the Americans stuck to the rules, the liaison was good, the entertainment was good. One time an American truck pushed a school bus off the road, through a fence and into my own garden . . . Next day a lieutenant, junior grade, was on my doorstep, a cheque book in one hand and all sorts of coloured forms in the other. Lavish compensation was paid, every pupil was medically checked, and the bus damage generously paid for. From our council they bought cement, metal pipes, etc., for the ablutions blocks, and paid well for it.

Personnel carriers await loading, Aotea Quay, Wellington, July 1942.
USA National Archives

We had the first vegetable dehydration plant in the area. Three thousand acres were taken up with growing spuds, peas, beans, beetroot — all for the troops overseas. One time there was strife on the wharves with the watersiders, so the roof was taken off the wharf shed and stores lifted direct from ship to store.

From my experience over two and a half years, I have nothing but praise. When they'd gone, by God we missed 'em. Colonel Shepherd used to come to my house for dinner, and he always wanted a shower first. I used to pass him a whisky through the shower door and he would say, 'Message received and understood.' He is ninety-one now and almost blind.

Years later I was in Hawaii and the customs man said to me, 'Ah, Noo Zillun. Do you know a place in Noo Zillun that starts with "Pie-"?'

'Paekakariki?' I said.

'That's right, Paekakariki, where we Marines were.'

'Take you back nostalgically?' I asked.

'What's that mean? But I used to have this thing on with a dame in Wellington called Smith. Do you know a girl in Wellington called Smith?'

I must have shown some of my incredulity, for he snapped my case shut and said, 'Have a nice time, buddy.'

Harry Woodward, Second Lieutenant in the Marine Corps 214th Coast Artillery AA Regiment, was back in New Zealand in 1987 and recalls how he first hit Pukekohe in the early days of October 1942.

> We were scheduled to go to Guadalcanal but there was a certain huffin' and a-puffin' by Admiral Ghormley. Guadalcanal was very shaky and there was a feeling we were about to give up the ship. Out at sea we were redirected to New Zealand. The afternoon that our ship docked in Auckland another young lieutenant and myself were given a jeep and told to go down the road and find the town of Pukekohe. Within a day or so our regiment moved in to bivouac on the Pukekohe racecourse. During that time Admiral Ghormley was busted and 'Bull' Halsey moved in. 'We're not giving up anything. Get back on that troopship,' he said and three weeks later we were on our way again to Guadalcanal. We stayed up there for a year and a half and came back to New Zealand for R & R. We got off the troopships and they sent us up here to Pukekohe and we bivouacked out at Helvetia Camp. We were here for about six months then. So you see, Pukekohe has a lot of history for me.

There was no electric light for the men camped in the pyramidal tents or in the two- and four-men huts. Every hurricane lamp or kerosene lamp in New Zealand (and candles when available) was bought up by the troops. One light that did shine was the Blue Light spoken of by the mayor of Pukekohe, the sign of the prophylactic treatment station for those servicemen who had within the previous few hours exposed themselves to possible venereal disease. The Blue Light must have been a familiar sight to the suburbanites of Auckland and Wellington, whether in the main street of Pukekohe, Goatleys Road Warkworth, the Auckland Domain, Victoria Park, or that vast conurbation of troops at McKay's Crossing and Camp Russell near Paraparaumu.

There were also the PX stores stuffed with American goods, and New Zealand goods where available, which some New Zealand civilians were able to get into (although they were not supposed to). For those servicemen shut out in some lonely enclave in the 'sticks' (or the boondocks, as the Americans would say), it was a dreary existence at night, with only the noise of the occasional opossum or call of a morepork to disturb the night. The boys who had only known the redbricks of American suburbia and life on the sidewalks were desperate to escape the loneliness, the slush, the cold and rain of a New Zealand winter — to anywhere where there were lights and warmth, liquor and women.

Bob Leiser of the 3rd Marine Division was camped out on the Francie Wech farm along Woodcock's Road, near Warkworth. He came back in October 1986 to look for his old camp site.

> I don't have any fond memories of my army service, but I do of New Zealand. New Zealand treated us so generously that I have never forgotten it. Life out in the camp was pretty miserable at times, it was cold, and

the louvres in the two-men huts let in the draughts, but on liberty away from camp in Warkworth it was fine. That was all we lived for, liberty and to get out of camp. Across the road from us was a farmhouse where we used to go for a meal. When we learned that they were really poor we used to pinch rations to take along. We felt really guilty about it when we found out this family was sharing their all with us when they couldn't afford it.

We used to go into Auckland to the Auckland Hotel, the Red Cross outfit, and spend our pay. Let's face it, we were a lot of stalwart warriors looking for women, and women were freely available. No wonder there was a bit of a fracas in Queen Street one time when the locals took to some of our boys.

Boot camp, or recruit camp as you would call it, was the most profound experience of my life — in fact I feel it altered my whole life. For three months we had no liberty and were confined to camp. Very few men failed — they had earlier taken the two physicals, which were rigorous enough. On my second physical the dental dispensary officer told me, 'Son, we will have to send you home,' this because my mouth needed so much attention. 'How keen are you to stay in the Marines?' 'Very keen, sir,' I said. I said this because my buddies and I had been given a send-off in our home town and I didn't want to go back with my tail between my legs. Anyhow I had eleven fillings and two extractions, all without pain-killer. Whether it was all part of the weeding-out process I don't know, but I survived boot camp and became a 'Gyrene', the vernacular for a Marine . . . 'Gyrene' is the equivalent of 'GI Joe', the latter referring to the ordinary Army man in the ranks. Because the Marines did not wish to be associated with other branches of the US Forces, somebody dreamed up this term 'Gyrene', 'Gy' being the equivalent of GI and 'rene' from marine.

The Americans touched thousands of New Zealand lives. Mention the Marines, army boys or sailors of those days to members of an older generation and the response is predictable: 'I remember when . . .' One woman talked of her social life in Pukekohe as a teenager.

I remember when another girl and I used to get around with a couple of US Army boys. I knew one of them was married, though my girlfriend, who was much in love with him, didn't. We went to the pictures in a cruddy old jalopy the Yanks had acquired. When we came out all four tyres were flat. My girlfriend's regular New Zealand boyfriend had seen to that. Our family had a Ford Prefect and we were only allowed two gallons of petrol a month. The Americans used to drive it back to camp. Next day when we got it back the tank would be full. We asked no questions. Looking back, we were just good-time girls whose appreciation of the American role in battle conditions was very sketchy. We saw them as being swallowed up in those thousands of Americans somewhere overseas. The sadness of it all I only came to understand in later years.

Phyllis recalls her memories of the Marines.

111

I remember the Marines, well how could we ever forget 'em. As the troops went by our farm gate the boys would throw sweets and chewing gum to the children. Of course the kids found the Americans tremendously popular. They were always very kind to the children. One time they put on a Christmas party for all the kids in the neighbourhood. They got their names and their ages. There was a present for every child and a ride in the jeep too. There were games and paper hats and a real feast afterwards. We used to have dances down at the Matakana Hall, only the Americans came and they picked you up in a jeep and took you home. In the winter time you wore your gum boots to the hall and changed there. There was Pop and Rex and Eva Collings and Chris Withers. They played the old time dances like the maxinas, the valetas and the waltzes. Jitter bugging had just arrived. Once in the hall you were not allowed out. The people who ran the dance were adamant about that. There was no booze inside and the local policeman was on duty to see there was none outside either. Of course some came in, gin in lemonade bottles or some kind of sly grog hooch. There were some pretty torrid love affairs I can tell you but I'm not going to gossip about those. The American captain saw that his boys behaved. Our husbands let us go to the dances, they knew they were strictly conducted.

Father Christmas arrives in a jeep. The Marines (3rd Division) turn on a Christmas party for the kids of the Matakana district, 1943. *A. N. Breckon*

Bill remembers life in suburbia when the Yanks were just down the road.

It was no use going down to the pub in the morning; the Yanks had drunk the pub dry. They used to drink it warm from the tankers. They would put their glasses down on the wooden floor, take out their sheath knives and fling them point down alongside their glasses.

There must have been 10,000 of them here in Warkworth at one time. It took a long while to drive your truck through them when they were out on route marches. They would give you anything, cigarettes by the thousands, clothes. Some of the women in the district used to do laundry for them. They only had to admire some piece of uniform and the Marines would supply them in dozens. Balloon-seated khaki-coloured underpants must have been worn by many local men. Shirts were the same, and boots; they asked you what size you took, and you had not one pair, but three. Somebody dropped a 40-gallon drum of petrol in my hedge one night. I was terrified to use it in case I was caught. Half of Warkworth was walking round in American clothing at some time.

When you went to a dance the Marines would ask you to come out for a drink. The local policeman was a strict disciplinarian. If you were caught drinking within a hundred yards of a dance hall he might well put you up in court. The Marines of course could do what they liked. Probably they were subject to the same laws as any New Zealander, but the police left them alone and relied on the military police to implement their own law.

Brandy came in from the United States for the officers in five-gallon kegs. One night some Marines pinched some brandy from the officers' quarters. In getting through the bush with their booty, the boyos lost one of the kegs of brandy down the hill and into a creek at the bottom. They tried for days to locate that keg but never could find it — neither could the locals who heard about it. It could be there still.

When the Americans departed, never to come back, the stuff they left behind was incredible. Some was bulldozed before they left, but things like blankets were left in their hundreds. One top sergeant Marine who I got to know brought back a revolver he had taken from a Jap officer. Before he took off again he said, 'Here, look after this until I come back.' He never did come back and I still have the revolver.

Charley was another local resident who benefited from the American troops. He describes his dealings, some slightly shady, with them.

Man, those Marines were big spenders; not so the Army, they were real mean, but the Marines spent up big. Something they ate was block cake, they might call it pound cake and we called it fruit cake. There was a constant and insatiable demand for it. I worked in the butter factory in those days and we used to take the back seat out of the Plymouth tourer and shove in packs of butter. The windows had curtains to them. We would drive into Auckland, hand over the butter and take delivery of the slabs of fruit cake, eighteen inches square and about four inches thick. It

113

was all very hush-hush, not to say illegal. You didn't want to get caught at the racket. There were still penalties for breaking the regulations. We considered we were helping the war effort. We may have also been helping our boss out too. We drove straight out to the American camp. The sergeant would blow his whistle and the Marines would line up and throw their dollars into a cardboard box. If you got your ration last week you didn't line up this week.

There were no shortages in that small town in those wartime days; sugar, petrol, cream, butter, steak, you name it and it was there. Much of it came out of the camps. The boarding house dining room, which held about thirty people, was in production day and night. It was always the same order, steak and eggs. There was no freezer in those days. The steak hung outside in the cooler in the shade of the macrocarpa tree. The Yanks liked their steaks long and fat. They loved sweet things. Bread and jam they ate with their steaks. The civilians had to surrender ration coupons for their meat, not so the troops. Well, they trained hard and they ate hard.

While they were waiting for their steaks to come up, they would be outside playing 'two-up'. There would be big dollars in the ring. Then the fights would start, they were invariably about gambling. The military police would arrive in their jeeps with a hiss and a roar. What a scatteration! Never mind the dollars in the ring, to hell with them, there were plenty of dollars. The Marines were frightened of the MPs with their long batons. Sometimes they would play 'craps' (rolling dice or the 'galloping dominoes', as they called them). Yes, outside the dance hall or the boarding house, that's where it all happened. They were great gamblers, but then they had the money. I asked one of them what he did in the States. 'Nothing. I was unemployed,' he replied.

They bought up all the clapped-out old cars and some good ones, ran them on the rims if the tyres had had it. Even ran them on the spokes and left them on the side of the road. One time we were taking a wooden butter vat to Kaipara Flats railway station. The boss reckoned it would be great for the Yanks to sit on. They were always looking for a ride to the station in order to go on leave in Auckland. There must have been thirty Americans sitting on this upturned vat when we went round a corner and a tie rod to the front wheel came off. Hell, there were Yanks flying through the air every which way. 'Goddamn it', I could hear them calling, 'son of a bitch' and all sorts of appeals to the Almighty as they picked themselves up out of the gorse. But someone fixed up the tie rod and on we went. At the end they would throw dollars into the cab, even silver dollars. They were very generous. I had an old Model A Ford Tourer in which I did a bit of illegal taxi driving. I would take it into the camp and the boys would say, 'Back 'er up,' and fill up the tank so I could take them into Auckland. The officers used to turn a blind eye. Strangely, the American transports were not allowed to pick up their own on the roads, or were not supposed to, so it was left to the locals to attend to the hitch-hikers.

One Marine has not forgotten the cake Charley mentions, even after forty-five years. George Unangst wrote the following letter from 1814 Bennett, Flint, Michigan.

> I was a Marine stationed at Warkworth and Pakiri Beach from February to July 1943. At the canteen the local women furnished coffee and pound cake for dances, etc. My request is for someone to locate and send to me the recipe for that cake. For a short while I could find ready-baked cake that was similar, but I guess due to the cost I cannot find even that anymore. Thank you.
> George Unangst
> PS. I enjoyed my stay in New Zealand.

Mrs Blakey was on duty down at 'The Hut', a recreational facility for troops in Warkworth run by the American Red Cross.

> The boys would come in to ring up their dates in Auckland. In those days it was a shilling a call, and I collected the money. At times 'The Hut' was jam-packed. They used to practise square-dancing and sometimes I was hauled in to make up a square. The music would knock your head off. I lived on Pulham Road and every morning at six o'clock the military band would play to wake the troops up. And so we got out of bed in those days to the tune of 'Praise the Lord and Pass the Ammunition'.

Most locals were more than willing to assist the war effort, but sometimes they were given no choice. The approach made to Alf Bell for the use of twenty acres of his Matakana farm was probably typical of wartime methods.

> They took twenty acres from my farm. The New Zealand Army officers came round and said, 'What about some of your land for an army camp?' I asked, 'What if I don't agree?' 'Well,' they said, 'it's all the same, we'll just take it, but we would like you to agree.'
> The camp was occupied by New Zealanders first — the 3rd Auckland Battalion. The Americans, who came later, were very well behaved — they had to be . . . One character pinched some mail so he was loaded up with bricks and had to march round the camp for a week.

Alf also remembers the landing exercises with the New Zealand Air Force.

> One American was run over by a landing craft and killed. I also heard about fatal accidents on Mount Tamahunga when they were on night manoeuvres there. They went for long route marches — to Wellsford and back. Sometimes they were away for two or three nights on training. There were 1100 of them here training for twelve months. It seemed an awful long time for troops to go on training.

And if you were young and in your teens, how did it strike you back in those heady days of early 1943? June tells her story.

Oh it was really neat when they came. There were no men around, they were all in the forces. It really set the town alight . . . I worked in a shop and sometimes we were invaded. They had plenty of money and nothing to spend it on. They bought biscuits and candy, probably to give away, for they had all they wanted in their own PX store. The dances were fantastic — they introduced the song 'I'm Dreaming of a White Christmas' to the town. (They happened to come just before Christmas, it must have been in '42.) 'In the Mood' was the big one of course. They played all the Glenn Miller songs — 'String of Pearls', 'Chattanooga Choo-Choo'. They were fantastic times for slumbering Warkworth. You can just imagine what the glitter of uniforms and first-class music right from the States did for us.

Ona is another woman who has fond memories of the dances.

I remember one night I danced with one GI all night. And did my father read the riot act to me! It was just not done to dance with the same guy all night — not in his book anyhow. I used to write to a lot of the boys when they left here. Of course we didn't know where they were, except that they were in the Pacific battle area somewhere. One soldier I wrote to after the war for a while, but I didn't get any reply. When my husband and I went to the States and were in Louisana and I took a chance and rang a number in the phone book. Strangely enough I got his uncle, who told me that my soldier friend had been dead for thirty-three years. 'No wonder you didn't get any reply,' he said.

Elsie did not have to go to dances to meet the troops; they came to her.

They were in my house from morning to night. I don't know how many meringue pies I must have baked. I used to get telegrams — 'Have a meringue pie for Saturday night, returning to camp'. There was a medical camp at the corner of Kaipara Flats Road and the State Highway, where the American doctors lived, colonels and majors. They used to come over to our house every night for cribbage or to sit around the fire and talk and laugh . . .'

Elsie still has letters that a few of the boys wrote back from the battle zones. Gene, Joe and Henry wrote what they could under the strictly censored circumstances.

We won our regimental colours a few days ago and they were going to be given us by Eleanor [Roosevelt], but they changed their minds (thank goodness) and had the general give them to us. A lot of the fellows, myself included, got their arms and wrists burned by the hot brass from the machine-guns. Boy, those guns were really red hot. I think this is about the hottest place on earth. Sweat so much you just wring your clothes out. I'm going to have to close now, because we're as busy as hell, and there isn't much to write about that wouldn't be censored, so I'll close hoping to hear from you soon. Take it easy.
Your friend Gene.

To begin with, it is impossible for me to disclose the facts concerning Buck's death. Many times he spoke of how he had been a bush soldier for three years and never had the chance to see the real thing. One day Buck's dream was fulfilled, hence he died a happy man.
[From Joe, Pharmacist's Mate, Second Class, US Navy.]

I have been rather busy since moving to this tropical island. The natives here speak a few words of English and live in grass huts — have not found any Dorothy Lamours running loose round here. I sure miss Warkworth and the supper hours and you people a lot. There is no such thing round here in any form whatsoever. We have movies quite often if not interrupted and that's about all, except mail from home. I sure did appreciate everything you people did for me. I am not such an expert at expressing my true deep thankfulness for the way you treated me and the rest of the boys. All my New Zealand memories center around the fireplace and the conversations that ensued. We all miss New Zealand and hope we come back there soon. There is no telling exactly from day to day, so we can only hope.
Your Marine friend always,
Harry.

Ina was young at the time, but has plenty of memories of the Marines.

There was a terrific girl shortage, every girl from thirteen up, grew up very quickly in those days. I played the piano for them. Girls didn't drink in those days. There seemed two groups of Marines, one group who were content with the local entertainment and the other which sought their pleasure in Auckland and what it had to offer. Mind you I was only fourteen and no doubt was blind to what may have been going on around me. The police used to meet the buses from Auckland and send the girls back in the next. There wouldn't be a family which didn't open its doors to the Americans . . . The Marines I feel looking back behaved according to the company they found themselves in. But what I remember most was the youth of the Marines. They were just kids in some cases, no more than seventeen and God only knew what they were going in to. It was all such fun but there were tears too, bitter tears when romances fizzled out, and even more sustained tears when the casuality lists came out.

Eva used to play the piano for dances held at the recreation hut on Smiths' (now Whistlers') farm for the Marines camped on the Whangateau Domain, north of Warkworth. The farmers' wives taught them the old-time dances. Eva said that the Marines used to go out in their jeeps to collect the wives while Dad stayed home and looked after the kids. I asked her if this had led to any broken marriages.

Not that I know of, though one or two were a bit shaky. When I was up at the piano I used to see quite a lot. I got some surprises, from the ones you'd least expect it too. Sometimes the Americans would come up to our house at night (I had three sisters) and I used to play for them. It got that I thought it best to pull the blinds. But I can assure you it was all clean

117

fun and no harm done. Time meant nothing to the Americans, they would stay till one o'clock in the morning, and that got a bit wearing after a while.

Eva was not the only one who found the Americans' expectations excessive. 'Once at a dance at Matakana,' said Sybil, 'a Marine said to me, "After the dance may I walk you home, ma'am?"

"But it's five miles on a country road."

"I'm used to that, ma'am."

"Yes, but I'm not,"' Sybil replied.

Sybil and George also entertained the Americans at Whangateau. George would give them a lift, take them home and give them a glass of milk, a slice of cake, and have a fireside chat.

> They thought that was real nice. Occasionally we asked some of the boys to stay and have dinner. Some didn't know how to use knives and forks. I usually said grace, a ritual some didn't understand. One night one Marine said, 'Say, sir, is it safe to start eating yet?" Some of them came from very deprived and humble backgrounds, others could only talk about 'outermobiles' and women. We had two lots here, the first came on R & R from Guadalcanal, and the second, the amphibian Marine Corps, practised in the lagoon and did landings on Omaha Beach. The tracks in the mud flats made by the amphibian units were visible for some years after the Americans left.

George could have been forgiven for wondering just what sort of soldiers these boys would make.

> We had an old ram, Old Tom we called him, who ranged at large, even came into the house. One day down a side road I came across a couple of Americans sitting on a stump where Old Tom had baled them up. They called out to me, 'Look out, sir, he's dangerous.' I knew how to get in close to Old Tom so that he could not charge you, which I did. 'Man,' said one of the Americans, 'we thought he was going to kill you, sir!'

George produced his visitors book of those days. Among those to sign were Lieutenant W. T. Whitaker of Springfield, Massachussetts: John K. Butler from Crosbie, Tennessee: Chas Stewart from Johnston, New York; and Captain Geo. Foot, USMC, the officer in charge of the amphibian unit.

Bruce used to look after a recreation hut, where the Americans came in in their droves to eat the apple pies (with full cream courtesy of local farmers), which were supplied at the rate of a thousand a day. His remarks echo the feelings of all the Warkworth area residents I spoke to who had contact with the Americans.

> They were naive in a way. 'We've come to save you from the Japs,' they would say. But they knew nothing about war, or what was in store for them. Very few had seen action. It was all very sad really; you couldn't help liking them.

118

Charlie gave a Marine's eye view of Warkworth. He was with the 21st Marines out at Kaipara Flats.

Initially I was with the 2nd Marines Division in Wellington. I had been there with the 6th Regiment for just a couple of days when we were given liberty. Some buddies and I went to Rotorua but we failed to get back on time and were placed on charge for being AWOL. They were going to give us a summary court martial, that is, sentenced by the colonel, who could give up to some years in some military jail back in the States. We requested a general court martial where we could have an attorney officer to defend us. This was really only a ploy to get out of it. Anyhow they transferred us to 3 Div in Warkworth, where we were regarded as the bad boys. It didn't worry us plenty. What the hell, we didn't care too much. Most of us were kept in such an uninformed state that we didn't know what the hell was going on anyhow. You had to be seventeen and have your parents' permission to get into the Marines, but several in our company were only sixteen. The authorities weren't too conscientious about checking up on your age.

We had boxing every week and everybody had to take their turn. We were separated out into weights and names were drawn out of a hat. If it was a terrible mis-match, you took a hell of a beating. Friday nights some of us made it into Auckland. There was sure nothing doin' on the sidewalks at night. We went down to the amusement park near the waterfront. They had a Ferris wheel and a dance floor too. Another good pick-up place was the railway station. If you could strike up a conversation with some girl, and that wasn't hard, you were in. But because we were so-called bad boys, we were on restricted leave. We weren't really bad, just unlucky.

At Kaipara Flats three of us went down to see the butcher, Mr Phillips. The issue meat was not too tasty and we felt in need of some steak. We had the money and we told Mr Phillips we wanted some meat. But he said he wasn't killing this week, there wouldn't be the demand.

'But we'll take the whole cow, Mr Phillips.'

'How soon did you want it?'

'We figured on waiting for it now, Mr Phillips.'

So we helped him kill the beast. He boned it and we struggled back to camp with the joints on our backs. We gave it to the cook and he almost ruined it.

Mrs Phillips chaperoned the girls down at the local hall for the dances. An Army truck went out to get the girls, and when it was home time Mrs Phillips used to stand at the back of the truck and count the girls back in; yessir, there could be no absentees, not with Mrs Phillips.

Our huts were two-men jobs and when we arrived the sheep were in them. When we went out marchin' the sheep would go back in because they had no doors. We had to knock up some sort of a barricade or hang a sack. The huts were cold, condensation formed and there were no windows, only a few vents in the gable.

The beer issue was pretty thin when I was in camp. We made our own raisin jack. We put dried fruit, a little sugar, some brewer's yeast (thieved from the cook-house) into a Lister bag (water bag). If it was hung in the

hot sunlight, it would work up real quick. It sure gave you a lift. Sometimes it gave too big a lift and put men into hospital. Somebody down the
road, Louie, I think, made wine, but to get wine you had to supply the
empty bottles and they were hard to come by in wartime.

We played cork ball, a game unknown in New Zealand. The ball, as
big as an over-sized walnut, was covered in leather, and the bat was about
the same diameter. The game was played something like baseball.

All in all, I consider we behaved pretty well. The boys in my outfit were
from good homes, though some were not mentally equipped for the job
ahead. I was very proud of the way they behaved in battle. I was very
proud to be part of them. I tell you this, very very few of them would have
got out of it without being wounded or worse. I was wounded at Bougainville and shipped back to the States, where I was discharged.

Looking back, a man was up to his arse in daisies one day, and then
sweating his guts out in full battle gear over the Kaipara Hills the next.
Of the good times, it makes my balls itch even today to think of 'em.
Occasionally it would all get too much for somebody and he would shoot
himself in the foot, and the old Chattanooga Choo Choo would have to
choo choo him home to a court martial and a dishonourable discharge.
Some guys may have got a heroic bang out of it all; but no the thing to
do was to survive, just to survive.

The 3rd Marine Division had left Auckland by 23 July 1943 to stay on
Guadalcanal until the opening of Operation Cherryblossom, a misnomer
for the landing at Empress Augusta Bay, Bougainville, on 1 November.
Bougainville could not be bypassed, for its six airfields, protected by
35,000 troops including the Japanese 6th Imperial Division, had to be
neutralised. The plan was to land on a lightly defended stretch of the
coast, build an airfield at Torokina and hold it. Doubts were expressed
that an airstrip could be built on the swampy ground there, but Halsey
said, 'It's Torokina, now get on your horses.'

Planning for this operation was interrupted when the 3rd Marine
Division commander, Major General C. D. Barrett, mysteriously fell to
his death from a third-floor window of the Nouméa officers' quarters.
General Vandegrift, then in Washington, was recalled to take control
of the preparation.

No bombardment of the bay was laid on. Diversionary bombing
attacks to the airfields at Buin and Buka were carried out. New
Zealanders from the 8th Brigade were to land on the Treasury Islands
to the south, and Americans on the island of Choiseul, at the same time
that 3 MarDiv went ashore at Empress Augusta Bay. The landing came
as a complete surprise to the Japanese, and just as well. They had
camouflaged pillboxes which gave enfilade fire down the beach and, if
fully manned, they could have wrecked a disorganised landing through
what proved to be heavy surf. Also, bearing down on the island was a
Japanese naval relief force with reinforcements from Rabaul, which

threatened to spell disaster for the Marines. A US Navy squadron got in amongst the fleet and sank the cruiser *Sendai*. Two other Japanese destroyers collided and the fleet retreated to the north. Halsey made a dicey decision to send in his two aircraft carriers, *Saratoga* and *Independence*, to bomb an assembling Japanese naval and air force in Rabaul. Ninety-six planes roared into Simpson Harbour to destroy the naval shipping there and the Bougainville campaign was saved.

The Americans had arrived from a bland New Zealand autumn, and an officer of the 21sts recalled that 'on Bougainville we were battling a jungle such as we had never dreamed of. For nineteen days we attacked this natural enemy with our machetes and knives, hacking our way through almost solid barricades of vegetation run riot. It rained daily from noon to dusk, fierce pounding tropical rains. If we had been lucky to hit fairly dry ground, we slept in foxholes six or eight inches deep. During the night water seeped through the earth. We invariably woke drenched.'

The Japanese were the enemy, but there were others too: dermatitis, dengue fever, malaria, ringworm, prickly heat and dysentery. There were battle casualties, but there were health casualties too, which only evacuation to a cooler climate could cure. The relentless rains drummed down in a never-ending cascade of depression. There were no lights at night, only a cacophony of insect noises. By day it was a morass of knee-deep mud where the bulldozers had cut in roads. For some men it was too much and they had to be removed to the psychiatric wards. No man could have stood it for too long.

The Australians also had a small contingent of forces in the campaign. One time General MacArthur paid a surprise visit to the Australians in their front-line foxholes. An astounded Aussie infantryman looked up to see the General over his shoulder. 'Jesus Christ,' he said, 'it's the Messiah himself.' Like everyone else in the Islands, New Zealand soldiers contracted skin diseases, particularly round the genitalia. Then it was off to the RAP (Regimental Aid Post) for a treatment with wintergreen. Wintergreen may have been good for ringworm but on the surrounding parts such as the scrotum it caused excruciating pain and a fandango on the part of the victim. All a soldier could do was to take his lemon-squeezer hat and fan the affected parts.

Within two weeks the 'Can Do' Seabees had a steel mat airfield down at Torokina and New Zealand pilots in their Warhawks and Corsairs were to fly off it. By the end of the year the Bougainville airfield and its perimeter was secure.

CHAPTER SIX

Tropical Lightning and
Winged Victory

The 25th Division US Army was in New Zealand for barely three months, from 7 December 1943 until 24 February 1944, and was stationed at Puhinui Camp (now the site of Nestlé's factory) in the Manurewa area with headquarters at Papakura Military Camp. The 25th, which had its origin in Hawaii, was first known as the Pineapple Division, with a shoulder patch of a pineapple on a blue and white background. Some months before war broke out, the division was reorganised and, under Major General 'Lightning' Joe Collins, earned the name Tropical Lightning Division when it took a ridge in the Guadalcanal campaign much ahead of the time frame laid down by overall command. Originally the 25th was a regular division, officered in the main by West Pointers. In September the unit, only partially at strength, received recruits from the States to bring it up to war establishment. Peter, an artilleryman now living in the Warkworth area, described what happened to his unit at this time.

They took cadres from all our different units and sent them back to the States as the trained nucleus to form a new division. About four months later this division was sent to reinforce General Douglas MacArthur's forces in the Philippines at Bataan and Corregidor. It was a doomed expedition from the start. The Japs vastly outnumbered our boys. Many of my buddies did not survive the death march or the prisoner-of-war years. I for one do not regard 'Dugout Doug' with affection. I lost too many buddies.

We were in barracks in Pearl Harbour when Commander Fuchida and his bomber squadrons dropped out of the skies and started strafing us. I can remember seeing the bugler being spattered with bullets as he sounded 'Boots and Saddles'. Somewhere else I could hear another bugler sounding 'To Arms'. We got a message that parachute troops were being dropped. This of course, though we were not to know it at the time, was false, but some Jap pilots did bale out when their planes were hit.

With our division again up to strength we trained for amphibious assault, up and down the nets slung over the sides of our transports. We left Hawaii on 3 November 1942 for Guadalcanal. Our unit was assigned to take Bloody Ridge, and it took us a month to do the job. Why did it take us so long? We had never been in combat before, and we were up against élite Jap troops who had fought in Mongolia against the Chinese soldiers. We experienced here the 'Banzai' charges, where they came at you naked except for a loin cloth. Armed with a sabre and rifle, they kept going till they died. They were doomed because the island was now blockaded. Any Japanese destroyers that came down 'The Slot' were now, because of superior American naval power, lucky to survive. The Japs took to cannibalism, and not only on their own troops.

After Guadalcanal some of our boys went up to Bougainville, some to Vella Lavella and then we moved back to Guadalcanal on the way to New Zealand. We arrived in Auckland in December 1943, supposedly for six months rest, recreation and some training but we stayed barely three. On the day we arrived we went on a route march from the pier to Mission Bay and back. From then on it was all play, but not quite. We refurbished our 'matériel', as we were pleased to call it.

With reveille at 6 a.m. we worked till noon, then it was shine up the shoes, get the creases right on the shirt, tuck the tie in below the second button, then either hitch-hike into Auckland or walk up to the Puhinui station for a ride into town.

I was a sergeant, and the top three grades of sergeants formed the 25th Jungle Division social club and took over the Silver Slipper in Customs Street. We had dances every night for our invited guests. The officers were along the street at the Waverley Hotel. But for the enlisted men and ourselves there were the Peter Pan, Metropole, Crystal Palace, Orange Hall, the El Rey out at Hillsborough, the Pirate Shippe over at Milford and Westhaven on the western waterfront. One night I poked my head into the Catholic Youth Centre and that's how I met my wife. Then there was the Downtown Club in Customs Street for all Allied servicemen. The famous Artie Shaw, who had worked with Bix Beiderbecke and Billie Holliday, came with his Navy band and played at the Auckland Town Hall. As a sergeant I had an overnight pass, but if enlisted men missed the last train, they could get a bed down at Victoria Park camp or up at Camp Hale in the Domain, and make it back to Puhinui in the morning.

Some Marines came here direct from the States and they were hardly dry behind the ears. Some were not trained troops, just the normal twelve weeks in boot camp. Some were not used to hard liquor, wine and fast women . . . In some instances, many probably, they were the product of Depression families who had barely survived those times. For the first time in their lives they had money, they had shoes, and by God they had something else they had never dreamed of, they had stature in the eyes of the public. For some this new-found glory was all too much and they stepped over the traces and found themselves drunk and disorderly in the arms of the military police. The MPs had not had too much training either, and clothed in all the authority invested in them, with their helmets with MP on them and their big long batons, they were only too eager to make their presence felt. And I can tell you discipline in the American forces was tough. Before you knew where you were, you could be in Leavenworth Jail back Stateside, serving out a two-year sentence. Towards the end of the war I was back in the States instructing recruits and on one occasion I failed, because honest-to-God I didn't see him, I failed to salute a major who was a provost-marshal in the military police. Only my overseas record saved me from being busted.

Captain L. N. Samuelson, a provost-marshal in charge of American military police in Wellington, went on record at the time as saying, 'The clubs my men carry are primarily for psychological effect. Only such force is used as is absolutely necessary. We try to have men who have been policemen in civilian life. We pick up staggerers off the street and keep them till they're sober. That way they don't get into trouble.'

'Ringing the changes'. US Army signal unit men getting their wires crossed.
Tudor Collins

Bill, a soldier who now lives in Ogden, Utah, described at length his experiences with the Tropical Lightning (25th) Division.

We left Ogden and headed for San Luis Obispo, California, where we were to have our year's training. What a hell hole, pigs lived better. It got no better during the winter, so much so that some fellows talked about going over the hill. San Luis was known as General Storey's concentration camp. A slogan was passed round — OHIO, which meant 'Over the hill in October'. Walter Winchell [the best-known columnist in the United States at the time] got word about the conditions and things began to change for the better.

I was sent to medical school and after three months of ten- to twelve-hour-day studying I graduated from William Beaumont Hospital as male nurse qualified in every field to assist doctors. I was all packed up ready to go on leave, went to the first sergeant's quarters to receive my pass, when word came that the Japanese had attacked Pearl Harbour — all leave was cancelled. Four years later, nearly five, I got home.

We left San Francisco Harbour on troop transports and headed for Hawaii, where some days later we landed at Kapow Kawai, Hawaii. I was sent to Kaneo Air Base as part of the nucleus that was to form the 25th Division. There were some regular Army men, National Guardsmen and the rest were made up of 'ductees' from all parts of the US, some of whom had never shot a gun or didn't know how to swim.

Again we were herded onto troop transports and, after days of sailing, informed that our destination was Guadalcanal, our mission to relieve the 2nd Marine Division. We made contact with the Marines and began the slow process of taking over. They were jubilant to see us Army fellows, they had been through hell. Hell wasn't the half of it. I've never in my life seen so much mud and slime, and mosquitoes by the trillions. Men came down with malaria and dysentery; paregoric [a tincture of opium used to relieve pain] was drunk like water.

After Guadalcanal was secured we moved over to New Georgia Island to secure the Munda airfield. We ended back on Guadalcanal where we were treated for worms in the intestines, malaria or whatever affected us as a fighting unit. The treatment for the worm was one capsule of tetra-ethyl-dia-chlordine. Half an hour later you drank a half-cup of Epsom salts. Believe me, you got cleaned out once and for all.

Orders came to board ship again and we learned we were going to New Zealand on R & R. We landed at Auckland on 7 December 1943 and were met by American Red Cross and New Zealand people. We were loaded into trucks headed north, though we had no idea where we were going, and settled in a camp north of Warkworth. It didn't take us long to get settled and meet the locals.

At first we were puzzled to see long lines of servicemen waiting to get into a small café in Warkworth, but it didn't take us very long to find ourselves standing in the same line to get food other than army chow. The waitress who took our order told us that all they were serving was steak and eggs. We thought we had gotten to heaven. When it was served there was a small steak, two eggs, tomatoes and tea. When we had finished, the

US Army men try out New Zealand beer with their 'chow', 1943. *Tudor Collins*

waitress asked if we wanted anything else. Yes, we said, bring us another order same as the first. I remember it as if it was yesterday. You see, that was the first fresh meat we had had in about a year and a half. We also visited a small ice-cream parlour and ate ice-cream as if it were going out of style.

We had pretty much a free hand at what we did. We could come and go as we pleased, just as long as there were enough people at camp to pull the necessary duties. My friend Joe and I got a ride into Auckland — what a beautiful city — visited some of the pubs, had a few beers with the patrons and very much enjoyed the associations. Another time we got on a train and took a trip to Rotorua, where we enjoyed meeting the Maori people. It was something like our Yellowstone Park here in the States.

After a while in camp we were asked if we would be interested in helping local people on their farms. Joe and I said we would just for the change. We went to the Langridge home the next day and stayed for a whole month. The only time we went to camp was for pay day. We helped with the milking (I was raised on a farm here in Utah), mowed hay, put it in the silos, mowed the lawns, slopped the hogs. It was not all work; we played tennis, Joe and I against the family, and had some good matches. I can truthfully say that was the best thirty days I've ever spent.

However, we knew it couldn't last for ever and about the last of January 1944 we received orders to move out. We went to the Langridges to thank them for giving us their time and home. They remarked that we would be remembered as their brothers Bill and Joe from the United States.

In Auckland we boarded the USS *John Pape* a 25,000-ton troop transport. Two days out we hit a typhoon. What a storm! We thought the end had come. We were locked down below for three days and two nights. The next time we saw land was coming into Nouméa, New Caledonia. We wondered what the hell are we doing there. Amphibious landings, forced marches from beach areas through the jungle, over mountain ranges from one side of the island to the other, we did it all. We were getting into shape, everyone thought, to hit the mainland, the homeland of Japan. Finally orders came for us to prepare to leave. We left New Caledonia, steamed out into the open sea and headed north.

Several days out the captain announced over the loudspeakers that for our information, and perhaps so that those who returned could tell their kids and grandkids, that we were part of the largest armada the world had ever known. It covered an area of 600 square miles. You could stand on deck and look in any direction and see ships, transports, tankers, battleships, destroyers and aircraft carriers. We were sure that this was the big one.

US Army men emerge from a liquid lunch at the Warkworth Hotel, 1943. The pepper tree on the right is still there. *Tudor Collins*

127

We landed in the second wave at Lingayen Bay in the Philippines. It seemed to me that the closer we got to the homeland the better the Jap soldier; they were better shots and were more willing to die for the cause. They had dug tunnels with tracks to handle rail-mounted artillery. To combat this our troops dismantled and hauled up on a peak overlooking this valley a 90 mm anti-aircraft gun and fired point-blank into the tunnels.

In early June 1944 Joe and I were relaxing in the camp area when Captain Hines came to us and said we were to be sent home. It seemed the Government had come up with some kind of point system, and with our long service we had qualified. On the ship Joe and I were put in charge of the psycho section, where some of the guys were really in bad shape. We stopped at Enewitok Island to bury one of the fellows from our section. Eventually we landed at Newport News, Virginia. We boarded the train and knew we were on the way home, Utah here we come. There wasn't much of a fanfare at Utah but we were glad to see our families. Finally we were discharged at Fort Douglas on 30 July 1945, after four years, ten months and eight days of service time.

One farming family near Warkworth came to know the Americans well because their farm bordered on the Woodcocks Road camps. Lilian and Winsome recalled life down on the farm in those days.

An American was wandering round the farm one day and introduced himself to my father. 'My name is Arnold.' 'So is mine,' said Dad. One of the boys offered to help with the hay-making. He had been a florist in civilian life, and at those days we made hay the hard way with hay forks. You should have seen the blisters on that poor boy's hands. The Americans used to visit our house and I remember the night before they left, they were up at our house sharpening up their knives — heavens knows whatever for . . .

One of the first contacts people would have with the troops was a knock on the back door and the request, 'Can I use your phone, ma'am?' It was either a taxi or a girl they were ringing, or both. Once I had a knock on the door and there was a master sergeant who said, 'Stay close to home today, ma'am. I'm looking for some of my boys who have been drinking hair oil.'

I corresponded with one of the boys for years after the war. He couldn't read or write, so his sisters used to write his letters for him. They were generous to a fault. At Christmas time we were loaded with presents.

Lilian showed me a photo of themselves and the soldiers round the table. On the back an American had written, 'Those were the days — congenial company and good food.'

Yes, they loved our food, roast meat and potatoes and especially roast kumaras. And the plum pudding — they called it pudding in the sack . . . Then of course we had tennis parties on the front lawn.

When the boys first arrived in New Zealand their hair was shorn to the scalp. They were amazed when they found a civilisation here with large

'Riverina', Warkworth headquarters of the 43rd division US Army units and also the 25th Division units in the district. 'Riverina' was built for Nathaniel Wilson founder of Wilson Cement NZ Ltd. Its owner today is Mrs Beverley Simmons. *Tudor Collins*

buildings. They had no idea what they were coming to — some had never even heard of New Zealand. Some of the New Zealand soldiers had been real rascals in this town. I will say this about the Americans, if they wanted something they offered to pay for it; our soldiers just liberated it. One time some Americans did pinch what they thought were watermelons but they turned out to be pie melons, and I understand down town Warkworth was littered with bits of pie melon. Sometimes we would join the boys on a fishing trip.

Les, another Warkworth resident, knew as much as anyone about the stay of the American troops in the area because he serviced their camps, attending to drainage, plumbing and kitchen problems.

The camps were built for the Americans, although the Haurakis were out in the Dome Valley on the Knoll farm, the 3rd Auckland Battalion occupied the Matakana camp on the Smith farm, and the Army Service Corps unit was camped in a bivouac at Anderson Road, Matakana. I must say that the New Zealanders did more damage in their short time than the Yanks did all the time they were here. The Americans were meticulous in the care of their surroundings.

They had plenty of money and for a while I'm afraid they were ripped off, but not for long, for they soon got to know the value of the pound. There was a certain amount of traffic in materials too, but on the other hand there was a great deal of waste by the Americans, particularly before they went off to a battle zone. They would dig a deep hole, dump full chests of tea and bags of sugar, pour petrol on the lot and set it alight. The Yanks hated mutton — 'Goddamned mountain goat' they called it. Sometimes they would cut off the legs and other fleshy parts and dump the rest.

One unit of Marines reckoned they were being done by the locals and threatened to take the town apart before they left. It looked a bit ugly at the time, so much so that headquarters up at Riverina homestead in Warkworth sent down two jeeps with 0.5 calibre machine-guns mounted on them. These took up station at each end of the main street to impress on the troops that if they started to get stroppy they knew the circumstances. This was the sort of justice they were prepared to dish out if necessary.

The military police were not above using their waddies on a few heads at times. Some of the other punishments round the camp — well, it frankly amazed me. We were not used to the things that I saw. I can remember going out to a camp on 'Canada' Edwards farm, on Woodcocks Road, where there was a heap of metal ready to go on the road. They had a couple of guys in bare feet — this was strange in itself, for the Yanks were never seen in bare feet — with a set of wheel chains over each shoulder, dragging them up and down this heap of metal as punishment for some offence. At Matakana there was a chap who had something to do with the postal section and he was found interfering with the mail — ratting money out of letters sent home. So they fixed him up with a great big canvas bag over his shoulders with a pocket in front and one at the back. This bag was filled with rocks and he had to parade round and round the camp from morning to dark with a notice pinned on his chest saying, 'I carry the mail'. Various camps reacted in various ways. Over at Matakana they had a prison, just a series of huts out in the paddock, no power on, or any convenience — the Marines called it the 'brig'. They were shoved in there for different crimes, tossed a blanket, no mattress, and at any time of the night, they would be called out by the military police. They were ordered to strip off, and all their clothes were thrown back into the hut. The prisoners would then have the job of sorting out their own kit in the dark. No sooner was this done than they were liable to be called out again and the whole performance would be repeated.

It got to the stage that when the troops were having their liberty days, the times were staggered so that there were not too many soldiers in town at the one time. They would buy a tin billy at the hardware store, go into the pub and say to the barman, 'Fill that up, guy.' The Warkworth pub organised their own billy can system. They hung them over the old wooden bar and painted on in red paint was 'This size five shillings' or 'This size seven shillings and sixpence'. Of course there was no top shelf stuff in the war years, so it was all beer. They could get all they wanted in camp but they were not permitted to take it out, so they bought up all the banana and apple cases round town and would sit on these and drink

High jinks outside a pub. The sergeant on the left has a billy-can of beer. *Tudor Collins*

their suds outside the pub. I think the funniest thing I ever saw was a Marine shouting for his mates, and pouring the beer out of a watering can.

We had a big gang of drain-layers in the district getting the camps ready. Our headquarters was in the Showgrounds and we worked seven days a week, sometimes an eighty-five-hour week. Some of the outfalls were miles long, or seemed so, and the septic tanks were half the size of a house. The Seabees were also in camp at the Showgrounds — they were all older men and generally tradesmen. They lived in khaki pyramidal tents with wooden floors and pot-belly stoves. After the war there were hundreds of these stoves for sale — but they were not designed to last a long time.

One of the Seabees had been a tree surgeon back in the States — we would call him a bushman. He wanted to plant a tree and selected a rimu twenty feet high. This was dug up and every little root system wrapped in burlap. Then they hitched this tree up on the mobile crane and came down the main highway with it. Everybody said that it will never live, but he carefully placed it in the prepared hole and it flourished like the proverbial bay tree by the waters of Lebanon. I would like to say that it is there today, but I am unable to identify it.

The Seabees were just marking time until they got the call to move into one of the Pacific Islands to put down a landing strip for aircraft and carry out all the ancillary construction work. For practice they decided to build a bridge on the Kaipara Flats Road. It was as cold as hell the night they

131

did the job, and these jokers would be in and out of the water and then warm themselves by the fire. They had arc lights on the job and by the morning they had a brand-new bridge there. They had everything imaginable in the way of portable tools driven by air — tools I had never seen in New Zealand. We dug our drains by hand — such methods for them would have been unheard of.

They built a picture show out at the Showgrounds, cutting up pine trees for seats and erecting a windbreak for the comfort of their patrons. The picture shows ran seven days a week and the proprietor was able to get late films through the good offices of the American command. We finished up with the latest in sound and projection systems.

Naturally the force had its own hospital — it was on the flat at the back of the present maternity hospital. When the war was over it was torn down and sold off. Every hut in the area was valued and put up for sale — the going price was about £12. The weatherboards were made from heart matai, the floors were rimu with heart rimu runners. A lot of the huts were made from heart totara — there was plenty of native timber round in those days.

Like many other local residents, Les remarked on the reticence of the troops who had been in combat: 'When they came back on furlough the boys were never keen to tell of their experiences — they would only say "It was hell".' Les has a brass shell case given to him by a soldier and inscribed 'Geo. E. Offendahl. Pearl Harbour, Fiji, Guadalcanal, Tulagi, Munda, Rendova. Where days seemed like years.' The last four place names were battle zones for the 25th Division.

The 43rd Division of the US Army was no newcomer to battle scenes. The 103rd Infantry Regiment, in the uniform of the 'Blues' of the North, was engaged in the American Civil War of 1861 against the 'Greys' of the South. The 169th Regiment is recorded as part of the history of the colony of Connecticut as far back as 1739, and the 172nd Regiment was known in Vermont in 1765 as the Green Mountain Boys.

Even before war was declared on 7 December 1941, the 43rds had been in training and on manoeuvres. They had been inducted into Federal service on 21 February 1941, and had been engaged in training in Camp Blanding and manoeuvres in Louisiana and South Carolina. One member of the 43rds who has lived in Auckland for many years said, 'We trained for seventeen months for desert warfare.' In February 1942 the division moved to Camp Shelby in Mississippi and spent the next six months in training before moving to Fort Ord in California. On 1 October 1942, minus the 172nd Regiment, the division sailed out of San Francisco Bay for a destination unknown.

The 172nd Infantry Regiment sailed direct on the *President Coolidge* to Espiritu Santo in the New Hebrides. On 26 October 1942, while entering Pallikula Bay, the ship struck an anti-submarine mine in the

US Army men move out. Wilson Road, Warkworth, 1943. *Tudor Collins*

Segond Channel and sank with the loss of one life, Captain Elward Euart of the 103rd FA Battalion. (He was posthumously awarded the Distinguished Service Cross and Camp Euart at Mangere Crossing was named in his memory. The liner is still in Vila Harbour and is a well-known attraction for divers.)

The Japanese on Guadalcanal may have succumbed to the attacks by the Marines, but there remained many pockets of hard-core resistance throughout the Solomons Group. Wherever there was an airfield in Japanese hands it had to be taken. Munda, in the New Georgia group of islands, was one such, and the task of taking it was handed over to, among others, the 43rd Division and elements of the 25th Division.

The 43rd Division arrived in Auckland on 22 October 1942 and most of the troops went to the permanent military camp at Papakura, with some in Warkworth. Some units of the division stayed in Auckland for only three weeks before moving on to Nouméa. By mid-December the whole of the Division had cleared New Zealand for Nouméa, and then went on to Guadalcanal for mopping-up operations in mid-February 1943. A month later the New Englanders began the war in earnest when their mission was the invasion of the Russell Islands, an operation known as Cleanslate. Their landings here were unopposed by the

Artillery units of the 43rd US Army Division 169th FA parade through
Warkworth, 1944. *Tudor Collins*

Japanese, but in New Georgia, Operation Toenails was to be another
story. For thirty-five days the 43rds fought for the control of Munda airfield. As yet inexperienced in the ways of jungle fighting, the division
was opposed by some of the crack fighting forces of the Imperial
Japanese Navy. The Americans were not experienced in jungle warfare
and had to learn the hard and bloody way. There followed more island
hopping to Arundel and Rendova Islands and then it was back to New
Zealand via Guadalcanal; a return for some to their old stamping
grounds in and around Auckland and to familiar camps in the Warkworth area.

They were here from 27 March 1944 until the last unit moved out at
the end of July 1944 to engage in Operation Persecution, an attack on
the Japanese at Aitape in New Guinea. With other forces, the 43rds had
a share in the bloody battle of the Driniumor River. It was here that
the Japanese, in an effort to break through the encircling American
forces, were slaughtered in their thousands as they attempted a crossing
of the swift-flowing river.

134

After the campaign in New Guinea, the 43rds drew a tough assignment, the invasion of the Japanese-held island of Luzon in the Philippines with a landing at Lingayen Gulf. While other assault divisions were moving south over comparatively easy terrain, the New Englanders had to fight their way through deep ravines against Japanese artillery units dug into caves. Wherever they were, even on small Pacific atolls, the Japanese dug themselves into the ground with connecting tunnels.

The 43rds later became known as the Winged Victory Division when they were commanded by Major General Leonard F. Wing. The division's shoulder patch features a black grape leaf because its original members came from the National Guards of Maine, Vermont, Connecticut and Rhode Island, an area called Vinland.

Harry of the 43rd Division remembers his first glimpse of New Zealand from a troopship bringing his unit to this country.

We found it quaint with all these small English cars, single-storeyed buildings, the red roofs on the houses. It was like a faded picture in a

Parading Old Glory. Units of the 43rd US Army Division march through Warkworth, Sunday, Anzac Day, April 25, 1944. *Tudor Collins*

135

geography book. We thought 'Oh boy, are they way behind the States.' But we found the people really genuine, most hospitable. We made friends everywhere. If we went to a local dance, everybody treated us like royalty. Some of us got a bit objectionable, I suppose, because of the way we were treated.

Tension with the locals was not a problem. Most of the tension was among ourselves. The Marines went into Guadalcanal in the first wave and suffered great losses. The 43rds were in the second stage, and when we got back to New Zealand for a rest it became a question of sorting out who won the battle. We had the war to fight all over again. Apparently there was the occasional scrap with Kiwi soldiers, but I personally didn't know of any. There were not enough of them around to be a problem.

There was also a certain amount of in-fighting in the upper echelons of the American command. There were Marine generals who did not want to serve under Army generals, and Army generals who did not want to serve under Marine generals, who, in turn, wanted no truck with Navy admirals. The politics of the hierarchy was of no concern to the GIs and the Leathernecks in battle, when their main concern was to survive. But when on leave, with time on their hands, some Army boys claimed that the Marines got more credit than they were entitled to, and that their Fancy Dan stuff was obscuring the contribution of the GIs. Molly had vivid memories of a US Army camp on her family's property on Woodcocks Road, Warkworth.

It was an American medical outfit we had in our front paddock for a start. When the GIs first arrived we had an armed guard outside our gate twenty-four hours a day. One day it poured with rain and they looked so wet and forlorn that I asked them if they wanted to shelter on our front verandah. So for the rest of the war we had an armed guard on our front doorstep. The outgoing guard would change over the ammunition with the incoming guard and occasionally a rifle would go off. At night, when they were doing this, I lived in fear and trembling that a stray bullet would come through the side of the house into my bedroom.

They were hungry when they first arrived, because they had had only two meals a day on the troopship coming over and besides they weren't too taken with the camp tucker anyway. They asked me to get them some meat so I pooled our meat ration coupons and got them a huge roast of beef. I told them it would take at least four hours to cook. At the end of an hour they were over to see if it was ready. In the end I took it out after two and a half hours and even then it was dripping red. I carved the roast up and they wolfed it down.

I suppose we had 1200 in our camps, with their enormous trucks going up and down the unsealed roads. There was dust everywhere, the bushes on the sides of the road were brown with it. And of course they all came over to use the phone. Don't ask me who they rang, I don't know, but they damn soon found out who to ring. And the next lot who came into the camps rang the same numbers too.

The gravel crunchers. Men of the infantry of the US Army on a route march in the Warkworth district, 1943. *Tudor Collins*

We had ten cows and a bull in those days, and the soldiers used to torment the bull. When one of them put a rope round his neck I was furious and went over to the back camp. 'Who put the rope on the bull?' I demanded. No one would own up. Zach and Lopez volunteered to help me get it off, but Zach backed off, saying, 'I'm only a city guy, ma'am, and when I sees them parting the groun', ma'am, ah knaw its time to run, ma'am.' They used to go into Warkworth, buy up billy cans to hold their beer and then walk home to camp. For a short cut they would go through the bull paddock and run like hell, at the same time trying not to spill their precious beer.

When they went on route marches all the dogs for miles around went with them. They were very fond of the dogs and made pets of them, giving them all the kitchen scraps. One of the dogs started to worry the sheep and my husband took his gun to shoot it. Unfortunately the 'ammo' in those days was not the best, and he only succeeded in wounding it. He followed the dog to one of the camps and said to the sentry, who was fairly bristling with guns, 'Put that dog out of its misery, will you?' The sentry replied, 'Ah bud, I guess I'm too soft-hearted for that.' The dog was a favourite with the GIs, and Ted judged it wise to make an early departure.

There were some protracted gambling games went on, and there were times when we heard the stray shot. Crime was not something we heard a great deal about. Nor did we ask. There were some extraordinary punishments used at times, including tying a chain to a man's leg and sending him round a tree. He would wear a rut in the ground with the chain. Occasionally women got into the camps and stayed there. But I will say this, the boys were very well behaved and always most polite and considerate to us.

One character bought himself thirty cockerels — thought he would fatten them. He found it was impracticable to do this in camp and so asked me if I would look after them for him. Then he up and left and I was left with all these chooks. Somehow I got rid of them.

Sometimes they played baseball in our front paddock. If you can imagine 300 soldiers on one side screaming at the pitcher and 300 on the other side screaming at the batter — well, there was a fair noise going up along Woodcocks Road. Oh and they loved babies — there was always someone to nurse our baby. Something else they loved was milk. But then an edict came forth that they were not to drink unpasteurised milk. One of them knocked at the door for milk and I said that I was not permitted to give it to soldiers. He looked at my daughter and asked, 'Does she drink milk?' 'Yes,' I said, to which he replied, 'Well, what's wrong with her?'

There was a great deal of chewing tobacco in evidence too. At a dance you would see soldiers with great wads of tobacco on the side of their face like a big gumboil. When it came to conversation there was a great deal of shifting the wad from one side of the mouth to the other. Any young girls round the place were like magnets to the troops. They would come to the door on any excuse. The girl herd-tester could well have gone to America as somebody's wife, but she resisted that temptation.

They had a game of gridiron football on the farm one time. That was a big event. Fences had to come down, hair had to be close-cropped. For a curtain raiser some of the local schoolboys played a game of rugby and the Americans were very impressed by the bare-footed kids.

Stan was closely associated with the Americans in Goatleys Road and has lively recollections of the GIs.

It used to be strange to go down the road and see Old Glory — the Stars and Stripes — floating over Ned Gibbs's paddocks. They used to blow taps every night at sunset and reveille in the morning. It was part of the daily ritual round here in those days. Oh, and they had a makeshift prison down here made from someone's old cowshed. But they were very good to the locals. I used to wander down to the PX store in bare feet and shorts, saunter in and get my fags at two bob a time — much cheaper than outside of course. At times we noticed great hostility among the troops themselves. I'm talking about North versus South, the Blues

138

versus the Greys. After all, the American Civil War had only been over eighty-odd years then. We heard talk of 'nigger lover' and 'nigger hater'.

Sometimes they were short on rations, and bullocks and vealers were bought around the district. Once they bought a vealer from me, and a group of them arrived bristling with knives. But when it came to the actual killing I was asked to do the job. Some of them looked like New York taxi-cab drivers and were not exactly used to slitting the throats of cattle.

When soldiers from the 25th Division arrived for R & R after being involved in heavy fighting for Guadalcanal, they looked like zombies. They had been through traumatic times and stuck to their camps and to their bunks. In some cases their companies had been decimated by the Japs in Guadalcanal. It took them a while to understand that we were offering them hospitality when we invited them into our homes. On one occasion when we had some of the boys here one soldier left a two-dollar note under his plate. But with time they got to know us and accepted us as friendly natives.

When the boys came back from the battle zones they were bristling with guns of all sorts and liked to go shooting for rabbits and goats. I took some of them with me on a rabbit-hunting foray over my own property now and then, but, man, they scared the shit out of me. Their guns were pointing in all directions and I reckon I was lucky to get out alive. One day I was coming in through my gate and I heard *plop, plop, plop* ahead of me. I knew someone was shooting nearby. I counted what I thought was a magazine full, then put my heels into my horse and went like hell for home. Yes, there was always some sort of activity going on, legal and illegal — life was never dull down our street in those days.

I remember one day watching a line of soldiers moving down our road and I could see the forward element moving over the brow of the hill a mile away. They must have had a battalion of men moving in single file in manoeuvres. Every camp had an outpost set up on the hills. Even today you can see the foxholes commanding a view of the road to the north. They had dispersal areas round the camp in case of air raids and there was a complete blackout at nights. The Navy had a station over the water from Leigh at Cape Rodney — obviously a radar unit. The house is still there, a great big place with big rooms to take many cots. The infantry were all through the Waiwhiu Valley on manoeuvres, up to the Wayby Valley, back through to Whangaripo over to Matakana and then home. I don't know how many miles they did, but they were always absolutely jiggered when they got back — really flaked out. They did night manoeuvres — you never knew when you were going to have them around you.

There were quite a few American troops killed here one way and another, with road accidents, two killed on a goat-hunting expedition, and there were a few shootings and knife incidents. But it must be remembered that these men had been brought back from sustained battle actions and some were under stress. I know I made a bit of a fool of myself one day. I had been away for a while and when I came back into one of the camps the soldiers were all looking very glum. Jokingly I asked, 'Who's dead?'

and was told, 'Oh, Private So-and-so shot himself last night.' Of course I felt as big as a grasshopper's knee.

Doris spent the war years out in Kaipara Flats near Warkworth. Her family, too, sold meat to the Americans and received frequent visits from both officers (chaffeur-driven) and men.

We used to write to their relatives and say that we had met Jim down the street and he was looking fine. On one occasion I wrote to a soldier's fiancée and had a letter back asking, 'Where the hell in the United States is New Zealand? I've never heard of the place.'

Once, when two Marines went AWOL, the military police got wind of them and followed up Gubbs's bus. They stopped it at Puhoi and got the offenders off the vehicle. Then they made them take their trousers off and left them in their underpants. This was their way of ensuring that they did not attempt to escape

The Americans were very fond of dogs. My pet dog defected to them because he was fed so well. For a start he used to come home to me, but gradually the generosity of the Americans suborned him away. Once I was talking down the street in Warkworth and I saw my dog accompanying an American officer. I greeted him and the officer said, 'Ah, you like my dog.' 'Well, it happens to be my dog,' I replied. 'Can't be,' he said. 'He's the battalion mascot.' On one of my rare trips to Auckland an American truck passed me in Queen Street and there was my dog with its paws up on the tailboard viewing the passing parade. He sure got around. Skeeter was his name.

On one occasion we went out for the day and when we came back we were confronted by an American officer who said, 'You can't come in here, ma'am.' I explained that I lived there, and when I did get in we found our row of 15-foot-high blue gums had been cut down to accommodate trucks. The officer said there was no gate and therefore he had considered it public property. We put in a bill for damage to the property and it was paid without any demur. The bill was for £25, but when our American doctor friend heard about it he was furious. 'You should have demanded £150,' he said.

When the New Zealand troops were in the district we used to take the kitchen wastes from the camps for the pigs. We had to pay cartage to the farm gate. But when the Americans took over they carted all the wastes to the farm for free. What's more, they supplied the labour — prisoners accompanied by armed guards — to spread the stuff.

Like most Warkworth residents, Doris stressed the generosity of the American troops, and she told a story which is fairly typical.

The Americans performed a kind deed for me one time. If you were a land girl you were issued with all the necessary equipment, including gumboots, breeches and wet-weather clothing. A couple of GIs saw me stuffing my oversized gumboots with paper to make them fit. A couple of days later they arrived up at the house with a pair of brand-new boots

140

for me. They had been through the PX store until they found my size and had bought them for me.

Sheila, who also lived on a farm near Warkworth, confirms that half of Warkworth wore American clothing. She, too, came to know those troops who volunteered to help keep the farm running, whether it meant haymaking, milking, or pulling a cow out of the creek.

The first day they arrived they were beating around the bush with knives and bayonets looking for snakes. There were an amazing number who had never been out of a city in their lives. They loved shooting; some of them would fire at anything that moved.

One lot came back from Guadalcanal, and for one soldier it was all too much. He wandered round the camp firing at random until at last he shot himself. But still the training continued. Sometimes I would ride along on my horse to see a neighbouring farmer, and the boys would be out on the road on manoeuvres. Once they were all lying on the road with their gas-masks on and I just had enough room to get my horse down the middle of the ranks. As I went by, the boys raised their gas-masks and said, 'Good morning, Mrs Stevens. Good morning, ma'am.'

At that time I milked twelve cows by hand. The GIs were crazy on milk and used to bring their own containers to the milking shed. When a bird got into the cream and I threw it out, one of the Americans said, 'One time a mouse got into mine and I heaved it out. Today if a horse got into the churn I would squeeze it out.'

That the presence of the American troops generated a feeling of security within the community was evidenced by the tremendous amount of goodwill shown to the visitors. No American serviceman hitch-hiking away from or to his camp at Warkworth, Pukekohe or McKay's Crossing ever lacked for a ride. Civilians conscious of their own security or even feeling guilty about it were eager to assist those who were about to move into the combat zones. When an American serviceman backed his car into a Warkworth farmer's car, the Americans offered to pay for the damage. 'Forget it,' said the farmer. 'You're going overseas to fight for me.'

CHAPTER SEVEN

The Home Front: Accidents and Incidents

Although New Zealand was not in the combat zone, casualties of war did occur on the home front. Apart from accidents on manoeuvres, there were several plane crashes, which were covered up at the time by the censors. One such case involved an explosion that rocked the western periphery of Auckland just after midnight on 9 June 1942 and must have set a nervous population wondering whether the Japanese were bombing the city. They would have turned in vain to a truncated morning newspaper or to the radio for information. So strict was the censorship that three and a half years would pass until details of the incident were released.

Some Aucklanders, however, were to learn by word of mouth that at 12.30 a.m. a Flying Fortress bomber (a B-17 named 'Texas Tornado') had crashed on take-off at Whenuapai, killing all eleven crew and military personnel on board. A full tank-load of high-octane aviation fuel had exploded, and two of the payload of four 500 lb bombs had detonated. Those killed were: Colonel Richard E. Cobb, Captain Joseph R. Bruce, Lieutenant Edward R. Hoffman, Sergeants Charles P. Brunson, Harry Cohn and Joseph R. Lopez, Corporals John R. Clayton and James Herriotts Jr, and Private Curtiss P. Childers, all of the USAAF; Lieutenant William E. Hurst of the US Navy and Captain J. Gilbert, a French Navy officier bound for New Caledonia to join the Free French forces there.

The cause of the accident can only be surmised. The official accident report gives the number of the aircraft as 41-2667 and states that it was taking off for Laverton, Australia, from the north-east/south-west runway at Whenuapai. It crashed on rising ground east of the main Auckland–Helensville highway on the farm of Mr. G. W. Sinton. The pilot was presumably Colonel Cobb with Captain Bruce in the co-pilot's seat.

The funeral service for the eleven victims of the tragedy was held at Waikumete Cemetery on 12 June 1942, and the New Zealand Government was represented by the Rt. Hon. J. G. Coates. Various officers from both the American and New Zealand services attended. The officiating clergy were the Rev. E. E. Bamford (Church of England), Father Kevin (Roman Catholic) and the Rev. W. Walker (Methodist). The caskets were later re-interred in the US Military Cemetery at

Waikumete when this was established. At the end of the war the bodies were removed for permanent burial in the United States.

Mrs L. J. Lucas, a WAAF driver at Whenuapai, was detailed to provide transport for the crew of the plane while they were on leave in Auckland. On the night of their projected departure from New Zealand, Mrs Lucas picked up the six non-commissioned men from a point in Auckland at approximately 10 p.m. to return them to base. The rest of the crew came out in private cars, probably with their hosts. She believes that take-off was scheduled for 2359 hours. One motor had been unserviceable and was not going until a short time before take-off. No test flight was made.

By this time Mrs Lucas had transferred to ambulance duties.

When the aircraft crashed I was at the scene immediately behind the crash tender as it led off across the tarmac and along the main runway straight through the perimeter fence. It took a course up Trig Road, which was a narrow, winding, country road, and because the precise position of the crash was not known, the route involved a six-mile detour. The time taken, however, made no material difference, as the occupants must have died immediately . . .

I was detailed to drive in the funeral cortège when the victims of the crash were transported from the mortuary in Auckland to the Waikumete Cemetery. No particular secrecy seems to have been involved beyond the fact that there was no newspaper coverage. I drove a flat-decked truck on which were carried the bodies of Colonel Cobb and Captain Gilbert, with both coffins openly draped with their respective country's flags. It was a very sad occasion.

The official accident report tells us that two of the 500 lb bombs detonated in the fire following the crash. The other two were thrown clear when the plane struck the ground and were detonated the following day by the armament section at Whenuapai.

It was the practice of the operations officer at Whenuapai to brief pilots on the existence of rising ground off the end of the runway in use, and this was done in the case of Colonel Cobb. Some trouble had been experienced with one of the plane's engines, and the B-17, fully bombed up and under full power, used most of the runway before it lifted off. No apparent attempt was made to gain further height and the aircraft struck the rising ground at the end of the runway. The B-17 skidded across the rise and over a depression to slam into a small hill.

Several houses in the vicinity were damaged by the blast, one being shifted off its foundations. Fragments of the aircraft were found miles away. The plane's fuel tanks were probably full, and high-octane aviation fuel makes as big a detonation as a bomb load in a crash.

No official finding about the reason for the crash has ever been made public, but many theories have been advanced, one being that it was common practice for US pilots of heavy aircraft operating out of the

US Navy nurses and medics parade for the opening of US Base Hospital at Silverstream, Wellington, 1943. *John Pascoe Collection, Alexander Turnbull Library*

Islands' airstrips to fly low over the sea after take-off. Whether the engine that had previously caused problems failed at a crucial moment of lift-off over rising ground at the end of the runway will never be known.

It was widely suspected that RNZAF planes flying back to the Islands took as much hard liquor as it was possible to acquire in Auckland, and there were rumours that the B-17 was loaded with whisky, but any suggestion of insobriety in the crew is entirely without foundation.

The secrecy that surrounded this tragedy at the time is understandable; that it continued so long is not. The plane's mission has never been revealed, and an aura of mystery has remained around the whole disaster. If the truth were made known, it is likely that there would be no revelations of cloak and dagger activities; the personnel were probably carrying out liaison for the invasion of American forces that was about to descend on an unsuspecting New Zealand.

The date the Flying Fortress landed at Whenuapai for the first time has not apparently been documented, but it has been established that the plane was on the tarmac at least twelve days before the tragedy of 9 June. Mrs Lucas remembers that it was parked over on the far side of the main runway and probably locked and guarded. 'The crew went immediately on leave into Auckland . . . They did meet civilians in Auckland and were given much hospitality. At some stage during the visit the aircraft went on a flight "down south", and it was my impression that there were civilians aboard, although this was not obvious. Whether it was "top secret" would be conjecture.'

Lilian lived on the farm on which the Flying Fortress crashed.

We were all in bed. I think I was asleep but then I heard this plane revving up its engines and I waited for the take-off. And then I heard this terrible noise. I thought it was a thunderstorm with lightning, or perhaps a ball of fire had hit the house. At one point I hid under the bed, the ceiling was collapsing, furniture, blinds and glass had been thrown all round the house. Father in his bedroom had been hurt. Then two bombs went off. They did not go off immediately on the plane's crash. I went to the back door, opened it, and there was what looked like the pilot's seat stuck in the ground.

The ambulance was there immediately; apparently it had been in the area at the time. There was nothing that could be done for the crew — there was no crew. The petrol from the plane had ignited and was pouring down the farm slope to the road. The plane landed in the bull paddock and next morning he was wandering round the farm. The marks of the three propellers could be seen where they ploughed into the ground and then the plane disintegrated . . .

We weren't allowed to go back and live in our house, the windows had been shattered, the chimneys twisted. That morning — the plane crashed just after midnight — Air Force people came and put sand bags round two unexploded bombs and detonated them. No one was allowed near the crash. We stayed with neighbours that night. The authorities brought in a Nissen hut for us to live in. They took the stove out of the old house. In the end we were quite comfortable. Fortunately we were one of the few in those days to have war damage insurance on our property. Gates, hedges, water-troughs and pigstys had all been destroyed. The Yanks paid for all the damage in the long run. We were picking up parts of the plane and worse for a long time afterwards, particularly when ploughing.

My brother, a mile away, heard the explosion and thought an ammunition dump had gone up. There was a huge hole at the time, but of course it has all been filled in. The late bus to Whenuapai that night, attracted by the blaze, went off its scheduled run, came down a nearby road, had to back and went into a ditch. There was nothing in the papers — Aucklanders could only talk about rumours about a big crash 'out your way'. People came to the farm looking for souvenirs, helped themselves to the vegetable garden, even took some of Mum's preserves.

The final words on the Flying Fortress crash come from an official of the Office of Air Force History USAAF who, when requested for information about the accident, replied: 'I must warn you that very seldom, if ever, does the Air Force release the cause of an aircraft accident. These reports are generated from a safety standpoint, and are used to learn from the mistakes of others. Therefore, any findings by the investigation board cannot be used to prosecute anyone for pilot error or other causes. This allows anyone involved to speak freely about their actions leading up to the accident without fear of reprisals.'

Two days after the Fortress crash, on 11 June 1942, a Hudson bomber, taking off from the same runway for submarine patrol, crashed at the end of it. Depth charges normally used on anti-submarine patrol went off and rocked Whenuapai and its environs. This time the crew escaped injury, though the plane was a write-off. That the event was not a ghastly repeat of the tragedy two nights before can only be put down to good fortune.

A little over a year later, on the night of 1 August 1943, another American plane crashed, this time not at the base, but near Whenuapai village. The aircraft involved was a US Army Air Force C-87 Liberator Express, radio call sign JD4. The Flying Control Officer at Whenuapai that night recorded conditions as poor, with moderate rain and blustery winds. His statement records the circumstances of the crash.

> I gave JD4 taxying instructions from his parked position down the flare path to the take-off point, this was at approximately 0225 hours. At 0235 hrs JD4 started moving with landing lights full on, and became airborne opposite the control tower, almost halfway along the flare path It climbed steeply then the landing lights were switched off and the aircraft seemed to be climbing normally with navigation lights on. At approximately 6–7000 feet the aircraft turned quite steeply, it appeared to me, and continued for a short period, then began to lose height. A great flash of light showed the aircraft's fate and the ambulance and fire tender started off immediately. I phoned the hospital for doctors and further ambulances, and the Fire Master for more tenders and crews, and then Group Captain Roberts.

The plane crashed at the side of a mangrove swamp near Whenuapai village. It was not high water, and for the rescuers who waded into the metre-deep mud ooze, some light was provided by a blazing tyre. The injured were taken to the Whenuapai station hospital, the dead to the mortuary. The plane was on one of those 'special missions', but as the rescuers discovered, there were a number of Japanese on the plane. The Americans apparently had entered into a prisoner swap deal, and the Japanese were destined for Sydney, where an exchange was to be negotiated. One local couple was awakened by three mud-encrusted Japanese who could speak no English. For a moment the couple thought the Japanese invasion had arrived.

Because the Liberator came down in the mud, some local residents living close by were unaware of the crash. Others used to the sounds of aborted take-offs may not have regarded the noise as anything unusual.

Consistent with US Air Force policy, no reason for the crash was ever revealed.

One other unusual air accident occurred in New Zealand during 1943. On 30 August a USAAF C-47 (call sign 16V402) left Tontouta, New Caledonia, for Whenuapai, with twenty-two crew and passengers. At 1455 hours the RNZAF station at Waipapakauri (near Kaitaia, Northland) contacted Whenuapai to say the postmaster at Mangonui had seen an aircraft circling in low cloud and drizzle for thirty minutes. The pilot advised Auckland at Musick Point that he was not sure of his position and was told to fly at 5000 feet. Waipapakauri advised Auckland that the C-47 had been seen circling three miles away looking for an airfield. Waipapakauri fired rockets and Very lights and used an Aldis signalling lamp but with no success in the heavy rain, with visibility down to nil at times. At 1640 hours, eight hours after departure, the pilot phoned Whenuapai to say he had landed in a field at Lake Ohia. All passengers and crew were safe, though the plane was partially damaged.

The loss of a USAAF C-47 (41-18675) on 23 November 1943 is of interest because among the passengers were three members of the RNZAF. They and the other sixteen passengers, from the US Marine Corps Torpedo Bomber Squadron, perished when the plane went down in the sea on a flight from Espiritu Santo in the New Hebrides to Tontouta in New Caledonia. Some debris, including personal effects, was found washed up in the sea at Nakety Bay on the east shore of New Caledonia.

Another accident occurred at Whenuapai in the late evening of 1 September 1945, when an RAF Transport Command (RY-3) on a flight from Sydney overran the airfield on landing. The five-man crew and nineteen passengers escaped unhurt, although the plane was a write-off after running straight off the end of the runway and coming to rest about 300 metres further on in a paddock.

Jim, a teenager at the time, related an occasion when the war came closer to home. He recalled a Japanese float plane flying over Auckland one night, 'launched, we learned later, from a large submarine in the Bay of Plenty'.

A submarine featured in another incident, which has never before been publicised. In the early hours of one morning in May 1942 some astounded New Zealand soldiers on coastal defence duty in the Pelorus Sound area observed a submarine on the surface. The defence unit was equipped only with howitzers at that particular time and their instructions were not to open fire until given permission to do so. Defence heads in Wellington were roused, but by the time intelligence had resolved whether the craft was friend or foe, the submarine had slipped out into Cook Strait. And so the howitzers never did get to fire a shot. Undoubtedly this was the Japanese submarine Jim speaks of. Indeed a plane flew over Wellington at dawn on 8 March 1942, and was seen the next day over Tauranga. On 10 March two reconnaissance planes flew over Auckland. All of this was kept secret from the public.

The presence of submarines and their float planes has been well documented following the post-war search of Japanese records. Float planes from the I-25 and I-21 submarines were over Sydney, Melbourne, Hobart (even in daylight), Suva, Auckland and the Hauraki Gulf, Wellington and the East Coast. New Zealand naval authorities had to wait until the end of the war to know the exact routes of the Japanese submarines during 1942.

Early in the war the Americans had envisaged Queen Charlotte Sound and Pelorus Sound as being fleet anchorages, but as the fortunes of war changed in favour of the Allies, the necessity for such a protected anchorage receded.

Net booms and anti-torpedo baffles were completed for Auckland by September 1942, though a New Zealand naval officer deplored that the work had to be done by the Americans. The American net tender

'I shot a shell into the air
It fell to earth I know not where.'
US Marine on the artillery range at Waiouru, 1943. *John Pascoe Collection, Alexander Turnbull Library*

Ebony was used as a gate-opening vessel until January 1943. The installation of anti-submarine devices took even longer in Wellington, despite Aotea Quay and the floating dock being particularly vulnerable. In the meantime crews manned anti-aircraft guns night and day on any ships in port.

Although New Zealanders did not experience the trauma of invasion, there was one so-called 'battle' fought on New Zealand territory — between American and New Zealand servicemen in Manners Street, Wellington. Over the years, the story of the Battle of Manners Street has become a mélange of truth, half-truth and pure fabrication. This could be blamed on the censorship of the time, and the playing down of the incident by the authorities. The fact that it happened at night in near black-out conditions would have made it impossible for witnesses to give an overall view of the brawl. The *New Zealand Encyclopaedia* has exacerbated the situation with its entry under 'Riots', which describes the incident as the ugliest riot in New Zealand history. Disturbance or fracas it was, riot it was not. That description should undoubtedly belong to the Depression riots in Auckland in April 1932.

The incident was in danger of passing into folklore in its inaccurate form, and this has only been prevented by the release to the National Archives of an official inquiry into the event at the time. A week after the disturbance the Commissioner of Police reprimanded rumour-mongers for their extravagant claims about the fracas. But, as the *New Zealand Herald* commented, this would not have happened had the authorities not attempted to hush up the affair.

A claim in the *New Zealand Encyclopaedia* that 'many American soldiers were injured during the affray and two were killed' is not supported by the facts. A statement on the affair in the file says that 'this disturbance was caused in the first place by three or four merchant seamen who had been drinking and made no secret of their intention to 'clean up the visiting servicemen'. This led to a series of fights in which US Marines and sailors, New Zealand merchant seamen and servicemen became entangled. The civil and military police no sooner got one disturbance under control than another broke out in a fresh place. One senior New Zealand officer went on record to say that 'when a sailor and a Marine went on to the street to fight, a collection of civilian loafers egged them on. Several drunk New Zealand soldiers became involved and Marines joined in. Disturbances broke out at the Royal Oak Corner, up Cuba Street and around Courtenay Place.' Looking for causes, a memo says, 'Police blame a rough civilian element which frequents the above localities and is always causing trouble.' Four arrests were made and the inquiry found that 'the presence of Provosts would help in this area about 1800 hours (6 p.m.) when

'I have a clue.' A US Army military policeman on his 'Indian' motor-cycle, 1943.
Tudor Collins

numbers of intoxicated troops provide good material for civilian fomentators of discord.' The major part of the fight lasted until 8 p.m., but some brawls went on later. In court on Monday a former RNZAF member was convicted, and fined £2 for being drunk and disorderly.

Time has undoubtedly dulled memories, but one New Zealand serviceman related the following version of events:

> From what I remember of the Battle of Manners Street, and I was there on the night, it all started from a steak house. Some Maoris in a steak joint objected because the Yanks were being served before they were, in their order for steak and eggs. One Maori was so hopping mad that he picked up a plate of steak just served to a Yank and let him have it in the face. This started a general stoush which spilled over into the street. The Yanks took off their belts with the big brass buckles and let fly. There were a number of Maoris in town that night on leave from the 10th Reinforcements about to go overseas. Also there were some from Ruatoria and they weren't the gentlest hombres around.

Perhaps the 'Battle of Manners Street' has lingered on in the memory because the phrase trips off the tongue; certainly the incident, and several others like it, suggests a simmering resentment felt by New Zealand servicemen towards their better paid, better dressed American allies.

New Zealand's archaic licensing laws, which failed to provide suitable places at night for the servicemen to do their drinking under civilian supervision, were factors in the confrontations. Some American officers solved that problem by taking hotel rooms in which to do their drinking and entertain their guests, a luxury unavailable to most local men. On a private's pay of seven shillings a day, the few young New Zealanders in uniform who were not overseas simply could not compete with the Yanks. Shopkeepers deferred to the Americans, and taxi-cab drivers could usually rely on a generous fare from the Marines. New Zealanders were economically out-gunned and they knew it.

With the passage of time and the absence of the protagonists, it is hard to establish whether the question of colour was really a significant contributing factor to the violence in Manners Street. That some US servicemen from the Southern states displayed an antipathy towards their own black troops is clear, and this antagonism may well have extended to Maori servicemen. There were reports of US servicemen being set upon by Maori men, so much so that the Officer Commanding American Forces, Manurewa, complained to Princess Te Puea at the Turangawaewae Marae that twenty-seven of his men were in hospital after alleged assaults. The situation was defused and sixty American officers were entertained at the marae. In March 1943 400 American troops went to Ngaruawahia for the annual regatta, where Prime Minister Peter Fraser presented Captain S. D. Jupp, US Navy, with a carved inkstand and a kumete for President Roosevelt.

Another incident that has passed into folk history is the Battle of Queen Street in Auckland, but this too is a misnomer. That there was a premeditated confrontation between a group of New Zealand servicemen and a group of American Marines and Army men is not supported by evidence. Flare-ups, yes, and plenty, but fights with battle lines drawn, no.

Clarrie is an ex-Navy man who was often called upon to attend servicemen involved in violent incidents in Auckland. He had his own theories about the causes of conflict between American and New Zealand servicemen.

> In a back street just off Queen Street, near Victoria Street West, was a Permanent Medical Dressing Station. All the New Zealand forces, Army, Navy and Air Force, were rostered to supply personnel to man this station for the purpose of patching up those who were injured in fighting or accidents in the city. We also treated Americans and got the impression they preferred to come to us rather than being manhandled by their own military police.
>
> I used to see some of these fights when I was going home on the Ponsonby tram, especially down from the Majestic Theatre in Queen Street.

Why the fighting? Booze, bravado, recklessness, frustration and the fact that the Americans had come from areas of violence and turbulence where no quarter was expected, no quarter given and often no prisoners taken.

Jim was a teenager in the war years, and this is how he recalls the Battle of Karangahape Road in Auckland.

There used to be a dive, the Dixie Club, where the Prince Edward Theatre used to be. The Yanks used to booze there, and the girls who frequented the joint would have been well known for their generosity to the troops. It was obviously a sly grog place, but the police probably turned a blind eye because it kept the Americans off the streets. I worked opposite, near the Family and Naval Hotel. As far as I remember, it was a no-no for New Zealand servicemen to go there. Also you never saw a Marine drinking with a 'doggie', an American Army man. But a stoush did erupt there one night and spilled out on to the streets; New Zealanders back from overseas versus the Yanks. It stopped the trams in Karangahape Road. But then the American shore patrol arrived and the MPs waded in with their batons. There were no beg pardons, and the Americans were heaved into the paddy wagons but not the New Zealanders.

I liked to see the Marines marching; they were the only American troops who could march. I found the Americans damned good. But there was crime, rapes may have been rare but there were some. My cousin, aged fourteen, was raped out at Pukekohe. Six negroes were involved. They pushed her off her bike and she was raped. She later identified them. She was from a very devout Catholic family and intended entering the church as a nun. It was all hushed up as far as she was concerned. What happened to the Americans no one knew. Another girl was raped and murdered in Victoria Park. Her body was found in an air-raid shelter. My mother was in Queen Street one night and the American MPs were chasing a soldier. One MP fired his .45 revolver over the head of the man. But he didn't stop, just kept going. Some Americans in civilian clothes robbed the Remuera Post Office and got away with it. I know that's true and there are people alive today who could vouch for it.

I had a hard-case uncle who drove an ambulance during the war years. He sometimes drove taxis too. Some taxis would have a jeep tyre on, tyres being so hard to come by, and American petrol in the tank. In his ambulance he would go down to the wharves to pick up shell-shocked servicemen, and also corpses, which he would take out to the American section of Waikumete Cemetery. Naturally there were accidents when American drivers got boozed and drifted to the right-hand side of the road . . .

Punishment for misconduct by the Americans was swift and severe, as one Marine remembers.

There were the robberies. I was going along one night minding my own business, and I came across a character, an American wielding a pistol. 'Keep going' he said. Down the alley I could see a US petrol tanker being

152

milked of its contents. Ask no questions just keep going was the story. It was the same with cigarettes . . . Serious crime, well what there was, and naturally there was some, was settled very smartly by court martial and before you knew where you were, you were back in the States at Camp 84, Mare Island out of San Francisco, a high security jail for US Navy serious offenders. I spent some time on duty there once. The prisoners were dressed in white for serious charges up to but not including murder, and grey for morals offences. One time I saw a smart platoon being marched in. 'Good,' I thought, 'our relief has arrived', [but] they turned out to be prisoners. No, the story in New Zealand about serious offenders was, get rid of 'em smartly back to the States. There were no rape cases that I was aware of, though there must have been some. Rape was regarded by the Marines as a very serious offence. I was unaware of any murders.

Those of us who were law-abiding Joes, and that was the vast majority of us, for leisure played cards, chess, bridge, volleyball, softball and throwing the horseshoe for 'learners' and 'ringers' and having the stray gamble on the side.

Marines while away the time on a route march with a game of poker, Wellington 1943. *John Pascoe Collection, Alexander Turnbull Library*

153

Although stories of the various 'battles' were grossly exaggerated, there was sufficient tension to give New Zealand Army Headquarters grounds for concern that there might be a clash between their troops returning from the Middle East on leave and the American troops in occupation.

The furlough scheme for battle-weary men of the 2nd Division of the 2nd NZEF, code-named 'Ruapehu', came to fruition in early June 1943. It had been rumoured for months that leave was coming up for the 1st, 2nd and 3rd Echelons, many of whom had been away for over three years. On 2 June the names of those balloted to go home were released. Middle East Command would have known from the mail being sent home, which was subject to the censor's approval, that the troops were worried about what was happening on the home front. A pamphlet entitled 'New Zealand As You Will Find It', distributed to the furlough draft, set out to explain the American presence and show the import- ance of their task to New Zealand.

On 15 June the furlough draft, under Brigadier H. K. Kippenberger, of 288 officers and 5799 other ranks sailed from Tewfik Harbour on the *Nieuw Amsterdam*. Some men were quartered five decks down below the water-line, obviously without portholes. A soldier's space was his hammock amid the heated, foetid smell of sweat, urinals, latrines and (in rough weather) vomit. The ship arrived in Wellington Harbour at dawn on 12 July 1943. For security reasons next of kin could not be notified in advance of the exact arrival date of their men and so received a telegram saying 'So-and-so will be arriving shortly from overseas'. A radio broadcast was then made which said, 'The day of interest to holders of telegram number . . . is . . .' The authorities in Wellington were concerned that New Zealand troops who hung round the city waiting for transport to their home towns might end up in the pubs, with the possibility of free-for-all fights with the Americans, so trains were brought on to the wharf alongside the ship.

The military authorities estimated it would take two days to dis- embark the draft. The wily Kiwi, with the scent of freedom in his nostrils, had other ideas. Some emerged from upper-deck portholes feet first and hanging on to knotted blankets for the four-metre drop to the wharf. A helpful sailor opened a watertight door and the Kiwis debouched en masse. What was to take two days, the Kiwis had accom- plished in one.

There was no march through the streets of Wellington. Any action that might precipitate a confrontation with the Americans was to be avoided. The men moved off by train to their various home towns and it was left to the local authorities to make their own arrangements for welcomes. So the Kiwis began their three-month furlough on full pay plus 4s 6d a day subsistence pay, and free rail and road services travel for the serviceman and his wife or mother. Thus there were about 6000 men on leave throughout New Zealand, and not necessarily concentrated in large numbers in those centres where there were American camps. Some furlough men, with the blessing of the Government, got themselves civilian jobs, many on the wharves.

George, an artilleryman who came back with the furlough draft, describes relations between New Zealand and American troops.

We hated their guts, with the stories we got. They kept us out in the stream for a day in the *Nieuw Amsterdam* when we arrived in Wellington Harbour. We were told no American troops had leave in Wellington on the day we came ashore; any strays were rounded up and sent back to camp.

In our artillery troop in the Middle East many of us got 'Dear John' letters. I got one a month before I was due to come back. One of our troops, a married man, knew that his wife was pregnant to an American. We were pretty bitter about it all. Generally speaking, we didn't have much time for the Yanks. In the Middle East an occasional American plane bombed us by mistake and, in one of the campaigns on the road to Tripoli, Rommel captured many Sherman tanks from the US Forces and later used these against us. We didn't get too uptight about the Americans and their fighting ability, but we sure were bitter about what was going on in New Zealand with our women.

I was one of those twenty-five per cent who went back after the furlough leave of three months. In a way I was glad to go, what with the wharfies striking for more pay for handling ammunition and we had been in Africa throwing it around for days on end at seven bob a day. It just turned me up.

I always went for the American clothing. Man, they had lovely stuff and what's more, it didn't itch. Their equipment would leave ours for dead. In Tripoli we worked hard at unloading the American ships, indeed we had the record for unloading time. We worked hard at pinching the stuff too; you name it we pinched it. We took it back to camp, hid it and lived the life of Riley for weeks. The MPs came looking for stuff but they never found any.

Mind you, the Yanks had a tough time in the Pacific. I would not like to have been on some of those landings on those islands, they got the rough end of the stick there. No, if there were bitter feelings about the Yanks it was only about one thing — women.

What had started as a happy reunion was to turn sour, for thousands of New Zealand families soon became involved in a highly emotive issue, one in which the tears of gladness were to turn to the dry tears of bitterness. As furlough time elapsed, it became evident that many of the draft had no intention of returning to action in Italy with the division. Those who had sacrificed so much as fighting men saw little evidence of equivalent sacrifice at home, particularly when they read of industrial troubles. But the nub of their argument was the fact that there were upwards of 35,000 Grade 1 men in essential industry who had not served overseas. The veterans considered that they themselves were well fitted to do those essential jobs. The public was on their side and womenfolk and family reinforced the resolve of many men not to return. New Zealand was remote from the war theatres, smug in its safety, and many people felt that the urgency of war had gone, the Allies were on the road to victory.

The Government, in view of an election two months away, was sensitive to the feelings of the electorate, and had no wish to alienate the overseas soldiers' vote. The Censor, on the grounds that it was not contributing to the war effort, suppressed public debate on whether the men at the end of their leave should be sent back to the Middle East. (He also censored any divorce proceedings in which an American serviceman was cited as the co-respondent as 'not being in the interest of the war effort'.)

After the election the Government decided that all married men with children, all men aged over forty-one and all Maori soldiers would stay home. This meant that of the furlough draft of 6000, over 1600 men were due to return to the battlefields. On 12 January 1944 680 men sailed away to another tour of duty, this time in Italy. Charges of desertion were pressed against those who failed to report, but they did not stick. During the six months of leave some men had found themselves jobs, some had married, and others were about to become fathers. To exacerbate the situation, another furlough draft of 1900 men came back, some of whom became involved in the whole sorry affair. The heroes of the Western Desert had become an embarrassment to the Government, which by the end of June 1944 had dismissed from the service 542 men for misconduct and insubordination. It was a penalty that the public felt was undeserved. That the New Zealand Government had to admit to insubordination among its own troops while foreign servicemen were on its soil, training and preparing to meet the common enemy, was a piece of irony it could well have done without.

The presence of American troops may have been an irritant, but it was not the major reason for unrest in those days. By July 1943 the 3rd Marine Division had left for the Solomons, and any servicemen observing the training of the 2nd Marine Division in the Wellington area would have known that their departure for a battle zone was imminent. It was difficult to justify a Kiwi soldier objecting to returning overseas because of the American presence in New Zealand. Indeed, in the middle of the fracas between the Government and the furlough men, the 2nd Marine Division landed on Tarawa, with tragic consequences, as evidenced by the casualty lists published in the Wellington dailies.

Bill was a Marine stationed in Kaiwharawhara, Wellington, in those days. When asked if he was aware of the arrival of the furlough draft, he said, 'I cannot recall any knowledge of it.' When told the trains were

156

taken alongside the wharf to avoid any confrontation, he replied 'Good God, first I ever heard of it.' The Americans, consumed with their own aspirations and the training that some day would land them on a Japanese-held island, probably had little concern for the domestic scene and its troubles. At no time in New Zealand did the Americans have a newspaper of their own, except for mimeographed unit newsletters.

In the end the furlough impasse resolved itself, but not without frustration and disillusionment on the part of the returning servicemen. There were arrests, men were confined to barracks, and courts martial were conducted, but finally the Government, which had vaccilated and was offside with the public, wiped the slate clean. Whether it wiped away the tears of those sorry days is another story.

In 1944 there were more agonising decisions to be faced by the Government on whether the 2nd NZ Division in Italy should be withdrawn, whether the 3rd NZ Division in the Pacific should be withdrawn to reinforce the 2nd Division, or whether emphasis should be placed on food production in this country. Politicking in the South Pacific with an eye to post-war strategies tended to squeeze the New Zealand forces out. But the New Zealand Government was adamant that it must continue to have a say in the Pacific. To further complicate the position, there were cries in the United States from politicians that American boys in their thousands were dying to protect New Zealand and Australia. All of these machinations, which involved protracted and frustrating discussions, were never aired in the press. Anything calculated to lower national morale was gagged by the Director of Publicity, and this of course included any derogatory comments about the American forces in New Zealand. When a Palmerston North editor published an editorial advocating the right of the public to complain in the press about wartime grievances, he was prosecuted under the Censorship and Publicity Regulations and convicted, a decision later upset on appeal to the High Court. A bomb 'brighter than a thousand suns' was to resolve it all for the immediate future.

A more serious incident than any of the previous domestic 'battles', but less publicised over the years, took place on 12 May 1945, only days after New Zealand celebrated VE day. The official inquiry states that an argument developed when a small group of Maori was abused by sailors off the USS *Transport* 75 moored at Aotea Quay, Wellington. On this Saturday night many of the 107 Maori soldiers on leave in Wellington from Trentham Camp had gathered in the Ngati-Poneke Hall in Sydney Street. Some went on to the Mayfair Cabaret in Cuba Street, where there were also men from the *Transport* 75. At 10.45 p.m. Army officers in Buckle Street received word that fighting had broken out in Cuba Street. The group of Maori complained that their hats had been stolen and they suspected the US Navy men were responsible. They sent for the Maori picquet (guard) at the Ngati-Poneke Club. Instead of quelling the fight, the Maori picquet jumped in to join it. Soon it was a free-for-all, with Maori soldiers, US sailors, and civilians both Pakeha and Maori battling in the street with broken chairs used as batons.

During one part of the battle, the *Transport 75*'s medical officer, Dr O'Grady, arrived on the scene in his jeep, which was attacked with stones and bottles. He left the jeep and told his driver to disappear fast. The jeep was overturned and in the ensuing brawl the driver was cut in the face. Dr O'Grady later told the police that it was no new experience for him to be followed and insulted by Maori in Wellington streets. The brawl ended when the American sailors were bundled into taxis and driven back to their ship.

A subsequent inquiry, conducted by senior Army officers, produced a memorandum commenting on the deep resentment felt by Maori over the treatment they received from some American servicemen. 'It is apparent,' reads the memo, 'that US personnel do not appreciate the standing that the Maori has in our community, and are inclined to treat him as they treat the American negro'. This was reinforced by a remark from one officer that 'Maoris from whom statements were taken allege that they have been insulted by the Americans and have been told by the Americans not to ride in the same tramcars and that they should walk via back streets, etc., that the Americans call them black curs, etc., and have generally insulted the Maori race.'

The Commissioner of Police later reported to the Deputy Prime Minister that no charges were laid because the fault lay with both sides, and that as far as the US servicemen were concerned, their fault lay in using abusive and derogatory language to the Maori. A brief report carried in Monday's edition of the Wellington *Evening Post* was headlined 'Fracas in Cuba Street'.

CHAPTER EIGHT

Tarawa: Prelude and Landing

Wellingtonians had a special interest in the 2nd Marine Division corpsmen, for they watched them arrive, observed them training and saw them leave within a space of eleven months. Thousands of Marines flooded into Wellington on leave from Paekakariki, Otaki and other outlying camps on weekends, and hundreds ended up marrying local girls.

When units of 2 MarDiv landed in Wellington in March 1943 there were gaps in their ranks. Some Marines lay buried in the cemetery near the Tenaru River on Guadalcanal, others on Tulagi, the island off Guadalcanal. Some had been evacuated home, others were convalescing in division hospitals at Silverstream and Wellington. During the Guadalcanal campaign 263 of the division had been killed, fifteen were missing and 932 wounded. Many of the personnel had been down with malaria, dengue fever, dysentery, jaundice or treated for dermatitis caused by a dank tropical climate. The 6th Marines had stayed briefly in Wellington in June–July 1942 en route to Guadalcanal. Some rear echelons of the division had been in Wellington since 1942. Not all the division was involved in the Guadalcanal campaign from the start, for some units waited out the landing in reserve in Espiritu Santo in the New Hebrides (now Vanuatu). The 8th Marines were called on by General Vandegrift in October and the 6th Marines in January 1943. The *President Hayes*, *President Adams* and the *President Jackson*, brought among others the 18th Construction Battalion (Seabees) to Wellington. The *Crescent City*, *American Legion* and *Hunter Liggett* brought the 8th and 6th Marines south. According to the historian of the 18th Battalion, 'Our first sight of New Zealand was Mt Egmont, our second, Wellington, and our third, of any importance, was women . . . New Zealand was excellent and the people were wonderfully friendly.'

After Guadalcanal, survivors of the campaign were told as they headed south in their transports that they were going back to Paekakariki for recuperation and training for the next assault, wherever that might be. The announcement was applauded wildly. American author Leon Uris wrote, 'A roar of cheers greeted the news, and there was a lot of handshaking and backslapping. We were going back to the land we loved. I couldn't help feeling soft about it, even after so many years of travelling from pillar to post in the Marine Corps.' Camp Russell was on what is now Queen Elizabeth Park (and the tramway museum line now runs through the camp site), while Camp McKay was

Marines march to attention, Paekakariki Railway Station, 1943.
Alexander Turnbull Library

sited on the high ground above State Highway One. There was a third
and smaller camp at Paekakariki close to the sea and bordering the
village. The Main Trunk railway line runs diagonally through the two
camps, and McKay's Crossing was where the points of the two camps
met.

Certain other troops came to this area in that same year, and they
were those rare birds, Japanese prisoners of war taken on Guadalcanal
and in surrounding waters. In all there were over 700 prisoners in
Featherston, half of whom were civilian airfield construction workers,
and the remainder mostly naval personnel. On 25 February 1943 an
insurrection broke out in the camp in which guards used machine-guns.
Forty-eight Japanese were killed and seventy-four wounded, while one
New Zealand guard died and six were wounded. No Japanese prisoner
of war ever wrote a letter home or received any mail from home,
although facilities for writing were in principle available. Many of the
Japanese assumed false names to hide their shame and prevent any
ostracism of their families back home.

With the 2nd Marine Division now brought up to strength, the object was to engage in intensive training for the next campaign. In July Admiral Chester Nimitz (Commander in the South Pacific) had issued a highly secret order for a Central Pacific offensive. The 2nd Marine Division knew their role was to go on the offensive somewhere in the Pacific and that it would be an amphibious landing, and probably opposed. Just where they were going was revealed only to a few when Vice-Admiral Raymond A. Spruance arrived in Wellington in August to tell Major General Julian Smith that his division would be spearheading the offensive with a landing on Tarawa. Night after night the lights burned late at Divisional Headquarters (the Windsor Hotel) as Smith, Brigadier General Hermle and Colonel Merritt Edson bent low over plans. The rooms were off-limits to unauthorised persons, and sentries were posted day and night.

Meanwhile out in the field the Marines got on with it. From the States came the first medium tanks of the Pacific War, General Sherman's mounting 75 mm guns, and though no juggernauts in comparison with later tanks, they were still a vast improvement on those used at Guadalcanal. On the Waiouru artillery range in the middle of the North Island, the 10th Marines carried out training in mass firing,

Oriental Bay, Wellington. It was here that personnel on the amphibious craft were trained and vessels serviced for the landing on Tarawa, November 1943.
P. W. Dept

161

five battalions shelling at once. While the engineers perfected their flame-throwers, the 2nd Tank Battalion sent hunting parties into the Tararua mountains after deer.

At Hawke's Bay and Paekakariki amphibious tractors practised landing exercises with troops aboard. The 'alligators' had been used before at Guadalcanal for supply and rescue missions, now they were to be used in wave assaults. Colonel Kenneth A. ('Duke') Jorgensen recalls, 'New Zealand was an outstanding place to train . . . The division required so many hours night training each month. We more than met this requirement by twice taking a week and having reveille at 1730 hours and working through the night, with dinner at 1530 hours. All training was done in the dark. The training at Waiouru was the greatest. The area was tremendous, restrictions on firing almost non-existent. It was interesting to watch all those fine young men develop, from awkwardness to co-ordination and skill, flab to muscle and strength, and increased confidence in doing their jobs.'

Some city dwellers may have thought that life for the American troops in New Zealand was one prolonged spree in which all was sweetness and light. But beyond the gaiety and partying was the unknown of some Pacific jungle, where an infantryman had to be fit, alert and lucky to survive. Out at Paekakariki, commanding the 2nd Battalion of the 8th Regiment, was the well-known and much-decorated Major Henry ('Jim') Crowe. Back in the Guadalcanal campaign Crowe had come on a group of Marines sheltering in a shell hole and had yelled, 'God-damn it, you'll never get the Purple Heart hiding in a foxhole. Follow me!' 'Follow me' became the motto of the 2nd Marine Division.

In order to fight a soldier has to make it safely to shore. It was critical that the Marines should have practice on the nets, followed by landings on the beach to consolidate initial positions. Some camps had vertical boards erected with nets on them so that troops could improve their debarkation drill. Some unfortunate Marines in the ensuing campaign against the Japanese were to spend hours in their landing craft, because command failed to give them the signal to go on in.

One day in mid-June, the division laid on a fortnight-long landing exercise in the waters off Kapiti Island. Out off the beach at Paekakariki were the personnel carriers USS *Crescent City*, *George Clymer*, *Hunter Liggett* and *American Legion*. The New Zealand Navy had Fairmiles there acting as an anti-submarine screen, while the RNZAF supplied Kittyhawks, Vincents and Harvards as part of an opposed landing. At the end of the exercises on 21 June 1943, two boats with Marines aboard were ordered back to their mother ship, the *American Legion*. One went on a sandbank, took on water from beam seas and was taken in tow. In the darkness and deteriorating weather men were thrown overboard by the heavy seas. Luckily the Marines still in the boat were able to throw lifebelts to those in the water. The towing boat was unaware

'Shall I put your name on it?' US Marine at artillery practice on the Desert Road range at Waiouru, North Island. *John Pascoe Collection, Alexander Turnbull Library*

of what was happening in the darkness. Twelve men and one officer made it to shore, but another officer and eight men, all Navy personnel, were drowned. All the bodies were recovered. Although rumours of the tragedy flew around the surrounding district, nothing appeared in the papers.

Lights continued to burn late in the Windsor Hotel. In early October another amphibious exercise was ordered. Brigadier Gen. M. H. Floom was to write later: 'In an attempt to deceive and confuse 2 MarDiv watchers, a cover plan for a Div Lex (Landing Exercise) on the west coast of the North Island was leaked in order to cool anxieties as to final departure and reduce speculation as to the next real landing target.'

One morning the residents of Opoutama and Mahia beaches on the Mahia Peninsula in Hawke's Bay woke to find their bay full of grey-blue

Marines of the Headquarters Battalion of the 2nd Marine Division relax outside their camp, Central Park, Wellington, 1943. *Wellington Public Library*

ships and small craft. Some thought the Japanese had arrived. For almost two weeks from 17 October, Marines from the 2nd, 8th and 18th Regiments were engaged in amphibious exercises, debarking down the nets from the *J. Franklin Bell*, *Ormsby*, *Harris* and *Heywood*. Also in the bay was the USS *Anderson* and Fairmiles from the the New Zealand Navy, while the USS *Feland* carried out night exercises off Long Point on the peninsula. Tanks and heavy equipment were brought ashore, smoke-screens laid and fighter sweeps made by RNZAF planes. The area was off-limits to the public, photographers and pressmen.

The exercise earned no plaudits from command. In the rough surf that prevailed at the time, boats were overturned, equipment lost, gear jettisoned and craft damaged on the rocks. Again there were stories of men being drowned, but these allegations were not supported by documentation.

A researcher who mentions the words 'American troops', even in very remote areas, will find that the Marines were very wide-ranging. One place the American boys pushed into was the Rerewhakaaitu country; translated, the name means 'to rush in foolishly to battle'. Forty kilometres south-east of Rotorua off the Rotorua–Taupo road, this area may not be remote today, but forty-five years ago, in the days when the cobalt deficiency of the land had yet to be discovered, it was undeveloped scrub country. Units of the 2nd Division came here from Wellington to use Lake Tarawera as a venue for amphibious landing exercises. It was no small-scale practice, for the marks of the tracked vehicles in the scrub were visible for years afterwards. Roads were pushed through and timber jetties were built onto the lake. Something the Americans did leave behind, although a rarity, was their contribution to the place names of New Zealand. Today the map of Rerewhakaaitu shows Yankee, Democrat and Republican Roads.

In the meantime other Marines, combat-loaded, sweated it out on Little Burma Road, as they called the Paekakariki Hill. It was 1500 feet to the top and there, as a reward for their pains was a view of farms laid at their feet and the Tasman Sea in the background. Whether this lent enchantment to the hike for the gravel-crunchers is doubtful. The fifteen-mile route march was a 'real pisscutter', as the boys would say, and not for the 'candy assed'. Tokyo Rose continued to bait the Americans on short-wave radio, saying the 2nd Marine Division had been issued with new tropical combat gear.

Landings from the *Feland* and *Ormsby* were made onto beaches within Wellington Harbour, including Petone, where the locals were treated to the sight of the Marines charging ashore 'a hollerin' and a shoutin'', over the sea wall and into the pub. A line of military police prevented such a repetition in subsequent exercises. 'It all looked so easy at Petone,' one resident was to say sadly later. Some 'amtrac' units went north to the reefs of Fiji to test their craft on submerged coral reefs. Where all this gear was to be used, still remained a secret known only to a few.

Many Wellingtonians have memories of this period. Len worked as an electrician for Camp Russell and Camp McKay. His description of life with the Americans differs little from stories heard in other parts of the country, and his recollections cover a great deal of 2 MarDiv's activity in Wellington.

> Let me say right from the start that the Americans as I knew them were gentlemen soldiers; they were professional soldiers and imbued with the Marine spirit. I had a store in the General's house, which was the old farm house. I had to have a bit of clout round the place because I had to give orders about electrical work. I had an apprentice to help me but it was almost a full-time job. They were a tough bunch of babies as far as electrical work was concerned. They thought nothing of shinning up a pole and attaching a wire to connect a toaster or a light. They always wanted electric lights in their tents, and they would rip out the fittings in the ablu-

US Marines of the 2nd Division line up for 'chow' in their 'fatigues' at Paekakariki, 30 August 1943. These men would have been in training for the landing on Tarawa. *John Pascoe Collection, Alexander Turnbull Library*

tion blocks in order to replace their kerosene lamps. There were several accidents in connection with illegal installations.

Len was on the patriotic committee at Otaki, and helped to organise weekly dances similar to those held in the Auckland and Warkworth areas. The locals here also entertained Marines in their homes, and found them to be extremely polite. Len remembers the route marches, the manoeuvres, and the amphibious landing in which lives were lost. He also has some typical tales of military discipline.

> Naturally there were some tough boyos in their ranks, after all they were soldiers. On one occasion three men broke out of the brigs, which were the size of enlarged dog kennels, and took to the Tararuas. They had a posse out for them, though a couple gave themselves up. The story was that if the prisoners got away the guards would have to serve out their sentences. The prisoners themselves would be court-martialled and serve their sentences back in the States, say on Mare Island.

166

One time the artillery had a shoot and for some reason, perhaps the wrong grid position was given, a shell landed in Paekakariki. A Lieutenant Zimmerman was court-martialled for this, but he must have been found not guilty, because soon after that he was on the General's staff. Minor misdemeanours were punished with drill on the beaches. One would see Marines with full pack on moving along the beaches or where the tramway is now in Queen Elizabeth Park.

Many Marines in the Wellington area managed to acquire cars, some in the 'bomb class', according to Len, which they parked outside the camp gates, since they were not allowed to take them inside. When they left for the combat zone, the vehicles went to girlfriends, families who had adopted their former owners, or to other people by arrangement. As usual, vehicles were not the only things left behind

> Food, if we cared to have it, was there for the taking. There were gherkins to burn. My apprentice's mother recently told me that she had just finished the 7 lb tin of mustard from the camp. A couple of local characters wanted to store jeeps in my garage. In the Seabee camp down the road refrigerators, washing machines, you name it, were run over by the bulldozers or burnt. Nothing was allowed to go on the market to be sold. If they couldn't take it with them it was destroyed. I was offered a mountain of empty beer bottles, the American stubbies of the day, imported Budweiser, Schlitz, etc., but how could I cope with a mountain of a quarter of a million dozen beer bottles?

While the American authorities may not have been able to keep total control over the disposal of their stores, Len recalls that they did keep a close watch on more directly military matters.

> Security was strict in the camp, no unauthorised person got inside. My apprentice once found himself in the guard house because he lingered too long in a security area. Outgoing mail was censored and troops were not allowed to disclose the country of their training. Of course girlfriends were able to write to the Marines' parents back in the States and in oblique ways tell where their sons were. It is said that the following formula was used by the troops when they wrote: 'Dear Mum, I am not allowed to tell you where I am. However, I find that I have lots of new zeal and energy.'

Naturally a considerable amount of construction work had to be done to accommodate the needs of American troops, and there are still some visible legacies of their presence in the Wellington area. Len recalled what he knew of the building activities.

> The Marines in Camp Russell and Camp McKay were housed in tents with wooden floors. The cases which brought out stores from America were scorched with a blowlamp and the timber used for the officers' messes. Between McKay's Crossing and Paekakariki the military built a bake-house, but it was only in operation for a week when it was burnt down, never to be replaced. The concrete foundation was used as the base

for a building used by a transporter firm. Alongside the school at Paekak was the first 'take-away' that I can ever remember, where the troops could buy sausages, chips, hamburgers, etc. It made a fortune. The only other American building I can recall that is still standing is the big storehouse at Paekak, which is now used by the Railway Society.

One person who remembers the original use of some of these buildings is Ngaire, who later married a Marine.

We lived in Lower Hutt, and in those days the heavy American trucks used to queue up in Waterloo Road waiting to be unloaded in the huge stores near the railway station. Day and night they were there, and all the residents along the road used to invite the Marine drivers in for a cup of tea and a bite to eat. It was winter time and it was cold out there in those trucks. Many many families got to know the Marines who packed in the stores to the depot . . . three of them married local girls. We all went to America, but mine is the only marriage to survive, though one of the other girls did have a large family.

Ngaire was sixteen when she first got to know the Marines, and remembers what it was like to be a schoolgirl in wartime Wellington.

The boys of my age group all served in the local Home Guard. Lower Hutt was a family-oriented community in those days. All we did was go to the pictures and there was the occasional dance for the Americans. I was at Wellington Girls' High, and of course the girls used to talk about the Marines. Some had Marine boyfriends. The principal was pretty stuffy and told us we were to behave outside like young ladies. We weren't allowed to sing 'Roll out the Barrel', but we did get into 'There'll Always Be an England'.

There were no Marines waiting outside the school gates nor at the business college I later went to. We used to get wolf whistles from Marines riding by on the trams, but we enjoyed that.

We had air-raid drill and practised getting into the dug-outs. We had to carry our survival kit everywhere we went, home and back to school. It consisted of emergency chocolate and a first-aid kit. We were shown how to wear a gas mask, though we didn't carry them, but they were there for issue if necessary. One time we were outside in the playground having lunch and a small plane flew overhead. Somebody began firing at it; I can distinctly remember seeing the puffs of smoke round the plane. It gave us all a hell of a shock. We never learned what it was all about. Probably some plane that failed to identify itself to ground control.

Barbara's memories were rather more ambivalent, reflecting the misgivings felt by many New Zealanders.

I remember very clearly, as a young girl in Wellington, my mother took me to see a film called *Bambi*, the story of a little deer. At one stage in the film Bambi gets lost and calls out in a thin piping voice, 'Mother, mother, where are you, where are you?' And a voice about three rows back from us called out, 'Gone out with a god-damned Yank!'

Captain S. D. Jupp US Navy welcomed on to the marae at Ngaruawahia, 1943.
US Pacific Fleet Public Relations, Alexander Turnbull Library

Wellington was absolutely swarming with Yanks, just swarming with Marines. We only saw American servicemen, rarely New Zealanders. The Americans were able to come in on the unit in their thousands, whereas I understand in other centres there was not the same public transport and troops had to rely on hitch-hiking. It was at this time I saw my first black man, and I can remember truck-load after truck-load of them going by with their German-style helmets on, staring out the back. I can tell you I was frightened. My mother told me that a friend of hers kept her two very pretty daughters at school until they were nearly twenty. Well, it was one way of taking precautions.

Jean was a training college student at the time, and she too had mixed feelings about the American 'invasion'.

Wellington was a very conservative town in those days and here were these crushes of Americans with their steam radios on the streets creating bedlam. I felt they were taking over the streets and I resented them. I felt that *I* was being taken over. And then one American told me Wellington was as dead as a cemetery, and that got on my wick. For a start I just loathed them, but with time I relented because I realised that they had their troubles. I was in several service clubs and we were always escorted at night to the trains in case we were caught up in any of the mêlées on the streets between New Zealanders and Americans. Individually the Americans were very nice but in groups they were very noisy. Whether they broke down the traditional conservatism of the Wellington of the day is a moot point.

Out at Oriental Bay the US Navy boys could enjoy a little doggerel:

> *To a gay little foreign port*
> *Where women and gin and original sin*
> *Are the favourite local sport.*
> *And all I ask is a cabaret girl*
> *And a quart of synthetic Scotch,*
> *A friendly patrol to see me off*
> *And a bud to do my watch.*

Taking the seaside air at Oriental Bay, Wellington, 1943.
Alexander Turnbull Library

The *Evening Post* in February 1943 was the vehicle for some ripostes concerning telephone conversations between Marines and the local girls. (The Windsor Hotel was the command headquarters for 2 MarDiv.)

From the switchboard at the Windsor
To the switchboard at McKay
You will hear 'Those lines are busy'
All through the whole darn day.
And then to Pauatahanui
And on from Judgeford too
You find those gallant switchboard men,
Are trying to get you through.
So, to make things so much easier,
While the boards buzz like a hive,
Don't make your calls at morning or noon —
Please make them after five.

Thank you,
The Boys at the Windsor.

More than one group of girls came back with a reply in kind.

From your captains to your corporals
All through the live-long day
Ten thousand of you calling us,
'Can I speak to my girl Fay?'
Your accent drives me crazy,
I can never understand,
As one by one you call us up
To put through your one demand.
So please, all brown-clad leathernecks,
Realise before you call
That we too, can be busy
AND DO NOT CALL AT ALL!

Thank you,
From one Insurance Switchboard.

Was it based on truth or fiction,
That spate of lyric diction
Adorning Column Eight,
Requesting some restriction
When girls communicate?
Are they jamming the exchange

In their efforts to arrange
For a Massachusetts mate?
Or are you going to tell us
It was penned by someone jealous
Who had failed to 'book a date'.

The Girls of Wellington.

Some Marines were camped as far north as Masterton, which also enjoyed the social life created by the Americans. With the end of the battle for Guadalcanal the 3rd Defense Battalion USMC came on to New Zealand to be stationed a thousand strong in Solway Showgrounds by 1 March 1943. They were there for rest, relaxation and re-equipping after the Solomons campaign. The advance party of the Marines had arrived at the time of the district's ram fair in mid-February, and some critics may have made this coincidence an opportunity for uncharitable remarks. The Marines were greeted with the sight of neat rows of bell tents barely adequate to ward off some of Masterton's freezing temperatures. 'These tents will be your accommodation,' said the top sergeant, 'and that is a girls' college. I'll *have* the first man I find going over there.' Other than that restriction the Marines were free to avail themselves of what amenities Masterton was able to provide. Dances at the Soldiers' Club in Essex Street and hot showers at the YMCA were the limit of these resources.

Wayne, a Marine who was stationed in Masterton, told of early days during the Americans' stay in that town.

I remember that when we landed in Wellington everything seemed so small. When we left Wellington in the train we didn't know where we were going. Near the summit of the Rimutakas the train engine wasn't powerful enough to get us over so we all had to debark, get behind and push. When we got to Masterton it was freezing, and all the clothing we had was what we stood up in, together with a couple of blankets and a camp stretcher. Needless to say, we went over the hill like shots into the town. I managed to get a beautiful eiderdown for a double bed. After that I was warm.

As in every army there were one or two who couldn't hack it. We had the occasional suicide. When one Marine shot himself at Camp Solway I was on duty about three tents away. Along with a will he left a typical 'Dear John' letter. His wife was having a baby back Stateside by another man and she was going to leave him.

There was sure a lot of money made by the Kiwis when we Americans were stationed here, particularly by the sly-groggers. Wine was all we could get, whisky was out of the question. We paid through the nose, £5 to the sly groggers for wine that cost a few cents to produce. But then I always remember the old A1 Café, where we could get a beautiful steak and eggs for 2s 6d. I think the exchange then was about six shillings to the dollar, which was pretty good to us. We enjoyed spending our money and it didn't mean a lot to you in those days. Live it up, tomorrow's another day was our thinking. This is the way the girls felt too. This is no degradation of New Zealand girls, but I think they were pretty fair game really. Most of them were good girls. Looking back, I see those times as lots of fun, but always at the back of our minds was the thought that soon we would be leaving, and leaving for what?

Robert E. Wickman, a Marine corporal who was in Wellington with 2 MarDiv, summed up his days in the capital.

By and large I suppose we behaved no worse and no better than troops usually do, taking with us enough memories to last a lifetime. For most Americans, 'down under' was 'good duty'. What Yank stationed in Wellington doesn't remember jitterbugging at the Cecil Club to the 'Jersey Bounce', 'Five O'Clock Jump', or 'I Don't Want to Walk Without You'? Who could forget riding back to camp in the rickety 'midnight special', when we were jammed in the aisles and even slept in the luggage racks? My personal recollections include the PFC [Private First Class] from H company who boasted that his old man was an engineer and therefore he could drive a train — easy. When challenged he locked the engineer and fireman out of the engine cab, and proceeded at full throttle to drive the thirty miles to Paekakariki, not bothering with the scheduled stops along the way. Then there was the pub in Willis Street where we used to drink warm beer and sing raucous songs until six o'clock closing; and the girls, the charming unaffected New Zealand girls who took us home to meet 'Mum' and have 'tea', which we found out, after loading up on steak and eggs beforehand, meant dinner.

Yes, there were memories — memories that for some ended in shallow beach graves. As we sailed out of Wellington for the last time, I remember the people waving white bed sheets up and down Seatoun Beach in a final farewell. We were on our way to Tarawa (but we didn't know it at the time) and I vowed then that if I made it, one day I'd come back.

All Wellington knew that the pot was beginning to boil, and that 'D-day' was approaching, when they saw a flotilla of transport ships assemble in the harbour. Few knew their names but for the record they were the *Zeilin, Heywood, Middleton, Biddle Lee ('Listing Lee'), Monrovia, Sheridan, La Salle, Doyen, Harris, J. Franklin Bell, Feland, Ormsby, Thuban, Virgo* and *Bellatrix.* On 28 October 1943 the Marines began boarding their transports.

Incredible as it may seem in comparison with New Zealand military procedures, the Americans ran liberty boats for the troops back to the docks at night. There, dressed in their dungarees, the Marines made their farewells to their girlfriends. There were few inhibitions, and it was no place for the Mother Grundys of this world as loving couples said their last goodbyes. The last liberty boat back to the ships was the last Wellington saw of the boys who were committed to this campaign. Tears would have floated it back. When Wellingtonians awoke on 1 November the ships were no longer there. They had slipped away at dawn and with them went the fears of thousands of Wellington women and the fearful wonderment of thousands more of the populace in every large and small town in the lower north. Their fears were proved to be well founded.

On the afternoon of 31 October Major Shoup, accompanied by Major General Julian Smith, hailed a taxi and told the driver to take them to Government House. There they said their farewells to the Governor-General, Sir Cyril Newall. They told him the 2nd Marine Division would not be back, but 'You're the only one in New Zealand who knows it.'

When the American armada sailed out of Wellington Harbour on that spring morning, suggestions were put about, and deliberately promoted, that the ships were again on the way to Hawke's Bay for further amphibious exercises. This was not an idea that endeared itself to the Marines, for there had been alarming reports of treacherous surf and fatalities in previous landings there. Another reason to spread false information was that some Marines, reluctant to leave the arms of their lovers, might have been tempted to stay behind had they known this was a final sailing; in fact only four did. Devious though they may have been, command did not fool radio propagandist Tokyo Rose, who was soon able to say that the Marines were on the way to Tarawa. But then she had been known to say accurately that a certain public clock in Wellington was two minutes slow.

The first landfall for the armada was Mele Bay, south of Espiritu Santo, in the island of Efate in the New Hebrides (Vanuatu) group, where Combat Team 2 practised landing on the beaches. Nearby in Havannah Harbour were the battleships *Colorado* and *Tennessee* and the cruisers *Mobile, Birmingham, Portland* and *Sante Fe*. There too was 'Old Mary', the battleship USS *Maryland*, resurrected from her temporary watery grave in Pearl Harbour. Flying his flag on that ship was Rear Admiral Harry Hill, who had already had numerous conferences with Major General Smith. On 14 November, 'D-day' minus six, Hill flashed a message to all transports: 'Give all hands the general picture of the projected operation.' The code name of the island was 'Helen' and the operation was called 'Galvanic'. The 2nd Division of the Marine Corps had been chosen to open the Central Pacific offensive by taking Tarawa in the Gilbert Islands.

In mid-May 1943 the Japanese had reinforced their defences with the Sasebo 7th Special Naval Landing Force of 2619 men, or *rigosentai* (marines) as they were called. Capturing Tarawa with its airfield would bring the Americans closer to the occupied mandated Marshall

Islands. If the Marshalls could be taken, the US would be 800 miles closer to the mainland of Japan, the ultimate objective. But for now, Betio, the small coral atoll in the Tarawas on which the airstrip was located, was the goal. This operation would also test strategies and equipment developed over the preceding decade.

The Japanese are fastidious in their personal habits, and nowhere more so than in the disposal of human wastes. Latrines on Betio were built out over the sea so that the tides could dispose of the solids. American intelligence, with the co-operation of its submarines, was able to count the number of latrines and estimate the number of Japanese using each unit. In the event they were only a few hundred out.

Many thought that Operation Galvanic would be a simple matter, more a demonstration than a fight. Some even called it the 'milk-run'. Others were not so confident. 'Remember one thing,' said Major General Smith at a staff conference, 'When the Marines land and meet the enemy at bayonet point, the only armour a Marine will have is his khaki shirt.'

The Japanese had nearly 5000 troops and Korean labourers on Tarawa. Part of their defence consisted of light tanks, concrete tetrahedrons on the razor-sharp reefs, with double-apron barbed wire in the water between beach and reef. The defenders themselves sat in low, massive, reinforced concrete bunkers, covered with layers of sand and coconut logs. Rear Admiral Keich Shibasaki, Tarawa's commander, was reputed to have boasted that 'This island could not be taken with a million men in a hundred years.' Said Admiral Howard F. Kingman, with the gunfire of three battleships, two heavy and three light cruisers and nine destroyers at his command, 'We do not intend to neutralise it, we do not intend to destroy it. Gentlemen, we will obliterate it.' How wrong both men were, the next few days would tell.

At 0507 hours on 20 November the Japanese opened fire on the troop transports with their fourteen huge coastal guns, including the eight-inchers captured from the British at Singapore. Fire was returned from the *Maryland*'s sixteen-inch guns. A message from the flagship was flashed to the *Zeilin, Middleton* and *Heywood*: 'All Marines lay topside to your debarkation stations.' Three thousand Marines of the three initial assault battalions climbed down the nets into their waiting craft. The Marines' hymn belted out from the *Zeilin*. Following the first wave of troops towards the shore, helmsmen were to confirm one ghastly fear. Some personnel of the initial assault battalions were able to cross the reef in amphibious craft, which could make four knots in the water and 20 mph on land. These 'amtracs', however, were in short supply and most of the Marines in the following landing forces had to use LCVPs (Landing Craft, Vehicle and Personnel), which drew three and a half feet of water. Major General Smith had been briefed in depth on the tides for the hour. Some planners felt there would be enough water (five feet) to float the LCVPs over the reef. Others expressed the opinion that predicted tide heights were not always dependable, and there could be as little as three feet. Smith decided to prepare for the worst.

The 3rd Battalion, 8th Marines, was instructed to move to the beach at 1018 hours. The entire battalion was embarked on LCVPs, which, it was found, could not climb over the reef. The troops had to clamber over the sides, hold their rifles above their heads, and wade the 700 yards to the shore. The carnage was unbelievable. Men drowned as they stepped into holes and were dragged under by the weight of their heavy packs. Those who did reach the shore were disorganised and exhausted, some having lost their weapons. Many of the unit's officers and non-commissioned officers were killed or wounded. Seventy per cent of the first wave died in the lagoon. Indeed it had all looked so easy at Petone. The land battle for Betio began at 0910 hours and 20 November 1943 and ended at 1330 hours on 24 November.

Tim, a Marine now living near Warkworth, went in on the first wave with the Marines on that fateful day. His memories give some idea of what they went through.

Tarawa was the most horrifying, the most horrendous thing in my life — in any man's life. It is etched on my memory like diamond onto glass. At the same time it was the most exciting thing that ever happened to me — but I could never go through it again. It was unbelievable, because it was all so unexpected. We had been led to believe that there would only be token resistance. We were due in at six in the morning, and the understanding was that it would be a pushover. Jesus, how wrong we were. In a matter of minutes, our buddies were floating face downwards in the water. Our battleships, the *Colorado* and the *Maryland*, had pounded hell out of the place, our aircraft had strafed the beaches, but all this was not enough, as we were sure as hell to find out.

We went down the nets over the side of the transport into our Higgins boat to go ashore. But our sailor helmsman was reluctant to go in. He could see what was happening ahead. Boats and their occupants were being machine-gunned out of the water. God-damn it, it was suicidal to go in, we were just sitting ducks for the Japanese and their machine-guns in their pillboxes. An LCT (Landing Craft Tank) pulled alongside us and we transferred to that, and this gave us some protection. The driver of this amphib only had a slit to see through to steer his craft. Suddenly the boat started to go every which way. We opened the door and the driver fell over dead, he had been drilled through the forehead. Just then the thing ran out of petrol, so it was over the side and wade ashore. Behind us men with full battle kit were in water up to their necks — no wonder some went down never to come up. The Japs just picked them off.

Somehow our unit, or what was left of us, got ashore. We hadn't used enough heavy bombs on the place. We had used 'daisy cutters' — parcels of grenades that exploded at grass level — but these were useless against the Japs in their pillboxes and underground defences. They had connecting underground galleries to their machine-gun pits, something we had never envisaged.

The whole scene ashore was unreal, just a gigantic shemozzle. Some companies had lost the majority of their officers. By Jesus Christ, I can tell you men were scared shitless on that morning. All around us were dead bodies of our mates. One man had gone beserk and we had to tie him up. A group of us got behind a concrete parapet, and I poked my head over. God-damn it, what did I see but a black V-8 Ford saloon! Somehow we inched our way forward. We would drop a couple of grenades down the stink tubes to the Jap burrows, but we soon learned it was insufficient to kill a Jap machine-gun crew — another pair would move along the burrow and take over — we also had to demolish the gun itself. Somehow we survived the day, and that night we burrowed into the sand for some sort of protection. The giant land crabs came ashore and joined us in our dug-outs. People started shooting — they didn't know if it was Japs infiltrating us or giant crabs. You can understand people being trigger-happy.

Next day we inched our way towards the airfield. A few Japs surrendered — very few. One group of three came out with their hands up. One was found to have a light machine-gun strapped to his back. He didn't last long. The next day we got to the edge of the airfield — the atoll itself was only two and a half miles long. We had dragged our .30 and .50 calibre machine-guns along with what was left of our company. Orders had come up from headquarters: 'Don't destroy the Zeros, save the Jap planes if you can.' The trouble was there were Japs in the planes using the machine-guns to pick our fellows off. We put some incendiary bullets into our guns and let 'em have it. We got five of the Zeros and while this was going on we got across the airfield. On this side was the airfield barracks, a thatched-roof affair — we had seen the Japs going in and out of this place. We put some incendiary ammo into the thatch and up it went. There must have been hundreds of Japs running this way and that — we took no prisoners and must have killed hundreds. That was the end of the second day and you could say the atoll was ours by then. Next day it was a case of mopping up and picking up a few snipers.

The engineers moved in with their bulldozers and scooped a big trench in the sand. The Jap bodies were pushed in literally in their thousands. No dog-tags were collected. It was a question of getting rid of bloated bodies in a tropical sun, otherwise disease might have claimed the rest of us. I saw twenty-three prisoners brought in, completely naked with their hands tied to the top of their heads. Hundreds of guards were detailed to protect those men for fear of what we might have done to them.

Yes, it was rough all right on Tarawa, but there was only one way to survive and that was to go forward, and that was what we had been trained to do. God, we had spent months training in New Zealand for four days on Tarawa. Of course we didn't know we were going there. The buzz was that we were going to Wake Island. Only after we left the New Hebrides did we learn where we were actually going.

We sat on Tim's lawn looking down on the Matakana Road. Not a stone's throw away was ground over which other Marines had trained — the 3rd Marine Division, some of whose corpsmen were to land on Iwo Jima for equally blood-letting battles.

Both sides made mistakes about Tarawa. Even the combined gun support of Admiral Kingman's fleet could not dislodge the Japanese from their subterranean bunkers on this speck of land. It took flame-throwers to do that. Joe of the 6th Regiment, 2nd Marine Division, described the method used.

General H. M. Smith ('Howlin' Mad') claimed that the island had been so pounded by Navy guns and Air Force bombs that we would just go ashore and have hot lunch! But we literally had to walk over our own dead in the surf in order to dig the Japs out of their concrete bunkers. The only way to get them was with sawn-off shotguns and back-pack flame-throwers. The shotguns were 12-gauge repeaters and semi-automatic, with the barrel cut off just beyond the forearm so the buckshot scattered in a wide pattern. The back-pack flame-throwers were just that, one man carried a tank on his back or shoulders. Of course this meant both the gunner and the flame-thrower had to go to the opening in a pillbox so they could work. Not a pleasant experience.

Wayne, who had been stationed in Masterton, was another lucky survivor who had believed that the Marines would meet with little opposition.

Tarawa? Well, they bombed and shelled it for about three days until they thought there was only rats alive on the place. But when we landed it was live all right. I went in with the seventh wave. The tide had gone out and we were stuck high and dry on the coral, so the coxwain dropped the front of our tank lighter. We were exposed to direct machine-gun fire and there was only one thing to do — go straight over the side. That will stick in my mind to the end of my days. I remember going over the side heavily weighted down with rifle, a ton of ammunition and all the other gear. I went straight to the bottom like a rock and was standing on the bottom of the crystal-clear water watching the men around me stripping off ammunition and rifles, everything that weighted them down, so that they could get back up. When we were able to pop our heads up above the water, *twing, twing, twing*, machine-gun bullets zipped around us. Some of us managed to dive down and retrieve our gear.

Fortunately, we were close to a huge causeway the Japs had built to bring supplies to the island, and once we were in amongst the huge chunks of coral we were pretty safe. I have never forgotten looking out over the water at the bodies floating everywhere.

We got ashore and then stuffed a petrol charge down the slot to one bunker, blew the door off and cleaned the Japs out. This bunker turned out to be the chief pay office for that part of the Pacific and held millions in paper money. Later we used it for playing poker and as toilet paper.

And what were the statistics of the battle for Betio? The enemy lost 4690 Japanese and Korean soldiers. Only 146 enemy soldiers allowed themselves to be captured. The Americans paid dearly with over 3000 casualties; 978 combat men (922 enlisted men and 56 officers) were killed and 2188 wounded.

Tarawa was not, in fact, the Marines' first experience of landing over a coral reef. Makin Island, which is just to the north of Tarawa was the object of a day-long raid of 17 August 1942 by the 2nd Marine Raider Battalion under Lieutenant Colonel F. Evans Carlson, was planned as a diversion to Guadalcanal. It was thought that this attack might induce the Japanese to divert reinforcements from there to Makin.

The transport submarines USS *Argonaut* and *Nautilus* rendezvoused off the reef and transferred 221 Marines to rubber dinghies. Although the pre-dawn landing was unopposed, it was not without problems. The submarines had to maintain their engines in reverse to avoid going on the reef, the roar of the surf on the reef made communications difficult, and some outboard motors failed. Fifteen of the boats managed to get ashore together. During the morning deck guns on the submarines sank two Japanese ships, then Japanese planes came over to bomb and strafe the Marines. In the sporadic fighting that took place, about forty Japanese were killed. Although one of the objectives of the raid was to take prisoners in order to gather information, this proved impossible.

Getting through the surf to rendezvous with the submarines that night proved almost impossible. A report commented that 'The ensuing struggle was so intense and so futile that it will forever remain a ghastly nightmare to those who participated.' Individual crews fought the surf for an hour, equipment was lost, and several men were drowned. Barely a third of the Marines were able to get back on board. The remainder were forced to stay ashore for another day, while the submarines were submerged because of repeated air alerts. Patrols were sent out to probe the enemy, but slowly it emerged that there were very few Japanese left alive on the island. An aviation dump was fired and documents were retrieved from the office of the Japanese commander, who had been killed. The Marines carried their rubber dinghies across to the inner lagoon, launched them that night and went through the entrance to meet up with the subs.

The Marines lost thirty men in this action; fourteen were killed in action, seven drowned and, unbelievably, nine were left behind on Makin. This did not become known to the US authorities until after the war, when it was revealed by Japanese documents. It is unclear how they were left ashore. Perhaps they were actually left on the island, or it may have been that they were in a boat that unsuccessfully fought the surf on the first night and drifted downshore. They were captured by the Japanese forces re-occupying the island following the raid and were executed after a brief captivity.

Critics later considered that the Makin raid had served no useful purpose, and had in fact alerted the Japanese to the command's intentions in the Gilberts, resulting in intensified fortification of Tarawa.

Wellington was to know the agony of that traumatic campaign. The Mayor of Wellington appealed to the American authorities to allow the publication of casualty lists in the *Evening Post* and the *Dominion*. A benumbed city could not believe the column after column of casualties. One day these men had been there in their thousands, bright-eyed and bushy-tailed, pouring out of the railway station on leave, intent on a good time, and three weeks later almost a thousand of their number, some only boys, had been buried in the sands of Tarawa. The tragedy of it all hit home not only in Wyoming, Ohio, and Tennessee but also in Khandallah and Lower Hutt. Suddenly some New Zealand girls had become American war widows, for over 500 of them had married Marines. Certainly there were New Zealanders who denigrated the Yanks at every turn, but the vast majority were grateful to an ally who was not only sharing the struggle but paying the ultimate price.

There were angry editorials back in the States about the Tarawa 'fiasco'. At the subsequent inquiry Rear Admiral Kelly Turner could only admit he had taken a calculated risk and lost. Lieutenant General Vandegrift, Commander of the Marines, said, 'There is no royal road to Tokyo. We must steel our people to the same realisation.'

After the war was over, the Wellington newspapers carried a number of sad advertisements: 'Harrigan, Harold, 1st Marine Division. Does any New Zealand girl living near Paekakariki have a portrait of my son killed on Guadalcanal. Family has none . . . Barnes, Richard Grant, 2nd Marine Division. Does any New Zealand family know my son killed at Tarawa. If so please communicate with his mother.'

Admiral Turner had insisted on the date for the Tarawa landing in spite of information submitted to the operation planners by Major Frank Holland, a resident commissioner in the area for fifteen years. He had lived on Bairiki, near Betio, and had spent a great deal of time studying the tidal cycles. The planners had suggested that there might be a problem getting the landing boats over the reefs. Holland agreed that this was likely and pleaded with lower-echelon officers to tell the top brass that tragedy would occur if the tide for the 20 November was chosen to go in on. He recommended the end of December. But an amphibious operation the size of Galvanic, once set in motion, was too complex to change.

Three merchant marine officers of the RNZ Naval Reserve, Lieutenants J. Forbes, G. J. Webster and S. S. Page, were seconded to the landing force because they had navigated in Tarawa waters before the war. Lieutenant Forbes piloted the US minesweeper *Pursuit*, which swept the channel into the Tarawa lagoon, and was followed by Webster and Page in the destroyers *Ringgold* and *Dashiell*. After the action Forbes, who knew the Tarawa atoll from his pre-war days in the Colonial Service, wrote to his daughter Alison, 'Since writing to you last I have been on the seas, over the seas and under the seas.' (A submarine had gathered intelligence by strapping a camera to its conning tower.) All three officers were awarded the American Bronze Star for their services at Tarawa. Forbes is also remembered for locating the hull of the passenger ship *Niagara* after she was sunk in January 1940 by a German mine laid off the Hen and Chicken Islands. He was a captain with the Auckland Harbour Board at the time, and after the war worked as a licensed compass adjuster and also as manager of the Devonport Steam Ferry Company.

Today at Tarawa there are several big derelict Japanese guns pointing the wrong way, a gutted plane remains on the beach, where the coconut trees have grown again, and snorkellers inside the reef dive amongst the detritus of war. On the fortieth anniversary of the landing, in 1983, a group of ex-Marines from the 2nd Marine Division came back to remember the landing. Near the beach is a monument, defaced by graffiti, with the inscription: 'Tarawa was the testing ground for marine amphibious doctrine and techniques. It paved the way for the island campaigning that followed and provided answers that saved thousands of American lives along the road to victory in the Pacific.'

Tarawa was a botched landing, the first but certainly not the last, as the Peleliu campaign (September 1944) in the Palau group off the south-east coast of the Philippines was to show. Tarawa was America's Gallipoli, but unlike Gallipoli, which was an unmitigated disaster, Tarawa was a disastrous victory.

There is another memorial plaque on Betio, which records the courage of some forgotten New Zealanders. Seven Post and Telegraph Department officers had in 1941 volunteered for coast watching in the Gilbert group of islands, some of which had no European inhabitants. Ten New Zealand Army men volunteered to go with them to assist in observing and sending reports of enemy activity on sea and in the air. In September 1942 these men, together with five other Europeans, were taken prisoner and removed to the Betio atoll. They were kept outside the Japanese commandant's headquarters, and tied to coconut trees for three or four days. For a short time they were required to work on the construction of the wharf at Betio. Then, on the afternoon of 15

October 1942, the island was bombed by a US warship and US aircraft. On the evening of that day the twenty-two prisoners were beheaded.

It was a chastened and bloodied Marine division that left Tarawa at the beginning of December for Hawaii, 2000 miles away. If the Marines anticipated another New Zealand break, and to be bathed in the euphoria of a victory on Tarawa, they were soon to be disillusioned. The site of their next camp was sixty-five miles inland from the port of Hilo on the island of Hawaii. Camp Tarawa they called it, but bare ground and stacked tents was all that greeted them. The Marines had not envisaged themselves in the construction business but this was now to be their role. New Zealanders may envisage Hawaiians as living in the glow of warm tropical off-shore breezes. This was not the case in Camp Tarawa, for winter brought high winds, chilly mists and freezing nights to the island's mountains. Sometimes it even snowed and skiing was possible.

Naturally the division needed many reinforcements, this time from those who were drafted into service and chose the Marines as their branch of duty. Training began again for another amphibious landing, on Saipan, in the Mariannas, where there were 30,000 Japanese defending the island. Strategists had learned from Tarawa, and this time Admiral Mitscher intended to pulverise the defences. Even so, the first day on Saipan cost the 2nd Division 238 men killed and 1002 wounded. The division's last active service role was on Okinawa, where 58 of their number were killed and 482 wounded. Finally the division went on to the mainland of Japan to Nagasaki as part of the occupying forces.

In February 1945 the Marines went ashore at Iwo Jima an island which lay 750 miles from the mainland of Japan. It had to be taken for it lay in the direct flight path of American B-29 bombers (Superfortresses) bombing Tokyo, consequently mainland air and land forces were fore-warned of coming attacks. Tiny Iwo Jima was the scene of the bloodiest battles in Marine history. Before 'Old Glory' was raised on the summit of Mt Suribachi, 4189 American servicemen had been killed, over 15,000 wounded. The raising of the flag on Mt Suribachi by the Marines has been commemorated by a well-known piece of statuary in Washington, DC. Okinawa Island, 360 miles from the mainland was to be the last bastion to mainland Japan's defence. In July Admiral Halsey's 1000 plane raids told the Japanese people the end was near. Four days after the dropping of the first atomic bomb Japan sued for peace.

The last American combat land force in New Zealand, the 43rd US Army Division, left in July 1944 en route for service in New Guinea and

An American naval captain addresses the gathering at a Remembrance Day
ceremony, Wellington War Memorial, 30 May 1944. Americans traditionally
hold remembrance services on the last Sunday in May. *Evening Post*

then the campaign in the Philippines. From then on the American presence in New Zealand became less and less. Indeed with the departure
of the Marines for Tarawa in November 1943, the large conurbations
of camps in the Wellington area remained empty, never to be used
again for offensive military purposes. The hospitals still received the
sick and wounded, and shore organisations serviced vehicles and ships.
When the peace bells rang out in Europe in May 1945 it could only be
a matter of time before Japan would fall. Different soldiers, airmen and
sailors started to arrive in New Zealand. The boys were coming home.

EPILOGUE

Thanks for the Memories

We do not see World War II in terms of the Rambo 'revenge and rescue' genre. Unlike Vietnam, where 'tag 'em and bag 'em' (meaning take the identification tag off the dead and shove the body in a canvas bag) was the terse motto, in this war there was glory and romance, there were bugles, winners and losers, heroes and cowards, no drug scandals and no armchair television strategists. There were proud parents back home in Kalamazoo, Michigan, who put a star in the window if they lost a son, and women who wore their husband's or boyfriend's military badges. The whole might of the USA was behind its fighting men, with war bond appeals, stage-door canteens, bands and flags, a united press glorifying and exaggerating its nation's victories, playing down the losses and accepting cooked figures from the military. Conscientious objectors were regarded as despicable, innocent Americans of Japanese extraction were treated with suspicion and in some cases interned for a considerable time. Purple Hearts were there to be won at the drop of a hat (or a coconut). Silver Stars were there for front-line men, and war correspondents were looking for heroes to enthrone in the eyes of an eager public back home.

For the first time in history someone had had the temerity to attack a bastion of US power, giving rise to the catch-cry 'Remember Pearl Harbour.' To see an armada of ships stretching as far as the eye could see, en route to some island landing, to watch hundreds of planes wheeling at different layers during their rendezvous prior to a strike, was to realise in part the might of the armed forces of the US. Even so, victory still depended upon the infantry platoon man up front in his cotton shirt, winkling out the enemy from his jungle bunker and winning ground yard by yard.

Some of those who survived the various battles in the Pacific returned to New Zealand arrogantly flushed with victory, others had been shocked by the trauma of front-line combat. Some young men who had never seen themselves as soldiers found they had been thrown willy-nilly into a kind of war with which they were mentally ill-equipped to cope and suddenly saw themselves as abject failures.

Is it any wonder then, that when the opportunity presented itself for GI Joe to get his feet under a table in Otaki, Khandallah, Kohimaramara, Masterton, Pukekohe, Warkworth or Manurewa, that he expressed his gratitude with lashings of flowers, cigarettes, Hershey bars and chewing gum? It was the nearest thing to Main Street back home that he would ever know in his war.

184

New Zealand troops in Fiji in 1941 were made very welcome by the white and Fijian population, but in French New Caledonia it was rare for a New Zealand soldier to be invited into a French home. As far as the French girls were concerned, the Kiwis did not even rate a smile. Contrast this with an outgoing, ingenuous New Zealand population living in blacked-out conditions, prepared to think the best of most people, in a country where muggings were unknown, houses left unlocked, and radio and visits to the movies the only entertainment one could hope for in a rationed society. The Americans brought colour to a drab scene and an air of optimism and confidence in the future, in spite of wavering success in different spheres of combat. It was unthinkable that, with the might of Uncle Sam on one's side, the war could be lost.

Seeking for the effect of the American occupation, one could look to the regrets expressed when the troops had departed. Gone was the vibrancy, the way things were done *con brio*, the excitement, the exotic touch to a society emerging from its colonial childhood. Had the troops been English, New Zealand would not have been surprised, because the country had been conditioned to look westwards to Singapore, that impregnable bastion which would hold back any invading hordes making a foray into the Pacific. That the troops should come from the United States, not just as an occupation force, but in the early days as a defensive measure, was a possibility New Zealanders had not contemplated.

It would be tempting to report that the Americans' visit helped lift New Zealand out of its colonial rut. But if there was any change, it came from within, for the Americans were not here with any messianic message, they had other things on their mind. To discerning Americans, New Zealand could be a land of expanding horizons and infinite possibilities. When the troops left there would have been many New Zealand men happy to see them go, glad to return to the norm. Some pipe-smoking males, in their heavy clothing and trilby hats, had not taken kindly to their facade of respectability being disturbed by brash newcomers, nor did they care for the standards the Americans set for the conduct of their womenfolk. If New Zealand housewives were 'frumps', by and large that was the way their men wanted it. Here they reckoned without the women, for it is they who, for the most part, remember the Americans with affection. After the American visit women were just not content with the standards set by New Zealand men. Somewhere out there was a brave new world and they were bursting to explore it. It was to take some time to shake the men out of the pallid conformity of their ways.

Travel, it is said, broadens the mind for some, while for others it merely lengthens the conversation. To a naive American soldier from a Tennessee mountain enclave, the war must have been the most traumatic experience in his short life. Even for those sophisticates of the big cities (whose knowledge of geography was likewise often non-existent), the limitless horizons of the South Pacific must have been a never-ending source of surprise. If there is one message that is constantly heard from American ex-servicemen returning to New Zealand on a sentimental journey, it is the kindness and hospitality extended to them during the war years. Almost all doors were flung wide for them. Only a very few were shut in their faces.

Joe of the 2nd Marine Division had some typical memories of his stay in New Zealand.

> Never have I found more friendly or nicer people than New Zealanders. Most of us had malarial fever from Guadalcanal and it did not take your people long to realise that Yanks who fell over shaking on the street were not drunk but sick. Of course, because Americans do not speak English but an American adaptation, there were times our expressions were offensive to the Kiwis, and at times your converstaion raised our eyebrows. But I believe that every man in the 2nd Marine Division who managed to return home has sung the praises of New Zealand and her people, and has wanted to return.

Ask the average middle-aged New Zealander today what the names Guadalcanal or Tarawa convey and you will probably get some vague reference to the war in the Pacific. Ask a New Zealand teenager the same question and you will probably draw a blank stare. But this reflects the priorities of our education system. Pupils can emerge from five years of secondary schooling and know very little about New Zealand history. Those who have advanced the subject to the sixth or seventh form will know about the origins of the American Revolution, the Age of Enlightenment, or the rise of nationalism in Europe in the nineteenth century. Ask about the Battle of Ruapekapeka, Sir George Grey, Colenso or pre-1840 times and the replies would be very sketchy. New Zealanders still downgrade their own history, apparently finding the past of other countries more exotic.

It seems incredible that in a small town like Warkworth upwards of 10,000 American Marines and soldiers could have lived and sweated their way over the countryside, and yet the present generation of school pupils are unaware of their presence, why they were here, or where they went to. The fault lies not with them but with the curriculum, which fails to teach about an important slice of New Zealand's history. The Battle of Guadalcanal in 1942 determined the course of Pacific history. The defeat of the American forces could certainly have raised the possibility of an invasion of New Zealand by the Japanese. New Zealanders should know about the grievous losses suffered by the Americans on Guadalcanal and the later carnage of Iwo Jima, the toughest battle of all.

It was once common around Anzac Day for principals of New

186

Zealand secondary schools to address pupils on the significance of Gallipoli, but no longer. Gallipoli has passed, like the Boer War, into dim history. The Pacific is different, for we should know about our own front yard, know its past, the present, and consider the future.

Nowadays, there are regular appeals from servicemen in the States to wartime sweethearts in New Zealand: 'Joan, where are you now? Forty-four years ago we sailed from Wellington for Tarawa. Though much too late, I nevertheless want to thank people, especially you and your family, for kindness shown this Marine during our stay in New Zealand. We live on Bear Spring Ranch in the foothills of the Chiricahua Mountains, Bowie, Arizona. If you're ever out this way stop in. Our latch string is always out.'

Few visible reminders of the Americans' stay here remain: a plaque at Aotea Quay, another at Queen Elizabeth Park (Camp Russell) and one at Pauatahanui. Out at Paekakariki there is a Tarawa Street, and someone has called his seaside cottage 'Leatherneck'. As for other relics of those days, one can find scattered around the countryside the occasional ablution shed now used as a haybarn, or the disintegrating concrete foundations of a latrine and a crumbling septic tank. Some farm animals may appreciate being able to stand dry-footed on old tent or recreation hut foundations.

Gone is the sound of infantry men crunching their way along rough metalled roads. Gone too are the bugle calls and the music of the regimental band. Nonetheless, it would be no exaggeration to say that hardly a day goes by without an American ex-serviceman arriving in New Zealand, accompanied by his wife, on a sentimental journey to visit the scenes of his training days and escapades. Because many veterans are now reaching retirement age, New Zealand can expect considerable numbers of such visitors in the years ahead.

Many veterans find that their memory has worn thin and they are unable to remember the exact whereabouts of their camp, a problem compounded when land development has erased familiar landmarks. Some ex-servicemen call on residents to jog their memories and to renew friendships of those days. Henry, now of Minnesota, returned to Warkworth to recapture old times.

I was with the 21st Marines, part of the 3rd Marine Division, an officer stationed at headquarters — Riverina homestead in Wilson Road. Later I transferred to the 1st Battalion (Infantry) down at Woodcocks Road. We were here for five months until late August 1943, and during that period we trained down at the Sandspit with the usual hikes into the woods for machine-gun and automatic rifle practice.

My main memory is the beauty of the countryside, the friendliness of the people, their outreach and warmth, and how they were prepared to share their precious petrol and sugar. We used to come into the village to the recreation centre, go to sing-a-longs at the church, play cards or go down to the little restaurant and clean them out of steak and eggs. I used to think how lucky I was to be in Warkworth with good food, kindness and friendliness.

If you were in Warkworth in December a couple of years ago you may have run into another American, pushing his trolley around in one of the supermarkets. Joe, accompanied by his wife, had come back to seek out his old stamping ground. 'People were kind when we came here forty-two years ago,' he said, 'and they're just as kind today.' Joe was with the 25th Naval Construction Battalion down in the showgrounds adjacent to State Highway 1. His unit was originally organised in Camp Bradford, Virginia, moved from there to California and arrived in Auckland in March 1943.

A sign proclaiming 'Camp Sheep Shit' indicated the whereabouts of Joe's outfit, and from there his unit used to commute daily to Auckland in Army trucks to work on Mob 6 Hospital at Cornwall Park, where Joe baked bread in the galley. Before the hospital was finished the Seabees were called away to Guadalcanal. After that it was Bougainville and then finally Guam.

Pacific Diary, published by Joe's battalion, is an account of the Seabees' campaigns and tells of their unit's arrival in New Zealand, and the memories that are inspiring so many veterans to return.

So this is New Zealand was the thought in our minds as our transport glided through busy Waitemata Harbour. This is the 'Land Down Under' where the summer comes in winter, and winter in summer, where the sun is in the north at midday and everyone drives on the wrong side of the street. We see modern docks, a city of red roofs against a backdrop of hills, hills which might make a San Franciscan homesick. Auckland a modern city. Why, it looks just like the good old States. It took some time to accustom our minds to this slightly left-handed country of inverted seasons and a system of money that just doesn't add up. As to the country, what's it like? Well, if you were to take a large American seaboard city with the rocky coast of Maine, mix it violently with hills of West Virginia, the trees of Oregon, the vegetation of Arkansas, and ferns out of another world, then you would have the countryside surrounding Auckland. It is beautiful. In Auckland we ate 'styke and aiggs' than which no beef could be better. New Zealand is now but a pleasant memory. It is with disappointment that many of us realise we may never see it again. As the years pass by, some of us may still laugh at the antiquated plumbing and the mud of Waikaraka Park. We still complain of those long rides by train and bus back to Kaipara Flats and that cold Sheep Ridge Camp. Some of us may have memories of the Domain, the Memorial Museum, Queen Street and of a few night spots. But the outstanding memory will be the people of New Zealand. We'll always remember their generous hospitality, those pleasant hours spent in family circles. We hope they remember us as favourably as we remember them.

188

US Marine Corps Units in New Zealand

1st Marine Division

(Wellington and vicinity unless otherwise noted)

Division Headquarters	14 Jun–22 Jul 1942
1st Marines	11–22 Jul 1942
5th Marines	14 Jun–22 Jul 1942
11th Marines (except 2nd Battalion)	11–22 Jul 1942
2nd Battalion	14 Jun–22 Jul 1942
1st Amphibian Tractor Battalion	11–22 Jul 1942
1st Engineer Battalion	11–22 Jul 1942
1st Medical Battalion	14 Jun–22 Jul 1942
1st Pioneer Battalion	11–22 Jul 1942
1st Service Battalion	11–22 Jul 1942
1st Special Weapons Battalion	11–22 Jul 1942
1st Tank Battalion	11–22 Jul 1942

2nd Marine Division

(Wellington and vicinity unless otherwise noted)

Division Headquarters	4 Nov 1942–1 Nov 1943
2nd Marines	6 Feb–1 Nov 1943
6th Marines	4 Nov–26 Dec 1942
	25 Feb–1 Nov 1943
8th Marines (except 1st Battalion)	16 Feb–1 Nov 1943
1st Battalion	6 Feb–1 Nov 1943
10th Marines	22 Nov 1942–1 Nov 1943 (Reg Hq)
1st Battalion	16 Feb–1 Nov 1943
2nd Battalion	4 Nov–26 Dec 1942
	25 Feb–1 Nov 1943
3rd Battalion	6 Feb–1 Nov 1943
5th Battalion	14 Jun–1 Nov 1943
18th Marines (except Companies A–F)	22 Nov 1942–29 Nov 1943
Companies A, B and D	6 Feb–1 Nov 1943
Companies, C, E and F	4 Nov–26 Dec 1942
	25 Feb–1 Nov 1943
2nd Amphibian Tractor Battalion (except	
Companies A, B and C)	22 Nov 1942–1 Nov 1943
Company A	6 Feb–1 Nov 1943
Company B	4 Nov–26 Dec 1942
	25 Feb–1 Nov 1943
Company C	4 Nov 1942–1 Nov 1943
2nd Medical Battalion (except Companies	
A–E)	10 Nov 1942–1 Nov 1943
Companies A and E	4 Nov–26 Dec 1942

	25 Feb–1 Nov 1943
Company B	16 Feb–1 Nov 1943
Company C	26 Feb–1 Nov 1943
Company D	1 Feb–1 Nov 1943
2nd Service Battalion (except Companies A–C)	9 Nov 1942–29 Nov 1943
Company A	4 Nov–26 Dec 1942
	25 Feb–1 Nov 1943
Company B	16 Feb–1 Nov 1943
Company C	6 Feb–1 Nov 1943
2nd Special Weapons Battalion (except Batteries B–E)	22 Nov 1942–29 Nov 1943
Battery B	22 Nov 1942–15 Apr 1943
Battery C	4 Nov–26 Dec 1942
	25 Feb–1 Nov 1943
Battery D	22 Nov 1942–29 Nov 1943
Battery E	9 Nov 1942–29 Nov 1943
2nd Tank Battalion (except Companies A–D)	22 Nov 1942–1 Nov 1943
Company A	4 Nov–26 Dec 1942
	25 Feb–1 Nov 1943
Company B	16 Feb–1 Nov 1943
Company C	16 Feb–1 Nov 1943
Company D	22 Nov 1942–15 Apr 1943

3rd Marine Division

(Auckland and vicinity unless otherwise noted)

Division Headquarters	7 Feb–30 Jun 1943
3rd Marines	29 May–25 Jul 1943
9th Marines	5 Feb–30 Jun 1943
12th Marines (except 1st–4th Battalions)	11 Mar–13 Jul 1943
1st Battalion	5 Feb–30 Jun 1943
2nd Battalion	28 Feb–23 Jul 1943
3rd Battalion	29 May–25 Jul 1943
4th Battalion	11 Mar–13 Jul 1943
19th Marines (except 1st and 2nd Battalions)	7 Mar–13 Jul 1943
1st Battalion	8 Feb–30 Jun 1943
2nd Battalion	9 Mar–23 Jul 1943
21st Marines (except 2nd and 3rd Battalions)	9 Mar–23 Jul 1943
2nd and 3rd Battalions	28 Feb–23 Jul 1943
3rd Amphibian Tractor Battalion (except Companies A and B)	7 Mar–30 Jun 1943
Company A	5 Feb–30 Jun 1943
Company B	1 Mar–22 Jul 1943
3rd Medical Battalion (except Companies A, B, D and E)	12 Mar–30 Jun 1943
Company A	9 Feb–30 Jun 1943
Company B	1 Mar–23 Jul 1943

Company D	11 Mar–13 Jul 1943
Company E	11 Mar–30 Jun 1943
3rd Service Battalion (except Companies A–B)	11 Mar–23 Jul 1943
Company A	5 Feb–30 Jun 1943
Company B	28 Feb–23 Jul 1943
3rd Special Weapons Battalion (except Batteries A–D)	7 Mar–30 Jun 1943
Battery A	11 Mar–30 Jun 1943
Battery B	11 Mar–15 Apr 1943
Battery C	11 Mar–23 Jul 1943
Battery D	1 Mar–23 Jul 1943
3rd Tank Battalion (except Companies A–D)	11 Mar–23 Jul 1943
Company A	7 Feb–13 Jul 1943
Company B	4 Mar–23 Jul 1943
Company D	7 Mar–14 May 1943
Company E	7 Mar–29 Jul 1943
1st Aviation Engineer Battalion (Auckland)	15 Apr 1943–12 Jan 1944
1st Corps 155mm Howitzer Battalion (Wellington)	12 Jul 1942–15 Sep 1943
1st Base Depot (Wellington)	21 Jun–22 Sep 1942
1st Parachute Battalion (Wellington)	11–22 Jul 1942
2nd Base Depot (Wellington)	27 Nov 1942–28 Feb 1944
2nd 155 mm Artillery Battalion (Wellington)	1 Aug–28 Sep 1943
2nd Antitank Battalion (Wellington)	12 Mar–1 Dec 1943
2nd Parachute Battalion (Wellington)	9 Nov 1942–6 Jan 1943
2nd Raider Battalion (Wellington)	9–18 Feb 1943
3rd Barrage Balloon Squadron (Wellington)	3–26 Aug 1942
3rd Base Depot (Auckland)	30 Sep 1942–30 Jun 1945
3rd Defense Battalion (Wellington)	16 Feb–6 Oct 1943
4th Defense Battalion (Wellington)	10 Mar–16 Jul 1943
5th Defense Battalion (Wellington)	3–26 Aug 1942
11th Provisional Marine Company (Auckland)	15 Jun 1942
Designation changed to:	
Marine Detachment, Headquarters South Pacific Area (Auckland)	15 Jun–19 Jul 1942
Designation changed to:	
Marine Barracks, Headquarters South Pacific Area (Auckland)	20 Jul–14 Nov 1942
Designation changed to:	
Marine Barracks, Naval Operating Base (Auckland)	15 Nov 1942–23 Sep 1944
2nd Marine Aircraft Wing (Auckland)	16 Apr–3 Nov 1943
Marine Aircraft Group 12 (Auckland)	10 Sep–2 Nov 1943
Marine Aircraft Group 14 (Auckland)	16 Apr–25 Aug 1943
Marine Fighting Squadron 121 (Auckland)	21 May–17 Sep 1943

Marine Scout-Bombing Squadron 141
   (Auckland)   20 May–17 Sep 1943
Marine Scout-Bombing Squadron 234
   (Auckland)   29 Aug–2 Nov 1943

US Army Units in New Zealand

43rd Infantry Division

Organic Units

103rd Infantry Regiment
169th Infantry Regiment
172nd Infantry Regiment
43rd Reconnaissance Troop Mechanised
118th Engineer Combat Battalion
118th Medical Battalion

Division Artillery

Headquarters and Headquarters Battery

103 Field Artillery Battalion (105 mm Howitzers)
152 Field Artillery Battalion (105 mm Howitzers)
169th Field Artillery Battalion (105 mm Howitzers)
192nd Field Artillery Battalion (155 mm Howitzers)

Special Troops

Headquarters
Headquarters Company
Military Police Platoon
43rd Quartermaster Company
43rd Signal Company
743 Ordnance Light Maintenance Company

37th Infantry Division

Organic Units
(as of 1 December 1943)

129th Infantry Regiment
145th Infantry Regiment
148th Infantry Regiment
37th Reconnaissance Troop Mechanised
117th Engineer Combat Battalion
112th Medical Battalion

Division Artillery

Headquarters and Headquarters Battery
6th Field Artillery Battalion (105 mm Howitzers)
135th Field Artillery Battalion (105 mm Howitzers)
136th Field Artillery Battalion (155 mm Howitzers)
140th Field Artillery Battalion (105 mm Howitzers)

Special Troops

Headquarters

Headquarters Company
Military Police Platoon
37th Quartermaster Company
37th Signal Company
737th Ordnance Light Maintenance Company

25th Infantry Division

Organic Units
(As of 1 December 1943)

27th Infantry Regiment
35th Infantry Regiment
161st Infantry Regiment
25th Reconnaissance Troop Mechanised
65th Engineer Combat Battalion
25th Medical Battalion

Division Artillery

Headquarters and Headquarters Battery
8th Field Artillery Battalion (105 mm Howitzers)
64th Field Artillery Battalion (105 mm Howitzers)
89th Field Artillery Battalion (105 mm Howitzers)
90th Field Artillery Battalion (155 mm Howitzers)

Special Troops

Headquarters
Headquarters Company
Military Police Platoon
25th Quartermaster Company
25th Signal Company
725th Ordnance Light Maintenance Company

The Battle Zones

Where were the American troops headed when they left New Zealand? Most New Zealanders would not have known at the time, and often the troops themselves could only speculate as to their ships' destinations. This is a summary of where they went on combat service after leaving New Zealand.

1st Marine Corps Division

This division (meaning only those elements that were in New Zealand from June 1942) went on to link up with the rest of the Division to spearhead the attack on the Japanese on Guadalcanal beginning 7 August 1942. The division did not return to New Zealand but went after the Guadalcanal campaign first to Brisbane then to Melbourne for R & R. Thereafter their campaigns were New Britain (Cape Gloucester), Peleliu (south-east of the Philippines in the Palau Group) and finally Okinawa.

2nd Marine Corps Division

Certain units that stayed in New Zealand later went to Guadalcanal for mopping up operations, sailing out of Wellington Harbour on 26 December 1942 to join the rest of the division, which had been there since 7 August 1942. The whole of the 2nd Division was back in Wellington by the end of February 1943, some units to occupy camps they had already used. The division remained in the greater Wellington area until 1 November 1943, during which time it trained for its next objective, Betio Atoll in the Gilbert Group. After leaving New Zealand never to return, the division's battle campaigns were Tarawa, Saipan, Tinian and Okinawa. The division's shoulder patch was a shield with five stars and a torch held aloft, its motto 'Silent Second, Second to None'.

3rd Marine Corps Division

This unit left New Zealand for its first Pacific campaign, the landing on Bougainville in the Solomons, November 1943–January 1944. Following this engagement, the division was involved in the campaigns on Saipan and Guam, (21 June–10 August 1944) followed by Iwo Jima (February–April 1945). Here the divison suffered horrendous losses, up to 60 percent battle casualties in some rifle regiments.

43rd Division US Army (Winged Victory Division)

This division took part in the final stages of the Guadalcanal campaign and then went on to the New Georgia (Solomon Islands) engagement. The unit came back to New Zealand at the end of March 1944, stayed for several months then left for New Guinea (Aitape). From there the division went on to the landing in the Philippines.

On 24 April 1989, a plaque recording the stay of the 43rd Signal Company of the 43rd Division US Army was unveiled by visiting US servicemen at the A.R.A.

Botanical Gardens, Manurewa, Auckland. The site of the gardens back in the war years was used for Camp Orford, home for hundreds of American servicemen.

25th Division US Army (Tropical Lightning Division)

This division was stationed at Schofield Barracks Pearl Harbour when Commander Fuchida emerged from northern skies to bomb the American Pacific Fleet on 7 December 1941. Almost a year later elements of the division landed at Guadalcanal to relieve the 1st and 2nd Marine Corps Divisions and later the Americal Division. Following the securing of Guadalcanal, elements of the division moved to Russell Island, to Rendova Island in the New Georgia Group, and were later involved in the attack on the Munda Airfield. There were mopping up operations in Vella Lavella, Arundel Island and Kolombangara Island. The New Georgia Group was declared cleared by October 1943. The division returned to Guadalcanal and prepared for movement to New Zealand for R & R combined with some training. The rear echelons had reached New Zealand by 5 December. There was training for a projected landing against the Japanese at Kavieng New Ireland.

By the end of February 1944 the 25th had quit New Zelaand and was en route to New Caledonia where it continued to train for Kavieng. This invasion was cancelled on 1 June. However, the division was alerted for participation in the Philippines operation. The unit left New Caledonia on 17 December 1944, practised assault landings on Guadalcanal, reloaded ships and sailed for the Lingayen Gulf, Luzon, in the Philippines, via Manus Island in the Admiralties, to arrive off the Gulf on 11 January 1944. The division was to spend the next six months in the mid-north of Luzon fighting the enemy down Highway 5 and over to the west coast at Dingalan Bay. By the end of June 1945, the Philippines campaign was over and again the division was alerted for its next objective, the invasion of the mainland of Japan. The Japanese circumvented this attack by capitulating, and so the 25th was designated as part of the Occupation Force of Japan.

37th Division US Army

This division first went into combat with the Marines at Munda, New Georgia, Solomon Islands. Following this the unit was a back-up division for the 3rd Marines Division at Bougainville and was later engaged in front line fighting against the Japanese in that campaign. From January to August 1945, the 37th was part of the invading forces in the Philippines and helped seize and liberate the walled city of Manila.

196

Tarawa

The battle order for the Tarawa landing:
Col W. M. Marshall succeeded Col J. M. Arthur as commander 2nd Regiment
Brigadier-General Thomas E. Bourke commanded 10th marines
Col M. G. Holmes succeeded Col Gilder Jackson, commander 6th Marines
Col Merritt A. Edson, Division artillery officer
Col Elmer Hall
Col C. W. Martyr, Engineers

The battalion commanders were:

2nd Regiment	1/2	Lt Col Wood B. Kyle
	2/2	Lt Col Herbert K. Amey
	3/2	Major John Schoetell
6th Regiment	1/6	Major W. K. Jones
	2/6	Lt Col Raymond L. Murray
	3/6	Lt Col Kenneth McLeod
8th Regiment	1/8	Maj Lawrence Hays
	2/8	Maj Henry P. Crowe
	3/8	Maj Robert H. Ruud
10th Regiment	1/10	Lt Col Presley M. Rixey
	2/10	Lt Col Geo. R. E. Shell
	3/10	Lt Col Lamar M. Curry
	4/10	Lt Col Kenneth B. Jorgensen
	5/10	Lt Col H. V. Hiett (105 mm Howitzers)
18th Regiment	1/18	Lt Col August L. Vogt
	2/18	Lt Col Chester, Z. Salazar
	3/18	(18th NCB) Commander L. E. Tull

On 28 October 1943 the Marines began boarding the transports. There were 12 APAs (ships used for transporting assault personnel), one AP and 3 AKAs (cargo ships used for transporting assault personnel). They departed on the following US Transport ships:
Zeilin 2/2
Heywood 2/8
Middleton 3/2
Biddle 2 Marine H/Qrs
Lee (*Listing Lee*) 1/2
The above group of Marines was named Combat Team 2 under Col David M. Shoup.
Monrovia 3/8
Sheridan 1/8
La Salle Division Troops
Doyen Division Troops

This was Combat Team 8
Harris 3/6
Bell 2/6
Feland 1/6
Ormsby Regimental Hqrs
This was Combat Team 6
Detachments from Combat teams 2, 8 & 6 rode on the AKAs, *Thuban*, *Virgo* and *Bellatrix*.

Camps and stores used by the Americans

Wellington

One of the memorable feats of World War II was the construction by the Public Works Dept of camps to meet the demand of the American command. In April 1942 the Government was given six weeks to have in place camps in the greater Wellington area to house 20,000 men. The department was already fully engaged on a hugh programme of works required for the defence of New Zealand itself. In six weeks, from a site where sheep might safely graze, sprang three camps with hot and cold water, drainage installed and cooking facilities ready to go on the boil. Planning had had to include roads, streets, paths, water supply, sewerage, electric power and vehicle parks. Practically all sleeping accommodation was in the form of tents erected on timber decks. Buildings were pre-fabricated in the South Island, marked, numbered and shipped to the North Island for assembly by local contractors. 150 Department tradesmen were employed, with over 700 contractors' employees in addition. Because the Wellington Hospital Board owned the property at McKay's Crossing, an Imhoff sewerage treatment plant was installed, with the idea that its continued use in peace time may have been a possibility. The sewerage for the Pauatahanui camp was run into holding tanks and discharged on the ebbtide into the Porirua Harbour. The first camps were ready for occupation on 16 June 1942, with the remainder ready about the middle of July.

Early in 1943 the original camp at Paekakariki (on the golf links) was increased to provide accommodation for an additional 2800 men. A new camp for 4850 men was built on the opposite side of the railway line from the existing one. It was known as Camp Russell. The erection of a number of recreation halls, each 90 feet by 30 feet, was begun in April 1943 for use in the larger camps.

There were 116 huts and 25 buildings with a total area of 81,040 square feet.

When finally completed, the military camps in the Paekakariki area were as follows:

Paekakariki	5200 men
Camp Russell	4850 men
McKay's Crossing	4650 men
Judgeford Valley	3800 men
Pauatahanui	2000 men
Titahi Bay	1500 men
Plimmerton	482 men
Paraparaumu	200 men

2728 buildings, 159 huts, 3401 tents, an aggregate floor area of 2,083,633 square feet.

Other camps and hospitals in the Wellington area were:

Silverstream Hospital, Silverstream, Hutt Valley

The original contract called for buildings to house 450 hospital and convalescent patients. This contract was for NZ Army patients. Then instructions were received, just before the contractors were ready to hand over the buildings, that the institution was to be made over to the US Navy and enlarged to accommodate 1200 patients, later to be increased to 1600. The completed hospital consisted of 46 buildings with a total floor area of 143,800 square feet. The hospital was in use by the US Navy from August 1942 until April 1944 during which period over 20,000 patients were treated. For short rush periods the accommodation was so taxed that the gymnasium, the theatre block and part of the staff quarters had to be used. The institution was later taken over by the Wellington Hospital Board for the treatment of long-term patients.

Temporary Hospital, Trentham Racecourse
In March 1943 a portion of the Trentham racecourse grandstand was occupied by the US Marines for the treatment of malaria cases. Two-men huts and four stores buildings with a total area of 5480 square feet were built to accommodate personnel of 340.

US Navy Barracks, Oriental Bay
It was necessary to provide servicing facilities for a large number of assault craft used by the Marines in their landing training. In all accommodation was provided for 350 personnel in Boat Harbour which entailed the construction of buildings with an aggregate of 22,000 square feet. After the US Forces left, the buildings were taken over and used as accommodation for junior officers of the Public Service.

Hutt Park, Lower Hutt (Home of the Wellington Trotting Club)
Accommodated in this camp by July 1943 were 1200 US Marines. 47 buildings were built and 229 huts erected. Buildings erected included a large new recreation hall.

Military Camp, Kaiwharawhara Park Road, Kaiwharawhara
Buildings with an aggregate of 27,000 square feet were constructed to accommodate the US Marines.

Military Camp, Anderson Park, Tinakori Road, Wellington
Instructions were received to prepare a camp for 4000 US Navy personnel. A hospital was built later to provide for 400 patients and the staff to attend to them. 27 buildings were erected with an aggregate of 50161 square feet. When the US Forces vacated the camp it was taken over by the RNZAF as a base camp and demobilisation centre.

Central Park, Wellington
Instructions were received by the Department to prepare a camp to receive 16 officers and 400 men of the US Marine Corps. Contractors were instructed to work over-time in order to have the camp ready for occupation by 22 November 1942. With time, increased accommodation was provided to house in all 540 personnel.

Storage (built for the Americans)

Aotea Quay	36000 square feet
Aotea Quay (Commissary)	25000 square feet
Paremata & Paekakariki Railway Stations bulk food stores	39900 square feet
Petone Railway Station (4 stores)	78400 square feet
Waterloo Station, Lower Hutt (5 stores)	92900 square feet
Park Road, Gracefield (13 stores)	291280 square feet

Seaview Road, East Petone (18 stores)	150000 square feet
Paekakariki	32200 square feet
McKay's Crossing	3000 square feet

Cool Storage:
Co-op Dairy Producers Freezing Co. Ltd, Aotea Quay
Frozen Products Ltd, Tennyson Street
Gear Meat Co. Petone

Residential accommodation
The 86-room Windsor Private Hotel in Willis Street was taken over under the Accommodation Emergency Regulations for the 2nd Division USMC in October 1942. The premises were vacated by the Americans in December 1943 but not released to the owners until several months later. The losses and damages alleged to have been sustained by the hotel during its occupancy by the USMC were the subject of a substantial claim by the owners. Other properties rented in and around Wellington included the Port Nicholson Yacht Club premises in Oriental Bay, which became a hospital and dispensary. Eleven furnished houses and flats were rented round Wellington in addition. Special arrangements were also made to board a number of US officers (up to 25) at the Hotel St George. Of the daily charge of 25/- per day, 16/- was met by the NZ Government.

Office Accommodation
Hotel Cecil, Lambton Quay, acquired compulsorily for the USMC. When the USMC vacated the premises in March 1943 the American Red Cross took over.
Union Bank Chambers, Featherston Street, acquired for the US Joint Purchasing Board.
Other office space was rented in the following Wellington buildings:
Hannah's Building, Lambton Quay
Levy Building, Courtenay Place
Bates Building, Victoria Street
Tisdall's Building, Lambton Quay
Vickery Electrical Building, Victoria Street
Lauchlan Building, Woodward Street
ASRS Building, Aitken Street
DIC Building, Lambton Quay
Ward's Building, Ballance Street
Kings Chambers, Willis Street
Co-op Dairy Products Building, Aotea Quay

Storage (Rented)
Wellington City Council Building, 139 Thorndon Quay
Murray Roberts & Co. Building, wool store, Thorndon Quay (18,700 sq ft)
Dalgety & Co. wool store, Thorndon Quay (13,000 sq ft)
Wright Stephenson & Co. wool store, Fryatt Quay (6200 sq ft)
R. H. Armstrong & Co. Building, Thorndon Quay (8832 sq ft)
J. B. McEwan & Co. Building, Featherston Street
Shacklock Building, Tory Street (10,122 sq ft)
Gough, Gough & Hamer Building, Blair Street (6600 sq ft)
Odlins Building, Cable Street (6036 sq ft)

Beresford Building, Molesworth Street (3000 sq ft)
Coca Cola Building, Hutt Road (3528 sq ft)
Green & Mathews Building (3880 sq ft)
Carrara Ceiling Co. Building, Daniell Street, Newton
Auld & Gleeson shop, Kelburn Avenue
Irvine & Stephenson shops, Brandon Street
Johnston & Co. Building, Ballance Street
H. M. Hayward's shop, Farish Street

Masterton Military Camps (Memorial Park & Solway Showground)
These camps were originally camps for the New Zealand Forces. Instructions were
received by the PWD to convert the camps into rest areas for the USMC.

Auckland
Camps for the personnel of the US Forces in the Auckland area were as follows:

Mechanics Bay
A barracks block of 40,620 square feet was constructed to house US Navy personnel.
Eventually 12 buildings were erected to provide accommodation for Navy men
stationed in Auckland and also for ratings off ships held here for repairs.

Military Camp, Auckland Domain (Inner)
The buildings erected here were similar in type to the barracks at Mechanic's Bay
and consisted of 8 large 'H' type dormitories accommodating 122 men. A total of
18 buildings were erected covering an area of 85,346 square feet to house 1000 personnel. Included also was an extension of a convalescent depot from Hobson Park
Hospital.

Military Camp, Auckland Domain (Outer-Camp Hale)
This camp was almost in front of the War Memorial Museum. It was a replica of
the Mechanics Bay barracks and was used by personnel of the US Army. Accommodation was made available for 750 men in 15 buildings spread over 53,005 square
feet.

Military Camp, Victoria Park
A total of 196 huts were erected lined with Pinex and lockers each hut 20 feet by
8 feet. Included among the buildings was a 26-bed hospital. The 205 buildings provided covered an aggregate floor area of 743,232 square feet.

Military Camp, Cambria Park, Puhinui
South of Papatoetoe and adjoining the Puhinui Railway Station, 64 buildings were
completed covering an area of 94440 square feet. The camp was used extensively
as a training centre and later as rest centre.

Military Camp, Waikaraka Park, Onehunga
Originally the camp was laid out as a tented camp but this was later changed to
provide dormitory accommodation. 32 dormitories, each 80 by 27 feet were erected
making a total of 57 buildings housing 2500 personnel.

Military Camp, Tamaki (Camp Bunn)
This camp, adjacent to the Glen Innes railway station, was used for personnel guarding the storage areas. Later the camp was enlarged to accommodate 4 'H' type dormitories, officers' quarters, a hospital and recreation building.

Military Camp, Mangere Crossing
At very short notice the PWD was requested to prepare a camp site of 80 acres adjoining Mangere Railway Station to accommodate 5000 US troops. 26 temporary cookhouses with ablution blocks, showers and latrines were erected. It was later decided to develop the area into a permanent camp. Fifty-five buildings were erected with a total of 115,328 square feet.

Military Camp, Western Springs
Altogether 31 buildings were erected providing accommodation for 600 men. After the war the buildings became a transit housing area for the Auckland City Council.

Hobson Park Hospital, Market Road
The first hospital project undertaken in Auckland for the US Forces was known as Mob 4 and was built for the US Navy. In all 68 buildings were erected covering an area of 250,000 square feet and providing accommodation for 1000 patients. The nurses' quarters were located on the adjoining courts of the Remuera Tennis Club. After 1944 the establishment was taken over by the RNZAF for use as a control depot.

Cornwall Hospital
This was built on a portion of Cornwall Park, One Tree Hill, facing on to Greenlane Road. A decision was made to erect a 1000-bed hospital for the US Army. Work commenced on 30 October 1942. Thirteen weeks later 62 doctors, 143 nurses and 500 male staff moved in, the first 500 patients being admitted four days later. In all 123 buildings were erected covering 367,000 square feet. The main hospital block was interconnected with covered ways and with subsequent extensions brought the total available patient accommodation to 1500 beds. The complex was built by four of the leading contractors in the city. 798 men were employed on the site at one time. After the war the complex was purchased by the Auckland Hospital Board.

Avondale Hospital
This was in the area bounded by Holly Street, Victor Street, and Rosebank Road. Early in 1943 instructions were received to prepare plans for a second Naval Hospital. As the site chosen was on Education Department land reserved for a future school, it was decided to design the main buildings as permanent buildings suitable for eventual use as a high school. The hospital was to provide for 2000 beds. Altogether 60 buildings were erected covering a total area of 388,000 square feet. Included among the buildings were an auditorium, a gymnasium, 39 class rooms, 22 wards. The first patients were admitted on 31 October 1943, nearly 16 months after the commencement of building operations. The maximum number of patients in occupation was 1050. During the peak of operations 450 men were employed, including approximately 150 men of the US Naval Construction unit (the Seabees) who assisted with the steel buildings.

Sylvia Park Stores
Sylvia Park is on the main highway between Otahuhu and Mt Wellington. This complex was built to house stores for the US Joint Purchasing Board. Altogether 48 stores were constructed, each 150 × 120 feet. The work was completed between April 1943 and May 1944. The total cost of the stores (873,174 sq ft), the largest group built in Auckland was £425,922.

Mangere Crossing
Like Sylvia Park, this site was chosen because of its ready accessibility to road and rail. The aggregate square footage built was 207,600 and the depot was used extensively by the Americans until vacated in 1944.

Tamaki Stores. Adjacent to the Glen Innes railway station.
These buildings were constructed for the handling of repair and maintenance work on vehicles returned from the Pacific. The buildings covered an area of 303,580 square feet. The work was started in May 1942 and finally completed in May 1944.

Old Dock Site, Quay Street
This building was erected for the US Forces on the site of an old dock site which had been filled in and was right opposite the Princes Wharf. The building covered a floor area of 79000 square feet. It was purchased from the Crown after the war by the Auckland Harbour Board.

Halsey Street Store, Freemans Bay
This area near to the wharves and the railway was developed for the storage of food. A total area of 50,280 square feet was built.

Medical Store Building, Mt Hobson Domain
This building of 32,000 square feet was built to supply the three hospitals in close proximity.

Fuel Tank Farm, Northcote
With the establishment by the US Navy of an operating base at Auckland, provision had to be made for the storage of some 20 million gallons of fuel oil on the slopes above Shoal Bay. The proposal was to provide for 50 tanks spaced about 3000 feet apart and set into the country on an irregular line following the foreshore. Owing, however, to the favourable progress of the war some of the original plans for storage were abandoned but not before considerable work was done on the project.

Radio Station
A receiving station was built at Purewa which comprised seven buildings covering a floor area of 9537 square feet and provided barracks for 60 men. The work was completed in December 1942. Simultaneously a radio transmitting station was constructed at Mt Albert involving the erection of eight buildings covering 1782 square feet. The Purewa Station was taken over by the RNZ Navy in December 1944.

Ammunition magazines, Motutapu Island (Hauraki Gulf)
Ninety structures were erected on the island the total area being 180,000 square feet. Each magazine of pre-cast concrete was 80 × 20 feet. A large store (360 × 120

feet) was erected at Home Bay. The work authorised was fully completed though the magazines were never actually required, and were eventually used for wool storage.

Magazines, Kauri Point (Waitemata Harbour)
Fifteen brick magazines for the US Navy were constructed between January 1943 and April 1944. The total area of all structures was 16,380 square feet.

Maungakiekie Rest Home
This was situated on the One Tree Hill Domain and adjacent to the Maungakiekie Golf House. The existing golf house was taken over and altered to provide lounges, kitchen and dining accommodation. Seven dormitory blocks were built. The project was to provide a rest home for US Air Force officers. The project was completed by November 1944, but due to the satisfactory progress of the war it was never used by air personnel. After the war the property was purchased for use as a home for blinded NZ sevicemen and as such became the New Zealand St Dunstan's.

Other units of the American forces to rent premises within the Auckland area were:
United States Administration Headquarters, Dilworth Buildings
US Naval Supply Depot, Government Building, Jean Batten Place
US Army Services Supply, Smiths Building, Albert Street
US Hospitality Centre, Endean's Building, Queen Street
US Officers Mess, Waverley Hotel, Customs Street East
US Marine Corps Post Office, Albert Street
US Fleet Post Office, Albert Street
American Red Cross, Hotel Auckland
US Officers Quarters, Hotel Arundel, Waterloo Quadrant
US Officers Quarters, Grand Hotel, Princes Street
Commodore's House, 62 Victoria Avenue, Remuera
Kia Ora Rest Home, Evelyn Firth and Russell House
Shore Patrol, 26 Airedale Street
Kia Ora Aviators Recuperation Centre, St Stephens Avenue, Parnell
Rest Home, 89 Gillies Avenue
Boat Pool, Princes Wharf
Johnston's Garage, Princes Street
Northern Automobiles Ltd, Central Auckland
US Army Range, Te Atatu
Camp Hillcrest, Hillcrest Ave, Northcote (now Stancich Reserve)
Camps in the South Auckland area used by the Americans were (owners names in brackets):
Grande Vue, Manurewa (D. R. H. Nathan)
Orford Camp, Manurewa (Countess of Orford)
Manurewa, Nathan's No. 1 & 2 (D. L. Nathan)
Pukekohe Racecourse (Franklin Racing Club)
Opaheke East (F. A. A. Parker)
Opaheke West (R. Kidd, G. Whitford)
Moult's House for senior officers, Pukekohe (Mrs Moult)
Hilldene (E. A. & A. R. T. Urquhart)
Karaka (A. F. Jagger, W. J. Potter, A. Wood)

Paerata College, Wesley College
Rooseville Park (Pukekohe Borough Council)
Helvetia (Ernest Schlaepher)

Camps in the Warkworth area were:
'Riverina' Headquarters, Wilson Road (3 camps)
Rodney Showgrounds, State Highway 1
Goatley's Road (4 camps: C. A. Kraack, N. Gibbs, H. G. Clayden)
The Knoll (J. Grimmer)
Camp, Old Great North Road (J. Hudson)
Camp (L. Beresford)
American Hospital, View Road (J. T. Ashton)
Camp, Woodcocks Road (Tucker's farm)
Camp, Carran's Road (H. Clegg)
Camp, Woodcocks Road (S. Edwards)
Wylie's Road (E. S. Wynyard, S. Edwards, A. W. Wylie)
Falls Road (E. S. Wynyard)
Perry's Road (Perry Bros, also Messrs Gubb, Holland, King and Fleming)
Matakana (J. J. Smith, A. Migounoff)
Camp Woodcocks Road (F. Wech)
Dome Camp (T. R. Blair), Kaipara Flats (J. H. Mason)
Whangateau Hall & Reserve
Anderson's Road, Matakana (C. G. Thompson, J. C. Cruickshank)
Artillery Range, Tapora
Pakiri Beach Camp
In the Whangarei area there were camps at Three Mile Bush and Maungatapere

BIBLIOGRAPHY

Buckner, David N. *10th Marines*. Marine Corps Historical Reference Series, 1981.

Capon, S. H. 'Hamilton Furlough Mutiny'. Unpublished thesis, University of Waikato, 1960.

Costello, John. *The Pacific War*. Collins, London, 1981.

Griffiths, S. B. *Battle For Guadalcanal*. J. B. Lippincott, Philadelphia, 1963.

Horan, James D., & Gerrold Frank. *Out in the Boondocks*. Putnam, New York, 1943.

Hammel, Eric, & John E. Lane. *76 Hours — The Invasion of Tarawa*. Pacifica Press, California, 1985.

Johnston, Richard W. *Follow Me*. Random House, New York, 1948.

Manchester, William. *Goodbye Darkness*. Michael Joseph, London, 1979.

McMillan, George. *The Old Breed*. Infantry Journal Press, Washington, DC, 1949.

Pacific Diary. Privately printed by the 25th Construction Battalion USN Veterans.

Santelli, James S. *8th Marines*. Marine Corps Historical Reference Series, 1976.

Sherrod, Robert. *Tarawa*. Sloan & Pierce, New York, 1949.

Strobridge, Truman R. *9th Marines*. Marine Corps Historical Reference Series, No. 33, 1961.

Sullivan, J. W. Article On Crashed Flying Fortress. Aviation Historical Society of New Zealand (Inc), 1968.

Upedgraph, Charles L. *US Marine Corps Special Units World War II*. Marine Corps Historic Reference Series, 1972.

Uris, Leon M. *Battle Cry*. G. P. Putnam, New York, 1953.

1st Marine Division and its Regiments. Marine Corps Historical Reference Series, 1981.

3rd Marine Division and its Regiments. Marine Corps Historical Reference Series, 1983.

Information was also gathered from the following newspapers and journals: *NZ Listener, Auckland Weekly News, NZ Free Lance, NZ Herald, Auckland Star* (especially Tony Potter), *Evening Post, Dominion*. Also used were accounts of camp construction by the Public Works Department and Air Force activities by David J. Duxbury.

INDEX